Go Stand Upon the Rock

From stories handed down by my grandmother
about how our ancestors fought to be free.

Buckhorn Press

Copyright 2012

ISBN-13:978-1494211561
ISBN-10:1494211564

For Maud, my first hero.

William Henry Ridley, Esquire
(June 12, 1867 – February 1, 1945)
Maud's father, my great-grandfather.

TABLE OF CONTENTS

TABLE OF CONTENTS

"This they tell,
and whether it happened so or not
I do not know,
but if you think about it,
you can see that it is true."

-- Black Elk (1863 - 1950)

The home of Cornelius Ridley
308 North Olive Street, Media, Pennsylvania.

PROLOGUE

308 North Olive Street, Media, Pennsylvania, 1921

THE OLD MAN climbed the stairs slowly; each footfall landing heavily on a narrow wooden step, revealing the weight of the heaviness in his heart. He mused to himself that the stairs seemed steeper every night, becoming a nocturnal ordeal. They creaked and groaned with every step, just like his rheumatic joints and arthritic knees. He was a small man by nature but had been sturdy and strong in his youth, which had enabled him to make an epic 300 mile walk to freedom. Now after 80 years of age and a lifetime of hard labor, including many years as a teamster loading and unloading heavy crates from a delivery wagon and piloting a powerful team of mules that demanded every bit of his strength and concentration, Cornelius had a deep and abiding fatigue that would only be assuaged by death - which was neither far off, nor did he especially fear it.

To the contrary, he welcomed the approaching eternal rest. His beloved wife of nearly sixty years had passed away just two years prior, finally freeing her from the physical and psychological trauma she had endured for nearly a quarter of a century as a slave during the first part of her life, over a decade of which was spent as a breeding woman on a plantation in the South. Now, a widower, Cornelius shared the cozy little two-story brick house they had proudly purchased together fifty years earlier with their devoted son William, a lawyer, who worked late into the evenings before returning home.

Despite overwhelming odds, their son was an attorney of significant standing, and the first of his color to break the racial barrier of the county's all-white court system in 1891. From his humble birth as a slave, Cornelius had become a man held in high esteem around the county; and this remarkable father and his remarkable son shared an unbreakable bond. The father was calm and wise, honest and soft-spoken. The son was handsome, bright, and passionate; and deeply devoted to his father. He had inherited his father's affable, engaging, courteous nature. These traits had served William well in his career in the courtroom. And like Cornelius, he was a good father.

It was on such evenings, when the night seemed particularly quiet; and the flame of his candle flickered, chasing shadows that danced up the stairwell before him; that he began to feel something somber, moody, and unsettling about this snug and once happy little home. Perhaps, he was infusing it with his own melancholia. Yet, he was reluctant to mention it to "Willy," for fear that his son would worry all the more about him. Cornelius was born in rural antebellum Virginia, where hauntings and apparitions were a part of Southern life and culture. However, he had never given them much thought because he never had the "gift" for seeing such things, but he respected earnest folk who did.

When he reached the little landing at the top of the stairs he would turn right, and look through the doorway into his room. On his feather bed in the corner where his wife had died, he would sometimes see a small boy awake and turn toward the landing, staring at him with dark eyes wide and filled with fear. He gazed back in disbelief with his thoughts racing and heart pounding. Though he had never met him, Cornelius felt as though he knew this boy. The child bore a convincing resemblance to his granddaughter - Willy's daughter, Maud. However, she was an only child, now nearly 30 years old with four young daughters of her own. The boy evaporated with the approach of light from his candle. The old man was thunderstruck; not knowing what to make of this timid little spirit or what to do about it. But it would not be the last time they would see one another.

CHAPTER 1

Uncle Robert

WEDNESDAY, April 10, 1839 seemed like another endless day - like every day, working in the fields. They needed no bell, no reminder, and no signal to tell them when to return to their homes. The sun was their sign. And they worked from sun up to sun down. They were slaves.

The overseer only occasionally rode by around mid-day to check on their progress because he knew they would always be there. There was no place they could go, at least not for long. Every slave knew it was better to keep your own pace, than to have someone else set it for you. It kept the overseer off their backs, and his mind on something else - like some farmer's pretty daughter over in Sussex County. That was better for everybody involved. Plus, one could never tell when he might ride by, looking for something he forgot, or coming out to relay a message from Colonel Ridley, and you had better be there, even if it was five minutes before sunset.

Aching backs, sore muscles, stiff joints, and tired, blistered feet carried them home. The burden of a day of drudgery weighed as heavily upon their shoulders as a sack of Southampton County cotton. Although it was as soft, white, and airy as angel wings, cotton was a brutal taskmaster. The respite of Saturday night and Sunday was still a long way off. Tomorrow was just another day in purgatory, and there was no getting out. The slaves shared this silent thought: "We was livin' in hell. And we was gonna die there. We all knew it."

The work crew had to get the fields ready for planting corn, cotton, soybeans and sorghum, and they were behind schedule because of the relentless spring rains. The work never ended and there were always trees to fell and lumber to cut. At least the slaughtering of the hogs and curing of hams wouldn't happen until the fall. That was hard work but it paid dividends, too, in providing extra meat for the slaves. The Master and his family "lived high on the hog," and always had the best cuts of meat. Smoked country hams produced in this region - referred to as Virginia hams or Smithfield hams - were arguably the equal of prosciutto from Italy. The leftover cuts would provide sustenance for the slaves, even though they could be a challenge to prepare and cook. Parts like ham hocks, pigs feet, hogs head, and pork rind had high fat content that served as fuel to help meet the caloric needs of people who worked 14 hour days. Hog maws, chitterlings, pig ears, souse and other parts had to be properly cleaned and often boiled for hours. These castoff parts had little nutritional value, but they added flavor to potatoes and greens and helped fill an empty stomach.

March hadn't gone out quite like the proverbial lamb, and what followed had been no gentle April showers. Winter had been cold and dry, and despite the almost daily downpours of late, the thirsty earth drank all the cloudy skies could bestow upon it. But the spring rains had finally ended. Now, while the Southern sun was sinking into the dusky fields, a crescent moon was just beginning to appear through the branches of the tallest pines along the windbreaks.

Like the oxen lumbering beside them, that plowed the fields and pulled out stumps and stones, their heavy footsteps made a steady cadence upon the ground. Too tired to talk, the slaves crossed the fields, as silent as the shadows that began to fall around them.

11

June Bug, a boy of ten whose eyes darted cautiously about their path - suddenly remembered that he didn't have to worry about stepping on snakes now. "Too cool for dem snakes, dis time of day," he thought. "Dey be on dey way home by now, jes' like us." It was chilly, even for April. The fire would feel good tonight. And the stars overhead would be bright.

As they turned onto the dirt road to Buckhorn Quarters - the slave quarters for the Bonnie Doon plantation - the smoke from the cooking fires wafted out to greet them, even before scruffy and burlap-clothed children could reach them to escort them the rest of the way. The grown-ups were always both happy and sad to see the children, because it was one of the few joys in a life of perpetual bondage. Yet it was also sad, because it was a painful reminder that this same life awaited the bright eyes, smiling faces, squeaky voices, and smooth little hands now pressed into the adults' worn and leathery palms to guide them home.

However, tonight was different. There would be a little cheerfulness around the village of old wooden shacks along a dusty dirt lane that was Buckhorn Quarters - about the distance of a good musket shot from the big house. Stars were coming out now and a baby boy had just been born. If only briefly, the occasion shined a little light onto their downtrodden world.

Uncle Robert always walked first in the work crew. He was not the tallest, but he was fit and strong for a man of over 60 years. No one knew exactly how old he was and he wasn't too sure, either. His skin was a rich brown - the color of baker's chocolate - and his hair was dappled gray. Although he walked as slowly as an old soldier from the toll that years of hard labor had taken on him, he was still as solid as walnut. He held no title; was elected to no office. He didn't

12

talk much, but when he did, others listened. Whatever he did say, he always said quietly but there was mettle in his words.

Uncle Robert was an unofficial leader of Buckhorn - though he would bristle at the suggestion of that. Like a revered Indian chief, he led by example, not by fiat. Children adored him. Women admired him, though he didn't have one of his own. The young bucks around the Quarters gave him respect, begrudgingly or not. Colonel Ridley thought well of him, and he was the one of the few slaves whose opinion the Colonel occasionally wished to know. If Uncle Robert said it, Colonel Ridley could depend on it being right as rain.

Uncle Robert may have been a slave but he was no fawning sycophant. He knew his place on the plantation and minded it well, never challenging any white man - but then, no white man ever challenged him, either. As much a fixture around the old plantation as the big house itself, he looked out for the folks in the Quarters as best he could and more than once, jeopardized his position to protect his people. He had developed a quiet courage in the face of constant danger, and was forced to make a critical choice that fateful August night eight years earlier when Nat Turner and his men came looking for recruits at Bonnie Doon.

Uncle Robert always seemed preoccupied by the deepest thoughts, and he was as inscrutable as the black waters of the Nottoway River, nearby. His avuncular face always looked stern, as if he was straining to see some faraway place or pushing back some painful memory. He often appeared to have storm clouds in his thoughts, except when he leaned down to talk to the children. He was a giant to them. His face would soften, his eyes would twinkle and he would speak tenderly to them as if he was their grandfather. Because of the routine breaking up and selling of families, he was the only grandfather many of these children had ever known. He once

13

had children of his own, and a wife, too, but that was long ago before he was sold to Colonel Ridley. Some say they were "sold down the river," to parts unknown - which was usually a plantation in the Deep South from whence slaves never returned. He never spoke about them and no one ever asked about them. He was serious, thoughtful, purposeful, and respectful. For all his outward stoicism, everyone knew there was a whirlwind deep down inside him that had been swirling for years.

No one could remember the last time he had raised his voice or fist in anger, nor did anyone ever want to make that happen.

And no one, black or white, slave or free, ever simply called him "Robert." Virtually everyone called him "Uncle Robert" - as Colonel Ridley did. Children sometimes called him "Mister Robert," until they were older. It was obvious that Colonel Ridley liked him, but Uncle Robert never traded on that, and always maintained his quiet, dignified distance. He knew his "place" - not because he felt he was inferior to anyone - but because he knew the havoc a vain and unpredictable master could cause any slave who didn't.

The folks 'round the Quarters often said: "One thing about the Ridleys - if they like you, they like you. But if they don't, you in for misery." Every slave knew the line between like and dislike, being favored or falling out of favor was an invisible and precarious boundary too easy to cross, often through no fault of one's own. The only assets for a slave, if there were any, were intelligence and dependability - but it was unwise to ever show the full extent of one's intelligence. A wise slave might be tolerated - sometimes even valued. A smart slave, however, was considered a crafty and dangerous one.

Slavery was a system that constantly assessed monetary and personal value. Slaves were costly to purchase, which is why many

14

Southerners did not personally own any, and the average slave owner owned five or fewer. A slave valued at $1,000 in the 1830's was worth approximately $30,000 by 2014 standards. Runaways – who tended to be strong young men and among the most valuable – were aggressively pursued and considered to be thieves who had stolen themselves – or, their master's "property." As the owner of over 300 slaves, Colonel Thomas Ridley III was one of the richest planters in Virginia. Contrary to some popular portrayals, few slaves were ever shiftless and lazy – even to be thought so, was a speedy invitation for the whip, or something worse. Therefore, slaves had to appear to be industrious and have worth. In that regard, they could be good actors at times, and despite their lack of formal education, slaves had to fully comprehend the politics and parameters of any plantation system or other places where they were held in perpetual servitude.

They had to be adept at quickly discerning the dynamics of any given situation, and be acutely observant of even minor cues of changes in a master's or mistress' tone and temperament. A slave had to have a fundamental grasp of logic and psychology, be psychoanalytic, and accurate at predicting the outcome of an event or interaction with multiple possible variables. Many were extremely intelligent. It was always best to appear attentive but limited, while imperceptibly vigilant to everything around one without visible reaction. One had to appear stoic, hiding any strong attachments to family, friends, or loved ones. Above all, a slave had to be perceived as docile, childlike, incapable of abstract thinking, never showing contempt for the institution of slavery or anger at the master.

There were two tribes that had lived in this region longer than anyone could remember – the Nottoway, who called themselves the *Cheroenhaka*; and the *Merherrin*. Local rivers carried their names.

"The Meherrin bein' farther away, and crossin' over into North Car'lina," as Uncle Robert might explain. "Nottoway Town, long gone now. Ain't many of 'em left 'roundabouts. A handful of 'em still live up'ta Assamoosick Swamp." Times were especially hard in the South for Indians, many of whom had lost their lands and livelihoods.

In the fall and winter, Colonel Ridley would let Uncle Robert go hunting with two local Nottoways - Black Turtle and his son, Little Horse - to bring home some fresh meat for the slaves in the Quarters. Uncle Robert would always be certain to bring back a nice buck or a couple of fat wild geese or turkeys for Colonel Ridley's table. Black Turtle's wife, Two Moons, had taught another Buckhorn slave - Mama Rue - about local herbs and roots. Sometimes on Sunday, Uncle Robert would help Black Turtle check the fish weirs along the river.

Uncle Robert could neither read nor write, yet his memory was as straight and strong as a poplar tree - therefore, even whites trusted his memory. He could lay brick, mend a wagon wheel, and shoe a horse if need be. He took pride in his work and it showed. He didn't do it to impress the Master. He did it to impress himself. "To be as good at somethin' as I can possible be," he'd explain. He labored as if the land was his, and in some ways it was. He and his forbears had paid for this soil many times over with their blood, sweat, and tears. And he wanted to teach the children by example, so that someday, if freedom ever came, they would know how to make it in this world on their own.

Although he had mastered the art of projecting the persona of a slave, Uncle Robert had a keen sense of self, and an inner compass that seemed to guide him. He was a dignified, dependable, and mature man who would brook no "foolishment," as he called it. Yet the fire for freedom burned silently inside him like ash-covered coals, glowing hot when fanned.

16

A lifetime of hardship and pain had made him careful and cunning as an old fox. He had felt the whip in his younger years and still had the scars on his back to prove it. At this point in his life he was resigned to dying a slave. "Hell, I got no kin, so where would I go?" he once asked. Even if he could have escaped, he feared what would happen to the others if he did - as they would be left behind to face the blame. He knew about retribution from personal experience. A vengeful master was as terrifying as the angry Old Testament God, and sometimes acted as if he was. Uncle Robert worried about the plight of his people and mourned the ones who were lost. Yet he never relinquished his hope of freedom some day for at least one of these children born in the Quarters. "At least one little baby, Lord, at least one," he often prayed.

As the children rushed up to meet the work crew, they breathlessly blurted out: "Uncle Robert, Uncle Robert, the baby's borned! The baby's borned! Colonel Ridley come by and seen him, hisself. He name that baby, Cornelius." Uncle Robert looked down into cluster of little brown faces, and smiling replied, "Well, I'll be..."

CHAPTER 2

Hoodoo Woman

Standing in the doorway of her cabin with a broom in her hands, Big Mama Rue smiled as she watched the ragtag army of little children rush up to the work crew sauntering down the dusty lane to Buckhorn Quarters. She didn't smile very often, or very broadly, but when she did it was sunny and as soft as clover.

She wiped the sweat from the brow of her brown face with the back of her hand. She was a broad and powerfully built woman of indeterminate age, with wisps of salt-and-pepper colored hair curling out from under the turban that was wrapped round her head. She wielded the broom like a soldier practicing the manual-of-arms with his rifle. Nobody around the Quarters - even the big men - were willing to take a cuffing from her powerful hands on wrists at the end of forearms as strong as the limbs of a tree. She often warned she was "not to be fooled with, and don't need no man lookin' after me." She could cut wood, plow a field, and hoe a row as good as any man - and better than most. If Uncle Robert had an equal, in respect and authority around Buckhorn Quarters, it was Big Mama Rue.

Her face was a history of hard times, but she had somehow survived. Her eyes were as sharp and observant as those of the hawks' that flew overhead, and a pair of "S"-shaped marks resembling snakes - one on each of cheek, facing the other - gave her wild and wizened look. The marks had been branded on her face thirty-some years ago down in the Carolinas by a master who discovered that she was using folk medicine to help another young slave - a breeding woman - to keep from getting pregnant.

"They was makin' that poor girl have too many babies too fast," she said. "Her body wasn't nearly healed from the las' one, before the next one come." But her master had been in a hurry to grow his slave population, because he wanted to expand his holdings. Raising a flock of little "pickaninnies" - he called them - at so little cost to him was as easy as picking fruit from a tree, he said. And he always had first pick of the healthiest young girls, until he was ready to move onto the next one. "Hell, it was good for 'em," he quipped.

One night, after a long pull on her tobacco pipe and a nip of dandelion wine, Mama Rue told her story to Uncle Robert.

"'Stead'a dis poor girl killin' herself - 'cause thass what she wanna do - me bein' a root doctor, I give the girl a potion to keep'er from havin' a baby. But Masta found out and he damn near kilt me. He said I 'was gonna rue the day that I was born.'" He tied her to a wagon wheel and had her whipped until she was nearly naked and bloody, forcing other slaves to watch. After he cut her down, the overseer branded those marks into her face so she would never forget. "As if the whuppin' wasn't enough to make me remember," she said bitterly. Her name had been Ruth. But after she was beaten and branded people called her, "Rue."

She nearly died from the beating and was comatose for several hours. Afterward, she was delirious for days during which she saw and experienced many otherworldly things. Her back, buttocks, and legs were crisscrossed with stripes, and she had internal injuries as well from being kicked. Blind in one milk white eye without an iris that could see through "the veil," Rue's grandmother - Mama Edo, an old and revered hoodoo woman - watched over her day and night, using all of her skills and powers to heal Rue's broken body and bring her back from the nether world, where her spirit was longing to join the

19

others it had encountered there. Rue cried for days when she awoke; partly from the pain, but mostly because she had survived.

Not long afterward, Rue was in a slave coffle tied by rope to a dozen others, staggering her way to Charleston to be sold at market to the highest bidder. Her master thought she would bring a good price from some farm down in Alabama or Mississippi – because they were in such desperate need of slaves at the time. As everybody knew, being "sold down the river" was a death sentence. On a plantation down in the delta, a slave would not last more than four years because of the intense heat, poisonous snakes, fire ants, voracious, disease-carrying mosquitoes, and the most brutal overseers in the South. Perhaps they were brutal because they hated being there, too. Since the U.S. had ended the importation of Africans 30 years earlier, plantations in the Deep South were always hungry for more slaves.

She later found herself standing on an auction block down at the wharf, still in a daze, remembering the face of another slave she knew who had finally drowned herself because she could no longer endure the life of a breeding woman. Rue had reluctantly resolved to do the same, when she began to feel woozy. Her eyes rolled in their sockets and the room grew dim. The auctioneer began speaking in tongues and the cacophony of the crowd faded away as a vision emerged out of a mist that surrounded her. She could hear the lapping of waves against a rocky shore, and a low, deep-throated, two-toned humming of an otherworldly choir seemed to well up from beneath the gentle waves.

Rue was now standing upon a rock at the edge of the ocean at sunset. Looking down at her ankle, she saw the shackle chaining her to a heavy iron ball had broken open, and she had slipped the bonds holding her to this earthly plane. She could see far across the water to the Bight of Benin, off the Slave Coast of West Africa, where her

20

ancestors had been bound in The House of Slaves, then shipped off to America - packed like eggs in a crate below the stifling, fetid decks of a slave ship. Schools of hungry sharks swam silently behind, waiting for the inevitable dead and dying cargo to be thrown overboard to safeguard the rest of the slave traders' investment. Like Christ the Redeemer she would gather their dispersed and troubled spirits, defiantly leading them home, marching like a phantom army carrying bows, war swords, and spears, to the sound of a thunderous corps of djembe drums, back through the Door of No Return.

But the vision was broken by the sound of the auctioneer's gavel slamming down upon the sound block, and she heard him shout: "Sold, to Price, Birch & Company!" Rue had been bought at a bargain price by slave traders out of Richmond who made regular trips through Tidewater Virginia to Norfolk, down to Charleston, and back. These traders were often used by the Ridleys, and they figured Bonnie Doon or Rock Spring could always use a husky black woman, if not for breeding, then for hard work. She could always be a mid-wife and care for the sick, and if that did not work out, they could always ship her west or farther south. Traders believed slave women were often a good investment, because many of them could work just as hard as a man, and have babies, to boot. They were less expensive to buy, usually less trouble than young men the same age, and they could always be used for personal comfort on a cold winter's night.

Rue had a few days' uncomfortable rest in the slave pen at Charleston. Slave traders were adept at hiding injuries and imperfections on their merchandise by using grease or tar, and she was given some extra food, water, and fresh clothes to wear. After that, they oiled her skin and made her brush her hair. She knew they weren't being kind - they were being smart. "They was jus' fattenin' me up like a cow goin' to market." They always made a better profit

21

on a slave who looked in good condition, than on one who looked poorly. A broken down slave was just another mouth to feed. Nobody wanted them. Certainly, nobody would buy one.

One day she arrived at Bonnie Doon on the back of a wagon, and was sent down to Buckhorn Quarters. Old Aunt Jo took care of her, told her about how the plantation ran, and taught her what to do. Like many slaves, Mama Rue had been split off from her family in the Carolinas, and she never saw them again, but she prayed for Jesus to watch over them. When she looked up at the stars in the night sky, she would mumble a few strange words in a language none of the others had ever heard before, to some spirit no one else could ever see.

She said her people had lived in the low country of the Carolinas harvesting rice and indigo for years. Some lived on the islands offshore where they caught and dried fish, and grew tapioca. Before that, her family had come from some island in the Caribbean - possibly Jamaica. It was from her grandmother that she learned to work the roots and make hoodoo - *Obeah*, some called it - and her people had other gods and spirits they worshipped and talked to, when whites were not watching.

Besides having mysterious skills and secretive practices, Rue was an excellent cook. She knew every root and herb in the field or forest and used many of them in her cooking, but she didn't cook like a Virginia woman. Sure, she could fry fatback or make the sweetest yams, tangy collards, cornbread, or black-eyed peas with the best of them. But she would also use onion grass and wild garlic, and mixed chicory in with her coffee. She cooked other things, too, that folks around there didn't eat much, like boiled crawfish from the creek, and okra and tomatoes she grew in her garden behind the cabin.

At that time, some people still thought tomatoes were poisonous, because they belong to the deadly nightshade family. A number of slaves like her knew about nightshade, wolfsbane, and jimson weed and toxic toadstools and fungi in the forest – though they would never admit it. "'Cause, one thing white people's afraid of, is a slave that knows how to use poison," she'd say. Even tapioca root had to be processed carefully to remove its cyanide toxin. So, it wasn't that the slaves didn't have the knowledge of how to kill – they just had the wisdom to rarely make use of it. Such a pyrrhic victory would quickly have become their funeral pyre.

Mama Rue also made her food spicier than the others. She liked cider vinegar, hot peppers, and Carolina-style barbecue, but it was the rice that truly set her apart from the others at Buckhorn. The other slaves ate a lot of yams and potatoes, but she loved rice when she could get it, and she'd gather wild rice along the creeks and rivers when it was in season. Sometimes the old Nottoway woman named Two Moons would go along with her.

Mama Rue was the best root doctor Buckhorn ever had. She knew how to cure tapeworm, break a fever, and make a poultice for snake bite. Even Doctor Baytop would rely on her occasionally to watch over some sick person. He claimed she was as good a doctor as he was. She had survived cholera back in the Carolinas, and she didn't fear sickness or death. She was the best assistant that he could find. Sometimes he'd even ask her to get him some medicinal herbs from the woods or along the river, when he couldn't get his supplies shipped down from the pharmacy in Richmond. The doctor and his nurse were often busy because a slave diet didn't contain the proper nutrition to protect them against common illnesses and diseases.

Some women are natural healers – perhaps because women have the power to bring forth life into this world. Due to her knowledge of folk medicine and gift for healing others, Rue became a person of some stature at Buckhorn Quarters, and people began calling her "Mama" or "Big Mama" as a token of respect. Unlike other cabins, hers had a low open platform porch in front that a few of her grateful patients had built for her. There was a large stone, almost fully submerged in the ground, the top of which had been worn flat over time that served as a low step onto the porch. However, there was something unusual about that stone, which may have been a sizable piece of granite with flakes of fool's gold or quartz.

When Mama Rue was settling an argument between two children, she would have them stand upon the rock, one at a time, and tell their side of the story. She told them it was "Solomon's stone," and warned the storyteller that dire consequences would follow if anyone ever told a lie while standing on that stone. It was a harmless but effective ruse, yet the stone did seem to have a certain aura which signaled this was the abode of a soothsayer and spiritualist. Perhaps this opinion was fueled in part, by folks who had occasionally seen her on nights when the moon was full, standing on the rock with her arms uplifted, communing with spirits. On those nights, moonbeams floated down, gently bathing her in an eerie pale light, making the stone beneath her feet sparkle and radiate a faint glow.

Visitors to her cabin would see that she always had herbs hanging from the beams. "Smelled good in there" they would say - not dank like the rest of the cabins. She also had some strange things in there for her root-workin' - or witchcraft - some folks said. Skulls of small animals were placed on a shrine in a corner, and she kept a collection of little bones in a box made from a turtle's shell. Sometimes, late at night, people hurrying past her cabin would say they could hear her in there "rattlin' them old bones, and then throwin'em down on the table."

Then "she'd be talkin' wit' de spirits an' da sprites." A few superstitious folks - black and white - were more than a little afraid of her. But she didn't appear to fear anything - not man, nor beast, nor the *duppys* (Jamaican patois for "ghosts") in the swamp. Spirits were regular visitors to the cabin of Big Mama Rue. The old folks at Buckhorn whispered that there were a lot of ghosts and spirits around Bonnie Doon, a place of so much misery where many had died in terror and pain. Everyone around those parts knew that they roamed the back country roads and lonesome little graveyards at night - especially when the moon was full. Mama Rue wasn't a pagan - she believed in Jesus, all right, but she also believed in other things that apparently no one else could see - nor did they especially want to.

But most agreed that Mama Rue was "good people." She minded her own business and wanted everyone else to mind theirs. She always had time for the children and watched over them like a mother hen. After all, she had delivered many of the babies in the Quarters and nursed the mothers back to health. Mama Rue also served as the local confessor, comforter, and counselor for the young women and girls who suffered sexual abuse at the hands of leering overseers or angry young bucks brought in from other plantation to mate with them. Misplacing their anger at being abused and exploited themselves, some young men believed they could exorcise their searing pain by inflicting it on another; usually, a young woman or a girl just past puberty who had no defense or escape - who would be tossed down on a bed of straw on the floor in a dark and desolate cabin. It seemed that nothing about such girls mattered to such men. Not their ages, feelings, physical condition, or whether they had children, sweethearts, or husbands they loved.

She was a pawn caught between a buck and his master. They were both victims. Slavery was slavery, whether in the field, in

25

the big house, or in the bedroom. Slaves had no say, whatsoever, in their lives. The only matter of importance about a breeding woman was how many children she could bear. The scars on his back would heal. The scars on her psyche might last forever.

If there were two people on the plantation that Colonel Ridley could depend on, it was Uncle Robert and Big Mama Rue. However, everyone understood that this was not out of friendship for one another. The master simply allowed key slaves the space to get along, as long as it facilitated peace and prosperity. In any penal system where inmates outnumbered guards, it was a necessary evil to make unnatural alliances at times to maintain order, which kept the plantation profitable. Like jail wardens, slave owners had to depend on a few slaves who understood the reality of their predicament and who, like them, did not want to see useless violence or bloodshed.

Big Mama Rue was there with Uncle Robert and many others that hot summer night years ago, when Nat Turner came calling at Buckhorn to recruit Ridley slaves for his ill-fated army. It felt like Judgment Day and there was an eerie light in the sky. She was afraid that night - not of Nat - but of what the white people might do after the *insurrection*, as they called it. To them, Turner's insurrection was just an excuse for crazy and violent slaves to go on a wanton killing spree. And she had good reason to be terrified that night - and for many more afterward.

As Uncle Robert trudged by on the way to his cabin, he greeted Big Mama Rue properly, and inquired about the baby and his mother. She told him the mother - a young and pretty octoroon - was faring poorly, but he could come round in a few days to see the baby. She said "it ain't good to make too much of a fuss around a little babe the first few days after bein' born. He needs time to get situated to his

26

new surroundin's. Birthin' is mighty hard work for a little baby," she explained. But Doctor Baytop had come by and pronounced the baby fit as a fiddle, she reported. "He looks like a Ridley," the doctor had said slyly. With a devilish grin and a twinkling eye, he whispered to Mama Rue: "But don't let Mistress Ridley know I said so."

Uncle Robert bid her goodbye, and she watched him fade into the shadows with a gentle look in her eyes.

CHAPTER 3

Daniel of the Lion's Den

After closing the door thoughtfully, she turned around to look at her frail patient and the old man praying over her. Mama Rue gave a look of approval to the young black woman sitting in an old hand-made rocking chair in the corner nursing baby Cornelius, because his mother was too weak to do it herself. Sister Sara loved children, and it was a good thing, too, because she was a breeding woman. She was a big, strapping girl in her late teens or early 20s, with a noble west African face, skin as dark as teak, teeth as white as flour and an absolutely radiant smile. Since she was almost always pregnant, she had plenty of milk to go around and served as one of Buckhorn's wet nurses. She and Mama Rue loved Brother Daniel, who was down on his knees praying over the pale, unconscious woman on the pallet.

The folks at Buckhorn were just like people everywhere. Some were sinners, some were saints, but most fell somewhere in between; or at times, were a little of both. But none had the stature of Uncle Robert and Mama Rue, with the possible exception of Brother Daniel. People always wanted to give him a title of respect, like "preacher," but Daniel discouraged that. He often said he was "just a slave servin' the Lord - like Daniel of old, who was thrown into the lions' den." He added, "when the Lord speaks to me, he calls me Daniel. And that's good enough for me."

However, on Sunday at prayer meeting, or when officiating at a funeral, or for some special occasion like a slave marriage - called, "jumpin' the broom" - he would allow himself to be called "Brother Daniel," because he was "doin' the Lord's work," he would say.

28

When he was "doin' God's work," a power came over him, as if the Lord had laid a sacred yet invisible mantle upon his shoulders.

Daniel was considered Buckhorn's pastor, and had a kind and gentle spirit. He was quite thin and now very old. A good, strong wind could have picked him up and carried him away on the currents like a child's kite. Had he been called up to Heaven, he would have been a very light load for an angel, indeed. Yet his eyes were sharp, his mind clear, and his courage, strong. In the Quarters, folks were a mosaic of colors and white people had a name for every shade of slave. Black, brown, copper, tan, high-yellow, redbone, dusky, quadroon, octoroon, and a dozen more. But Daniel appeared to be white - or nearly so. Folks said that he and his sister Aunt Jo, who was long gone now, had to be Ridleys because they looked so much like them.

Only a few Ridley slaves like Cornelius and Daniel were mulatto. Although Daniel's hair was now silver, it had been straight and red in his youth; and like Cornelius, his eyes were green. It is difficult to fathom how some white masters could own and sell slaves who were actually more kin than strangers to them. It was often hard to tell precisely who was black and slave or white and free, especially when a slave resembled his master or had as little as 1/16 or less Negro blood. Sometimes no one could be absolutely certain, but family resemblance is difficult to deny.

Big Mama Rue would say, "But it don't bother'em no how. Didn't matter who the daddy was or who mix wit' who - white, black, or Indian." The law said that if the mother was free, the child was free. It was as simple as that. If the mother was slave, the child was slave - forever - or unless they were freed. And that seldom ever happened.

When he wasn't preaching on Sundays or helping Mama Rue with the sick and old folks, Daniel would often be up at the big house, especially when Colonel Ridley had visitors. Daniel fit in well there, because he was soft-spoken and refined. The white folks liked him but he never debased himself for them. After serving cigars and brandy on the veranda, or mint juleps in the summer time, sometimes one of the white gentlemen would slip him a coin, which he would use to buy clothes or blankets for someone in the Quarters who needed them - because the one set they got each Christmas would sometimes not last the entire year. In his youth, Daniel had been the carriage driver, but later accompanied Tiberius, who replaced him, on his rounds to pick up passengers or supplies for Bonnie Doon. Now up in age, Colonel Ridley relieved Daniel of that job, letting him retire and continue ministering to his flock, which was an invaluable service.

Colonel Ridley was fond of Daniel and his late sister, Aunt Jo, who were undoubtedly related in some way by blood, and the Colonel made it clear that no one - black or white - had better lay a hand on either of them. Perhaps it was his way of acknowledging their kinship, or merely deference to their longevity. Daniel was circumspect about it, and knew that slavery made for strange relationships at times. For whites, their slaves were more than just servants. They were also their maids, guardians, nurses, babysitters, companions, lovers, and sometimes their kin.

Big Mama Rue lit the oil lamps as Daniel struggled to his feet. Few in the Quarters had oil lamps but Rue had two, because of Dr. Baytop. Since she often cared for the sick, he needed light so he could see well enough to treat them. Hers was also one of few cabins to have a wood floor made of old planks. She sometimes had a little fire in the fireplace at night for cooking as well as for light, and the fire helped to keep the dampness out.

The light flickering across Daniel's face revealed a look of deep concern, reflecting the goodness that glowed from somewhere

30

deep inside him. He spoke barely above a whisper. "Rue, I'm worried 'bout this here girl."

"I know, Daniel," she replied with a heavy sigh. "I've tried everything I know to help her. Somethin's drainin' the life outta her, but I just don't know how to fight it. Even Doc Baytop's not hopeful. He ain't sure but he say it might be the 'wasting disease'."

Daniel shot her a look of alarm. "They ain't no cure for that," he said. "I know," Rue responded mournfully, "I know. Colonel Ridley come down here this mornin' to see'er, hisself. He powerful fond o' that girl, an' Lil' Rosa look jes' like'er. Colonel say he want to move'er up to the big house if she don't get no better. But Lord, is he tickled with that baby," she mused. "He look just like his sister, Lil' Rosa, plain to see. The Colonel say they never be sold off here. They somethin' special, all right."

Daniel smiled sagely. "Well, I hope so. White people say one thing when it's a kitten but another when it's a cat. But they didn't split up me an' Jo – God rest her soul – that's for sure. And hopefully, they won't split up little Cornelius and Rosa, neither. But what would be even better, (his voice lowers to a whisper) is if one day, these chil'ren be free." He paused for a moment, then asked: "Where is Lil' Rosa, anyway?"

"She up the big house," said Mama Rue. "Mary Mae watchin' her, since I got my hands full down here. An' I don't want'er to see her momma sufferin' like this." Daniel smiled sweetly as he thought of Rosa. "That little girl ain't no bigger'n a bedbug," he said. "But she's a spunky little thing, that's for sure. I'll say a prayer for her tonight, too. If anything happen to their momma here, we're goin' to have to see to it these chil'ren are brought up right." Mama Rue nodded. "You know I'll do my best, Daniel," she said.

31

"All right then," he replied. "I gotta get up the big house now, an' look in on Rosa." He picked up his straw hat from the rough-hewn wooden table. "Thank you kindly for stoppin' by to see this poor girl. I can tell she know you're watchin' over her," said Mama Rue. "And you let me make you a salve for that knee of yours. I can tell you got some rheumatis' in there."

Daniel smiled. "Cain't nobody slip nothin' by you, can they, Rue? Alright, I'll come by tomorrow and you can give it to me then. I 'preciate that." Turning to Sister Sara, he said: "Sister Sara, you take care, dear." She replied lovingly: "Thank you, Brother Daniel, and you too." He walked to the door that Mama Rue held open for him. Taking a parting glance at the young woman on the pallet, he said: "And thanks for all you're doin' for her, Rue." Mama Rue bowed her head humbly. "We all family here, Daniel. One way or another." And he walked out the door.

CHAPTER 4

Black Turtle

Black Turtle was now somewhere past his 60th year. His face, wise and weather-beaten, was a noble and peaceful visage that belied the fact he had once been a fierce warrior. His chestnut skin stood in stark contrast to the silver hair that reached down below his shoulders. Once as black and shiny as his eyes, he wore his hair in braids in the summer, but let it hang loose in the cooler months, when he often wore a hat. Like many Natives, he was a man of few words, and disdainful of unnecessary talk. "Why ask a question if you already knew the answer?" he would sometimes say.

Black Turtle had traveled the entire width and breadth of Virginia and deep into North Carolina and Tennessee on foot during the course of his remarkable lifetime. His bones ached on cold, damp mornings from too many nights on the trail. And he was still occasionally nagged by old war wounds inflicted decades ago.

Like Colonel Ridley, Black Turtle was the son and grandson of warriors. His grandfather, Standing Bear, had fought in the French and Indian War. His father, Blue Heron, had fought on the American side against the British during the Revolution, as Colonel Ridley's father had done at the Battle of Brandywine, in Pennsylvania.

In his youth, Black Turtle had faced the Powhatans, the Chickahominy, the Monacan, the Occaneechi, and the British. Of all of them, he had greatest respect for the Chickahominy. They were fearless warriors and enemies with honor who were never conquered by the mighty Powhatan Confederacy and they had considered him a worthy adversary. As a young man, he had fought with the war club, the knife, the tomahawk, the bow, and the flintlock. He had fought alongside other Indians in the Chesapeake Campaign against the British during the War of 1812. One of his prized possessions was a .75 caliber "Brown Bess" musket and bayonet that he had taken from a Redcoat he had killed in hand-to-hand combat. Black Turtle had admired this enemy. In his grandfather's day, he might have eaten the vanquished warrior's heart as a sign of respect, to acquire his strength in battle. In the white man's war, Colonel Ridley's grandfather was given a gold pocket watch by a British officer he had mortally wounded at the Battle of Brandywine.

Recruited by Cherokee kinsmen, Black Turtle had fought alongside the renowned Chief Junaluska at the Battle of Horseshoe Bend in Alabama in 1814, because he believed it would help preserve the Cherokee homeland, which would serve as a buffer for his own. He was wrong. General Andrew Jackson became a traitor to the Indians, and forced many of the loyal tribes west of the Mississippi. Black Turtle knew what had happened to his Cherokee cousins on the Trail of Tears - or, *Nunna daul Tsuny* - "the trail where they cried." Although he had to interact with them, he never trusted whites again after that, because they never kept their word.

With the war a distant memory, he now only hunted wild game with a trusty percussion cap musket, but his eye was sure and steady as ever. Thought he was older, he could still move as swiftly and silently as a shadow through the trees. He was not a man to be taken lightly, even in the autumn of his years. However, it had become increasingly difficult for the dwindling number of Indians in the region to make a living because with endless fences the big plantations dominated the landscape, and the relentless felling of trees in the forests for the growing lumber and paper industries interrupted game trails and destroyed natural habitats. The fur trade

34

that had marketed millions of deerskins and beaver hides had peaked long ago. The eastern states were becoming increasingly more crowded, animals had been over-hunted, and now cotton was king.

Black Turtle was a perceptive and intelligent man who always knew when to make himself scarce when whites were angry, because whites would often vent their rage on any convenient target. Like some Indians, he at times felt more of an affinity with blacks - or the *Bluefoot* - as he called them, than with domineering and discriminatory whites. Runaway slaves sometimes headed South instead of North, seeking sanctuary among the lower Creeks who were also called Seminoles. Several former runaways had become warriors of that tribe who had fought under the great chief, Osceola; and the collaboration between these two groups created a formidable enemy that made parts of Florida impervious to invading federal troops.

Although they were free people, Black Turtle and his little family still had to be careful. Long ago his tribe, the Iroquoian Nottoway - who called themselves the *Cheroenhaka*, or, "the People at the Fork of the Stream" - had numbered roughly 1500. His wife Two Moon's people, the *Meherrin* - another Iroquoian tribe living along the river to the south that shared their name - numbered half as many. The Nottoway still had two small reserves in Southampton County just west of Jerusalem, the county seat. In the time of Black Turtle's father and grandfather, a traveler was more likely to meet an Indian along the Virginia frontier, than a white man.

Black Turtle would not help track slaves because of what had happened after Nat Turner's Rebellion. After witnessing the whites' brutal and excessive response to the violence committed by General Nat and his troops, he preferred to remain neutral. But to him, it did not seem unreasonable for blacks who suffered so much at the hands of whites to eventually rise up and make war against them.

35

That seemed natural to him, especially since there were so few whites and so many blacks.

Virginia is a land of many spirits, and Black Turtle believed that Nat Turner's ghost would forever wander along the turnpike and through the swamps where he had camped, looking for his severed head. There seemed to be many troubled spirits wandering these roads at night, trying to make peace with their disquiet deaths. Two Moons knew how to make charms to protect them from the wrath of vengeful spirits. Her friend, the slave woman Rue, also knew how to make magic so that she could travel about unmolested by ghosts who roamed the back country roads on moonlit nights. A greater danger for a slave or an Indian, however, was to be caught at night by the vigilante *paddyrollers*.

Though he had once lived a Spartan life on the warpath, Black Turtle often wondered how a slave could be expected to work such long and hard hours with broken bones or dozens of throbbing lash marks cut deeply into his back - especially, on so little food. Whatever food they did get, he would never eat. It didn't make sense. As with a good horse, why not channel a slave's spirit instead of breaking it? It not only seemed cruel, but wasteful, and that's how he viewed most whites - cruel and wasteful. They killed too much wild game for sport - not because they needed the food. That was why deer and particularly black bear were much less plentiful. And the forest buffalo on this side of the Mississippi had been hunted out back in his father's time.

The whites had been crazy for beaver as well. They didn't understand that if you killed too many, their numbers could not replenish. Everything had its season or its moon. When the beaver were plentiful, one could take more, but when there were fewer, one had to take less. That was the way the Keeper of the Woods had intended, Black Turtle reasoned. There were some good years and bad for all - men, crops, and animals alike.

To Black Turtle's way of thinking, whites often killed and maimed recklessly, without reason. They killed snakes merely because they feared and disliked them. They did not seem to care that snakes are wise and brave, and that if they killed too many, mice and rats would invade their barns. They killed many rail birds to practice their aim with a musket, making the woods grow quiet while insects attacked the crops. It did not make sense him. Why did they dump their waste in a stream, he wondered? Didn't the whites realize that people miles downstream might drink from that very same flow, making them sick? Did they not care?

The *Bluefoot* - the blacks - he could better understand. They often talked or sang to their god every day, and they had much joy and much sorrow in their hearts and songs. They remembered their ancestors, and cherished their children. They always had so little that they valued every scrap of meat or piece of cloth they could get. And they enjoyed each other's company and loved to laugh when the whites were not watching them.

He especially enjoyed the company of the one called Uncle Robert. They were nearly the same age and visited each other periodically. Always polite and respectful, he would never simply walk up to Uncle Robert's cabin and knock on the door. No, he kept the old ways. He would wait patiently outside, clear his throat or make some little sound to announce his presence.

Upon hearing this, Uncle Robert would open his door and welcome Black Turtle inside, gratefully accepting the gift of fish or pheasant the Indian would bring. In the summer, they would patrol

37

the creeks and swamps catching fish in weirs. In the fall, they would spend hours hunting deer, turkey, rabbit, duck, geese, quail, or pheasant. Their favorite time was the Hunter's Moon in October, when they would hunt with old muskets or sometimes use a bow and arrows, instead. Uncle Robert was surprisingly handy with a bow, but neither were as good as Black Turtle's son, Little Horse.

When he was not away courting some Cherokee girl in the western part of the state, Little Horse would often join them. The three of them would sit by the fire in front of Black Turtle's lodge, savor a quiet smoke, and share the deepest of thoughts with the fewest of words. Black Turtle would tell stories about the wars and adventures of his youth. Then Uncle Robert would tell the tall tales that enchanted the children of Buckhorn. He was a great storyteller. All the while, Little Horse would listen intently, his black eyes sparkling, savoring every tale like a choice piece of meat soaked in saltwater and slow-roasted over an open fire.

CHAPTER 5

"Angels Watchin' Over Me"[ii]

Life on the old plantation for an illegitimate son of the master of Bonnie Doon was as privileged as it could possibly be for a slave. Although he had no memory of his mother or when she died, he grew up among Uncle Robert, Daniel, and Mama Rue who loved him, and he spent hours with Black Turtle on Saturday afternoons and Sundays, catching catfish and black bass in the Nottoway River, or tracking game along its banks. He got along well with the other slave children despite his nearly white skin and preferential treatment, perhaps because his status was due to an accident of birth and not a preordained position of privilege. But he seemed to understand all this early on, never flaunting it over his peers.

The slave offspring of a master was often resented and rejected by his sire's family because it served as living proof of the master's infidelity to his wife, but Cornelius reported that was treated well. By this time, Rosa had been sent to Rock Spring plantation - the nearby home of Robert and Ann Ridley. Robert was the brother of Colonel Thomas Ridley. Although the distance between the plantations was not great, the move nevertheless proved to be a barrier for them and Cornelius never saw his sister often enough. Yet, the distance made him love her all the more. Cornelius could, however, take some comfort knowing that his Uncle Wilson could watch over her at Rock Spring, since he could not; and Cornelius looked forward to seeing them both on Sundays and holidays.

Unlike other slave children, Cornelius didn't work in the gardens or fields; instead, he spent his youth growing up around the stables, learning to care for the horses. Born with a quiet and sunny disposition, he had a natural way of disarming people as he walked between two worlds. He was a little gentleman, always polite and respectful, and one couldn't help but enjoy his company. He had a knack for making people feel important and for putting them at ease. He was bright and even-tempered, and took on any task given with an alacrity and attention to detail that won over any skeptic. He was inherently fond of horses, and those same skills served him well with people, too.

He saw intelligence, strength, beauty, and loyalty in horses, and each one had a distinct personality. It was true that with enough pain, both slaves and horses could be tamed or even broken. Some were destined to pull the plow for a lifetime of drudgery as if they had been born for no other purpose. But others were like him. They may have been owned by another but they had some secret place inside of them, seldom shown, where they remained free in spirit.

When he was older, he was allowed to go on fox hunts with Colonel Ridley. Like the mythical Pegasus, his horse would unleash its soaring spirit, nearly flying across the wide green fields, leaping over fences and hedgerows – especially when it had a laughing, red-haired boy bouncing on its back. The equines also enjoyed the serenity of quiet country mornings and were always eager to seek some far off place, the location of which only they seemed to know on the maps in their minds. They were noble, dependable, and kind to him. They loved him and he loved them.

As he grew, so did his knowledge of horses. He first learned how to clean the stables and care for them from Tiberius, the old slave who now served as stable master. He learned about their muscles and joints, and he would listen carefully when they cantered so he could tell by the sounds of their hoof beats if one had a sore knee or ill-fitting shoe. From Black Turtle, he learned how to think the way a

40

horse might think in order to better understand and communicate with them. Two Moons taught him how to make a poultice to put on their stiff joints and sore muscles.

Big Mama Rue sometimes told him stories about when he was little, and how she would carry him on her back up to the barnyard to look at the horses and stroke their foreheads as they stood along the fence. He would laugh unabashedly when one would study him in mutual awe with big brown eyes then suddenly flick its ears to ward off flies. He was a boy who had been born in the eye of a storm, with angels watching over him. They were his mothers, fathers, family, friends, but one guardian angel stood taller than all the rest.

He was called "Big Man." No one knew if he had ever had a real name. Big as a bear and the color of cowhide, Colonel Ridley's father bought Big Man from a neighbor years ago as a favor for a perpetually cash-strapped friend. But the purchase turned out to be the best deal he ever made.

Big Man was mute. No one had ever heard him speak, nor did they believe he could. Much like his origins, the reasons for this were unknown. Most people thought he was slow-witted and some said he heard voices in his head. There was nothing wrong with his hearing - in fact, it was acute - and his eyesight was exceptional. Out in the fields, long before he could see it, Uncle Robert could always tell when a rider was approaching because he would notice Big Man suddenly alert like a pointer. "Boy, you can really see that far?" he wondered aloud. "Or, did you hear it first?" Big Man would only respond with a Sphinx-like smile.

He may have been different from the others at Buckhorn, but Uncle Robert and Mama Rue saw nothing deficient about Big Man. To them, he was simply shy, and gifted in different ways. It's true that

41

he never spoke but he understood English, and could, or would respond with a respectful "yes," or "no" nod of the head, rarely looking anyone in the eye. He had a secret smile reserved for those few he considered his family, like Uncle Robert, Big Mama Rue, and the little red-haired boy, Cornelius, for whom he had an instinctive protectiveness and deep devotion. For these few would he also communicate by using hand gestures at times.

Big Man was known for his legendary strength, and had once picked up a colt that had gotten stuck in a mud hole. He lifted it up from the muck with both arms and carried it back to its grateful mare. When they were out in the fields, if Big Man stood over someone pulling up collards or peanuts, he would block out the sun like a cloud casting a shadow over the workman.

He could not tell time but every morning just before dawn when Uncle Robert opened his cabin door, Big Man would be standing there quietly in the dark like the silhouette of a mountain, waiting for his friend and mentor to emerge – sometimes startling the old man.

"Boy, don't you ever sleep? Make a noise an' let somebody know you're out here" Uncle Robert would admonish him. "You 'bout to scare a body half to death," he would add grumpily. Walking up the path behind Uncle Robert, Big Man would respond silently with a faint smile on his face.

As childlike and docile as the giant appeared to be, he had one more look that few ever wanted to see - a look that resembled the face of a mother bear about to defend her cub. It was a narrowing of the eyes and a dead-on direct stare at his target. It was a look of steely, unwavering rage, without care or concern, slowly seeping through his bristling body like a poison; down through massive muscles

42

tightening up in his sleeves, cascading down into enormous hands that clenched into fists of their own accord. It was such an unsettling, primitive stare, that no one ever wanted to provoke him. Even the paddyrollers gave him a wide berth, because, besides his inhuman strength, many of them thought he was "touched" in the head.

He always walked a step or two behind Uncle Robert and never beside him – except when he thought the old man was being challenged in some way. Then, he would step up, looming even larger. This self-deprecating behavior perplexed Uncle Robert, but he accepted the giant's peculiarities, allowing the possibility that perhaps Big Man walked behind him because he felt he needed extra space to avoid stepping on someone accidentally. But there was no one else Uncle Robert would rather have at his back.

When Cornelius was a toddler the two would often be seen together, when Big Man would escort the boy up to the mansion. They made a whimsical sight – a behemoth leaning to one side so that his long arm could reach down far enough for the tyke to grasp a big paw to hold on to. At other times, Big Man would hoist the boy onto his shoulders, gently holding onto the little legs around his neck with his massive hands, which gave the appearance that Cornelius was sitting in the upper branches of a lumbering tree. A soft lullaby-like humming would emanate from deep inside Big Man's barrel chest that expressed an elusive joy and contentment, as if he was carrying his favorite teddy bear.

On one occasion, when they were walking to the barn, a buckboard wagon loaded with heavy crates and barrels approached them. As the wagon passed by, the right-front wheel hit a partially concealed rock that cracked the wooden spokes, suddenly tipping the wagon toward them. With incredible speed, Big Man leaped between the wagon and the boy, and with arms as stout as the branches of an oak, kept the wagon from falling on them. The seams of his work shirt split as his powerful shoulder muscles flexed, and beads of sweat burst from his forehead, while a low feral growl welled up from his throat. Not only did he stop the wagon from falling onto them, he was beginning to push it back upright. Farmhands rushed to help him and with force and fence posts, propped up the wagon until the wheel could be replaced. Onlookers were stunned by spectacle they had seen. The gentle giant was the best guardian angel any child could have.

CHAPTER 6

Fortsville[iii]

Fortsville Plantation was owned by the absentee master John Young Mason. An 1816 graduate of the University of North Carolina, Mason served terms as U.S. Secretary of the Navy under President John Tyler, and as U.S. Attorney General under President James K. Polk. Like his gentleman-planter neighbor - Colonel Ridley - Mason also served as a judge. In 1819, after studying law in Connecticut, Mason was admitted to the Virginia Bar. Colonel Ridley's brother - Robert Ridley - studied law under Mason, as was the tradition in the legal profession at that time. Mason also served as U.S. Minister Plenipotentiary to France (a diplomatic post below ambassador) from 1853 until his death in Paris in 1859.

When he married Mary Ann Fort in 1821, he became the new owner of her father's Fortsville plantation, commanding 2,000 acres of land that produced corn, cotton, peanuts, and melons. Although Mason had a distinguished legal and political career, when it came to managing a plantation he was not a financial and organizational genius like his colleague Colonel Thomas Ridley, III. Perhaps because he lived beyond his means, had encountered a number of financial setbacks, or was distracted by affairs of state, Mason often had to rent or sell off slaves to satisfy his debts. His slaves suffered because of it and constantly feared being shipped a thousand miles west to his plantation in Coahoma County, Mississippi, along the Mississippi River, run by Mason's able and dependable son, Lewis E. Mason.

Though plenty of them existed in the South, Lewis E. Mason was not a brutal slave master, and appeared to have viewed slaves as human beings with human needs and families. In a letter to his mother he expressed concern for the health of their slaves because of the "wetness" of the region that receives 43 inches of rain a year, their predisposition for cholera, and their need for coats in the winter. Because of his administrative expertise, he managed the Virginia and Mississippi plantations for the Mason family, and he was a meticulous record-keeper noting the names, ages, and valuations of each slave along with their family groupings, in an attempt to keep families together. That is not to say that he was not a prudent Southern businessman as well, but he contradicted the stereotypical image of the evil slave master. However despite his best intentions and financial prowess, even Lewis Mason was not able to avoid selling off slaves.

In stark contrast to Ridley's astounding population of 300, in 1840 the Masons held 60 slaves at Fortsville and another 54 slaves on their plantation in Mississippi. Since their slaves were often rented out to other farms for profit, this may be the reason why there were only 11 slaves remaining at Fortville by the 1850 Census, nine of whom were children and of far less monetary value than the two females of breeding age on the list. Their male slaves had probably been rented out or sold off earlier.[iv]

CHAPTER 7

"Mary don't you weep, Martha don't you moan."[v]

It had been over a year now since the mystery that made her a young woman had occurred. Although it surprised her to see a bit of blood on her underclothes one morning, Martha Jane had been gently warned in advance to expect what her mother called her "monthly visitor." But she had also been not so gently warned by her mother to never say a word to anyone about it – particularly, the overseer. If he asked her about it, she should say "no, not yet." This troubled and puzzled her, but she had learned long ago never to question her mother's judgment, even regarding things that she did not fully comprehend.

She had noticed her mother's demeanor inexplicably changing over the past year, and thought her mother would be happy to see her finally pass into womanhood. Martha Jane would then feel she was on equal footing with the other women at Buckhorn, who would no longer consider her a child and shoo her away from their adult conversations. Yet over these past few months a sinister shadow hovered over her mother's heart, reminding her of a Red-tailed hawk hopping along on the ground behind the plow to catch mice suddenly uncovered in the freshly turned furrows.

She saw no reason why things should change. She worked hard in the fields and she could pick, carry, and chop almost as much cotton as the other women. True, some slaves had been sold off, but not that many and not all at once. She had a family and their little garden behind the cabin kept them fairly full. One day she hoped to have a husband – a man she could give her heart to – with a little baby

47

and a cabin of their own. From the snatches of conversation she could pick up from gossiping grown-ups, the Masons were not bad masters – not as bad as some – and slaves on other plantations had a much harder row to hoe.

The obvious worry etched on her mother's brow troubled her. Her father had not been the same since he had gotten kicked in the head by an ill-tempered mule, as he was trying to reconnect it to the chain fastened to the fallen tree it had been pulling. He wasn't in pain but he barely spoke and wasn't much help on the farm. Some said he was crazy now, and he often paced around the cabin at night mumbling to himself in Yoruba. But Martha Jane couldn't decipher a word of it because her family had lost their language and culture of origin years ago. Since her mother was now in poor health, she and her brother, Andison, had to work twice as hard to make up for their parents, so no one would complain about them.

As she was walking home to her cabin, she could hear the heated argument a good distance away. It wasn't the first time that Redmond, the overseer, had been to their place, and she didn't know why he came to see her mother at all. He wasn't like the Masons, who were educated and had a refined air about them. Redmond was a pock-marked, sallow, somber man who seemed perpetually angry. He abhorred slaves and hated often having to work alongside them. He had worked his way up from field hand to foreman to overseer from farm to farm, a long way from the rough-hewn backwoods cabin in Arkansas where he was born.

She only heard the tail-end of the argument. It really wasn't an argument at all. It was a set of orders being barked out with her mother on her knees pleading for mercy. "You been stallin' me long e'nuf, Mary. You better have that girl in that cabin next week when

48

that buck comes, or y'all get a good whippin' a'fore ya get shipped down to Coahoma County!"

He stormed out the door, his face red with rage, knocking into Martha Jane with a curse as he brushed by. She could see her mother, still on her knees crying, through the open door, and she climbed up the steps as slowly and fearfully as if she was ascending the gallows, which she later thought might have been a kinder fate. Her mother closed the door and began the talk she had been dreading for years, forcing out the words a few at a time as if they were stuck in a logjam in her throat. Martha Jane listened in growing horror and disbelief. Afterward she ran out of the cabin and hung over the hitching post on the side, sobbing and heaving until there was nothing left for her stomach to give, and her eyes were out of tears. However, the appointed day came quickly and there was no escaping her fate. Her mother led her to the breeding cabin like a sacrificial lamb. They walked in silence, there was nothing more to say.

There was intense pain, unimaginable fear, and suffering that she could never have imagined. On that night, she was the slave of a slave with no hope of salvation. Perhaps worst of all, she was alone. She spent her mornings crying and in pain, and her afternoons welling up in terror. She was still just a girl but the men were big, strong, and rough. Some barely spoke to her. They asked her nothing; and just conducted their "business" as if they were avenging some past wrong or insult done to them. Most were cold and careless and there was nothing remotely romantic about the entire experience for her. To ask for pity was to incite violence.

During these assaults, she would sometimes simply lie on her back and stare at the black ceiling, dissociating from what her body had to endure, and feeling her dreams slipping away like a boat on a fog-bound river. Some days, she would scrub herself raw with harsh

49

soap made of lard, pine oil, and sassafras; but she could never erase from her memory the stench of sweaty farmhands, who seldom shaved and hadn't bathed in many days.

Martha Jane became cold and distant, even to those who loved her. She drew back, even from her mother's touch - she wanted no one touching her at all. She tried to feel nothing - it was easier that way. She often had to be forced to eat. She saw no beauty, heard no birds, noticed no flowers, and saw no stars or sunsets. That life was gone forever. What the bucks did to her was bad enough, but even some of the women resented her now because she worked shorter hours in the fields and occasionally got an extra piece of fat back for her pot. A few old crones whispered loud enough for her to hear what they thought of her - a big lazy girl whimpering when she should be chopping cotton like the rest of them. Some made fun of her fear.

She wished she was dead. Cold, hard, hate grew inside of her like a tumor. She wanted revenge, and the target of her revenge was the worst of the bucks who were sent to impregnate her. He was a tall, broad-shouldered, hot-tempered bully named Goliath. To plot her revenge, Martha Jane would need the advice of a smart, tough, fearless woman who had once endured and survived the same hellish fate. And that was Big Mama Rue, in Buckhorn Quarters. She would send word that she wanted to see the hoodoo woman come Saturday night.

CHAPTER 8

Serpent and the Apple

From noon on Saturday until late Sunday night, slaves were generally free to do want they wanted, within reason. Most chose to spend time cultivating their gardens, earning a little money, spending time at home, or visiting family on neighboring plantations. But they couldn't travel far, and they couldn't travel at night without a pass. Even with a pass, it was dangerous to meet the Southampton Militia or the paddyrollers on the road at night. After the weekend break, if slaves were not back at work in the fields or elsewhere on the farm by dawn on Monday morning, there would be hell to pay. That was the reason why most runaways left on Saturday, because it gave them a day and a half head start before they were reported missing.

It was late in the afternoon on Saturday when Mama Rue spotted Martha Jane coming down the lane in Buckhorn Quarters. Rue was sweeping dirt out the front door of her cabin, and she paused to take a long thoughtful look at the girl who might have passed for her in earlier years. As Martha Jane walked up, the big woman gave her broom a rest and with a sigh of compassion, said "come on in chile, I been expectin' you."

For a woman known for her toughness, Big Mama Rue had a remarkably tender side, too. They sat at a little rough-hewn table made from remnants of floor planks and on chairs crafted from leftover lumber and bent tree branches. Rue had made some sassafras tea and this token of human kindness and sisterhood between two black women who had shared a common fate warmed Martha Jane's heart. She let down the blockade that held back her emotions and kept others at a safe distance, confiding to the older kindred spirit

51

who held her hands gently and looked deep into her eyes. Rue spoke to the young woman in dulcet and reassuring tones, and for the first time in longer than she could remember, Martha Jane felt a refreshing stillness that eased her mind like a washcloth dipped in cool water, and placed upon a fevered brow.

A consummate psychologist, Mama Rue tried to exorcise the demons that plagued this younger version of herself. They talked until the last of the afternoon light, with each one first listening then speaking her piece. The words welled up from deep within them with anger and anguish that lost much of their power and terror the moment they left their lips and hit the air like smoke drifting away. This was a balm for the soul that each of them needed, and they helped to heal one another. It had been years since Rue had allowed herself to be vulnerable to another human being, but the only way to help this young woman was by taking an equal leap of faith. Once the catharsis was over, each felt a quiet joy and a bond that was nonexistent before. Eventually, they stopped to have supper.

Mama Rue lit her oil lamps while Martha Jane brought in some branches to feed the fire. They continued to talk while they worked, with the conversation growing more lighthearted. Rue brought the roast catfish and potatoes from the fireplace and placed them on wooden plates. From an iron pot resting on the coals, she ladled boiled collard greens seasoned with wild onions and pig foot. Hoecakes baked among the coals and drizzled with honey would serve as dessert.

After dinner they tidied up then sat outside to watch the stars come out while Mama Rue smoked her pipe, thoughtfully. The beauty and serenity of the stars showered down upon them like a sprinkling of gentle rain. This was not an escape from slavery, but a new beginning that brought hope and friendship to them. Martha Jane

52

finished her story by saying, "Goliath the worst one, and he comin' back soon. What do I do, Mama Rue?" Rue took a long pull on her pipe. As she finished formulating her plan, her eyes narrowed to slits like a snake's, and she smiled darkly. "This what'chu gonna do..."

"First," she continued, "you get good and strong. You don't haf'ta work so many long hours in the fields right now. But carry water, wood, anything that's heavy. Make yourself even stronger. Make your back and your body strong. An' you kin make yo' woman muscles strong too." Martha Jane looked quizzically at the older woman. "You do that when you pass water. First, drink a lotta water, every day" said Rue. "An' when you gotta go real bad, first you start, then you stop. An' hold it, long as you can. Start an' stop, start an' stop, 'til you done. And there's other things you can do, too.

"Next, you gotta git control of the situation, best you can. You be forceful an' hongry - like a black widow spider. You attack that man two ways: one to his body, an' t'other to his mind."

"How, Big Mama," Martha Jane asked. "There's good mens and bad," Rue said. "I ain't talkin' now 'bout the good ones like Daniel nor Robert," she said with a soft smile. "I'm talkin' bout the bad ones that acts like they own you. But they don't! It's like they poundin' the drum - and you the drum. But you don't let'em do the way *they* wants. You make'm do the way *you* wants." She could see the puzzled look on the younger woman's face and smiled warmly.

Rue sauntered into the cabin and brought out a little brown jug and two tin cups. "Dandelion wine," she said with a wink. She didn't ask Martha Jane if she wanted some, she just handed her a cup and poured some in both. Rue sat back down, and took another long puff on her pipe. The Quarters were peaceful now. It was dark and quiet and the lights from candles made of rendered hog fat

53

twinkled through open windows and doors like fireflies along the lane to her cabin. Both women savored the moment. "There is a God, chile, yes there *is* a God." Martha Jane nodded yes, "but it sure don't seem like it sometimes," she confessed.

Her elder responded, "Jus 'member one thing - no matter how long it takes, one day, deliverance will come. One day, deliverance *will* come," she said emphatically. Rue took another pull on her pipe and exhaled the blue smoke slowly, blowing it reverentially upward to the sky, as if it was carrying her silent prayers toward Heaven.

"Now, as I was sayin'," she continued, "bad ones like Goliath, always want to be in control, and they wants to punish you. But there's more'n one way of makin' rebellion." A devilish grin spread across Mama Rue's face. "But I'll git back to that, later."

Rue went back into the cabin and emerged with a little pouch of dried leaves. "Now, this firs' part you gotta be extra careful 'bout, 'cause you a breedin' woman and thass your job now. Yo' Masta find out about this, be big trouble for you *an'* ole Ruth." Martha Jane looked at Rue as if she were a sorceress. "Plain fact is," Rue continued, "you gotta have *some* babies, an' somma them prob'ly gonna be sold - can't save'm all, daughter. But you can slow down how many you have, or stop havin'em for a spell when you need to. To be born to a life like this? Maybe better not to be born at all," she said wistfully. "God forgive us what we gotta do. But it ain't our fault. He knows it."

Her voice grew stern and serious again as she held up the pouch. "This a special tea, made of wormwood, parsley, and ginger. You drink a lotta this befo' your monthly time and you won't have no babies for a spell." She could see the look of worry and guilt on the younger woman's face.

54

Martha Jane began feebly, "but Mama Rue I don't wanna..."
Rue cut her off brusquely. "I know you a good girl, and this hard for
you, honey. You ain't no harlot, neither was I. But if they know you
got a fertile field, they gonna plow you all the time – won't give you
no rest. They gonna keep sendin' bucks 'til you broken down or too
old to have babies no more. This life an' death, girl," she reprimanded.
"An' nobody's comin' to no slave cabin in the night to save you.

Martha Jane sighed in somber recognition of this inevitable
truth. "I'll give you root medicine to slow the men down, or make'm
drowsy, if you sufferin' an' can't go through it some night. An' I got
somethin' special in mind for Goliath," she said with a sinister smile.

Once you start mornin' sickness, they'll leave you alone 'til
after the baby's born. But don't expect no long rest. They gonna try to
make the most of you in your breedin' years. After they done with
you, they'll send you back out to da fields jus' like the rest. Your real
money-makin' days be over by then." Martha Jane nodded solemnly.
Her face looked as if she had just taken a bite of the apple from the
Tree of Knowledge. It was knowledge she wished she didn't have.

Mama Rue grabbed Martha Jane's arm with an urgency that
startled the younger woman. "Now, you look at me, child, you take a
good look." The women stared at each other's faces intently. You see
these marks on my face? Look like snakes?" Wide-eyed, Martha Jane
nodded timidly as if noticing them for the first time, realizing the
history they represented.

"Why did they do that to you?" Martha Jane asked reluctantly,
dreading the answer. "This what they done to ole Ruth when they
caught me helpin' another poor girl like you," she replied ominously.
Seeing the faraway look in Mama Rue's eyes, Martha Jane watched the
older woman journeying back in time, and she now regretted asking

55

the question. With her eyes now staring into the past, the old witch spoke with a disembodied voice, not her own. The tale she told sounded something like this one...

"Back in the Carolinas, I worked on a farm owned by a terrible man named Blackshear. He was a devil - had no soul if you looked in his eyes. He did things to some of the girls that I won't speak of today. Some of the girls had babies, and it was hard bein' a young mother and workin' the fields every day. So, 'Blackshear had them take their babies with them to them to the field and it was two or three miles from the house to the field. He didn't want them to lose time walking backward and forward nursing. They built a long trough like a great long cradle and put all these babies in it every morning when the mother come out to the field. It was set at the end of the rows under a big cottonwood tree. When they were at the other end of the row, all at once a cloud no bigger than a small spot came up and it grew fast, and it thundered and lightened as if the world were coming to an end, and the rain just came down in great sheets. And when it got so they could go to the other end of the field, that trough was filled with water and every baby in it was floating round in the water, drowned. They never got nary a lick of labor and nary a red penny for any of them babies."[vi]

"That why I started usin' the roots to keep somma those girls from havin' too many babies in too short a time. But don't let'em catch on to you. For God's sake, don't let'em catch you usin' these herbs, or you'll get worse'n me. An' they surely come for me, too. To them, if you ain't makin' babies, you stealin' from'em. You stealin' from the master and costin' him profit. An' that'll be the end of me.

"But turn that leaf over and 'member this too... Any man hurt you real bad, wanna mark you up, maybe cut you or beat you - you tell your master. You tell your master that boy be damagin' his
56

property. An' ain't no buck allowed to do that. You like a prize mare to your master. An' you tell them young men you gonna do it, too - if you have to. But remember, you can't 'cry wolf' too often.

"But like I say, some buck gonna hurt you real bad - you tell your master that boy thinkin' 'bout runnin'. An' they'll believe you 'cause mos' young men natchally think about runnin' sometime. Jus' so you know, if you say that, somethin' bad might happen to him. You gotta do that to save yourself or your baby, then you do it. But jus' know what might happen to him." Her tone was circumspect now.

"I don't allow no man to hurt a woman, but you never know what another slave's been through, neither - even them young men. Sometimes they do terrible things to *them*, too. Maybe they was raped when they was a boy. Or maybe they saw they mama raped or killed. Maybe they was forced to mate wit' a woman, in front'a some white men, all drunk and laughin'. Maybe they was abused somethin' terrible. You never know. You jus' never know. But no slave got a right to make you *his* slave, neither. You gonna be a growed woman soon. An' maybe someday, you be married. Have a baby, a husband, a family of your own. So, you have'ta take care of yourself." Martha Jane couldn't speak after this sermon. Bitter tears fell from her eyes.

"Like I said, there's more'n one way of makin' rebellion," Rue sighed, looking back at Martha Jane with misty eyes. "Come on, chile, it's gettin' late. You stay here the night and walk back in the day light - I'll see ya half way there. Paddyrollers be on the road at night, and they'll gang rape you if they catch you out alone."

They blew out the oil lamps and climbed onto Mama Rue's pallet in the corner of the room, each one's back facing the other. Martha Jane's thoughts were spinning with all she had learned tonight. There was so much more she wanted to know from this woman who was part witch, part fairy godmother. She thought of the ordeals in store for her and wondered if she would survive years of heartbreak and abuse as her mentor had done. How many men and how many babies she would she have? And how many babies might be taken from her? What good man would want her after all that? Rue's mind was racing too, trying hard to shut the flood gates that had unleashed a torrent of painful memories. She could feel Martha Jane's body quivering as she cried silently. The youth was now a breeding woman, 14 years old. Rue turned over and cradled the young woman - still just a girl, really - in her arms, as if Martha Jane was the daughter she lost many long years ago. Clinging tightly to one another, the women wept quietly in the dark.

CHAPTER 9

Goliath

Over the next few days a passion play, of sorts, unfolded. Resigned to her fate, Martha Jane was determined to exert some influence over it. She now had a quiet strength and steely temperament she hadn't had before. She just wished she hadn't waited so long to see Big Mama Rue; but the women now shared a bond, a special knowledge, and a history that made them family. No matter how seldom they saw one other, each carried the other in her heart.

The bully buck of the county was coming back to the cabin again, after his "victory tour" of the region, boxing other young bucks and impregnating other females. The first time he raped her he was ferocious, but after her bite of the apple and the serpent's wisdom, she was ready for him. In fact, she was looking forward to this night of reckoning. She was the huntress now, and he was the game. She had knowledge and knowledge is power - *woman* power.

He expected another spirited night of rough sex when he saw her from afar, standing outside the door of her cabin. His ego told him she was probably coming out to greet him to assuage his contempt for this now muscular farm girl, who needed to be taught another painful lesson. It was still very hot on this late afternoon and his brow dripped with sweat as he strode defiantly down the lane to her cabin, his feet kicking up dust each time they struck the ground.

As he walked up to her door, he ignored the pleasantries of a proper greeting, and simply demanded water - "an' it better be cool," he growled. "You want some water, Goliath?" she asked sweetly.

"I'll get you some water." She turned and walked inside with him following behind, as he again wiped his sweaty brow.

She lifted the lid of a clay pot and ladled out water into a large tin cup - much larger than the wooden cup she typically used for herself - and handed it to him. Like a tree standing in the doorway of the cabin blocking the light, the hulk greedily guzzled down the water in one long gulp. "Gimme more," he growled again. But he didn't see her smile as she dutifully complied. The water was cool and he drank the second cup more slowly. He paused for a moment as if trying to remember something, while making a clicking sound with his tongue against his palate. He peered into the cup. "When's da las' time you wash dis cup, girl? Tastes a little tinny," he griped.

As he stood there in extended contemplation, the light in the cabin seemed to dim and he swayed on his feet. He rubbed his forehead.

"Damn, it's hot out dere," he said. She grabbed his muscular arm and led him to a little wooden chair.

"You been out workin' in the fields all day, Goliath? Sun's powerful hot today. Better sit down." As his legs buckled under him, he dropped onto the chair like a sack of flour hitting the floor, and mumbled something unintelligible.

"Don't worry," she replied, "Martha Jane take good care o' you tonight." The sun was setting as she slowly closed the door without fear. The eerie creaking sound it made drew Goliath's widening eyes toward it as a shadow of doubt fell across his face.

Everything was dark, except for the buzzing of the bees. "But it's almos' night time," he thought. "Ain't no bees out at night." His head rolled like a cannonball on his broad shoulders and felt just

60

as heavy. He hadn't even noticed that his eyes were closed. As his eyelids open slowly, he squinted at the candle sparkling before him.

His breathing was heavy and labored as his chest heaved slowly trying to pull in more oxygen. He felt paralyzed, and he couldn't move his arms or legs. There was a tingling in his hands and feet as if they had gone to sleep. When he looked down he didn't understand why he was now tied to the chair. It didn't make sense. Maybe he was dreaming. Martha Jane came into view carrying a candle, looking demonic as she seemed to float toward him. She had a frightful grin on her face, black smudges under her eyes, and she was humming a weird, otherworldly tune, soft and low. His eyes bulged. His mouth was dry as cotton as he tried to speak, but he couldn't because he'd been gagged. The rag in his mouth had a bitter taste. His breathing grew shallow, and his head ached as if he'd been hit with a horseshoe. He had never felt so weak.

When the demoness spoke he was mesmerized. "Now Goliath, you 'member the last time you was here?" A chill crept through him like an overnight frost. A flurry of pictures flooded his mind. He saw his face contorted with cruelty and anger, shirtless with shoulders heaving. Next he saw Martha Jane younger looking and gripped with fear of the realization that she could not stop what was happening to her. He made some nervous grunts as the images washed over him like hot water. He remembered hitting her hard and her screaming, as he threw her down and pounced on her like she was one of his opponents. His breathing grew rapid and his heartbeats louder now as he saw images he didn't want to remember – of her powerlessness, of what he had done to her with his brute force. His grunts became groans as he began to remember what she had never forgotten.

"Oh, you remember now, don't you Goliath?" she whispered.

"Why she keep sayin' my name like dat, an' hissin' like a snake?" he wondered. His groans became whimpers as his foggy mind slowly pulled the together the pieces of the puzzle. He could hear her distant pleading now echoing in his ears. His muffled words were muted by the gag in his mouth - the mouth that had threatened and screamed and sneered at her. But he wasn't sneering now.

Goliath struggled against his bindings but it was of no use. He was bound tightly to the chair with his arms behind him but the bonds were actually unnecessary - because he was nearly paralyzed by the poison he had unknowingly ingested. He could not have lifted his hand in anger, even if had he wanted to do so. There was no anger in him now. It was extinguished.

The buzzing had finally stopped in his head. However, Goliath now heard the rattling of what seemed like a million cicadas outside the cabin's open window which made his head ache. Twenty miles away in her dimly lit cabin, Big Mama Rue was shaking her turtle shell box and rattling the bones inside. She was mumbling mystical words spoken in a dialect from some country far across the sea. She threw the bones down on the table with a flourish, and began deciphering the foreboding tale they told.

One stood out among the rest - a dark piece of petrified wood positioned awkwardly in the center of the display. She smiled when she whispered the words, "the condemned man." She then closed her eyes to commune with her "sister-daughter" Martha Jane, who had since become a strong young woman - if not in years, now in spirit. "Show'im the doll, daughter, show'im the doll," she whispered more loudly this time.

Martha Jane had her prisoner's full attention now. Gone was his arrogance, his rage, and his contempt for women. However, the

62

lesson had just begun and the night would be long – the longest of his life. When she threw it down on the table his eyes grew as big as saucers. He didn't believe in *Voodoo* – or at least he didn't *want* to believe in it. Yet when he saw the little straw man, with its male appendage protruding, he realized how deeply he was in danger. He knew many slaves believed in it, and their secret ceremonies with blood rituals, speaking in tongues with foaming mouths, and spirit worship were disturbing. In that state they were capable of anything. His mind raced through a dozen possibilities each more horrible than the one before. His eyeballs danced wildly in their sockets.

"This you," she said, holding doll. He moved his head slowly left and right to signal "no," and a muffled "unh-unh" came through the gag in his mouth. "Oh yeah, Goliath, this you." He disagreed again, but more politely this time. She held up the doll. "You the one with the big sword. Use it to hurt me, and a lotta other girls, too. Ain't that right?" He made a confused "yes" then "no" sound that sounded like a dog whimpering. "You don't remember how bad you hurt me last time?" Her voice was creepy and giving him goosebumps.

He whinnied a sound that resembled, "no." She drew out a large knife and continued, "You remember how you said I had to eat that?" He made a more emphatic whimpering sound to indicate "no!" He was terrified of what might come next with this crazy woman and he knew he had to surrender to her and answer carefully now. She held the straw man down on the table and with a decisive blow, cut off its private part. The noise startled him and so did the message.

His muffled moan sounded like a lonely hound, as she pushed the little table out of the way with a sinister and disconcerting smile on her face. She was beyond anger and seemed grow larger as she loomed over him. His gulp could be heard across the room.

With movements as slow and deliberate as a panther, she prowled toward him with the knife and knelt down in front of him, between his legs. She looked up at him with inquisitive eyes. "Do I have to eat it again now?" He shuddered on the chair as if a winter wind had just blown in through the window, and wiggled his head back and forth with short "unh-uns" an octave higher to assure her that was not necessary. Her eyes never left his as she deliberately untied the rawhide strap that served as his belt and pulled it from his waist. With his eyes pleading up toward Heaven, he shimmied like a snake trying to shed its skin, but the poison weighed him down like chain mail and the bindings held him tight like a vice.

She tore open the few wooden buttons that held the front of his pants together, which produced a muffled squeal from her victim. "You like to hurt girls don't you?" she asked accusingly. He eked out a three syllable response that resembled, "no I don't." Now, starkly confronted by all the fear and suffering he had inflicted upon others, his "chickens had come home to roost."

Although she loathed touching him, the lesson had to continue. And she would scrub her hands clean later. It would be her only chance to prevent future abuse from this brute. To her own surprise, Martha Jane continued coolly, "Well, this is what they do to bulls that shouldn't mate no more." She lifted his "family jewels" and put the strap around them. He was in full panic now, squealing like a piglet caught in the jaws of a fox. "You sure you don't want me to eat this now?" He emphatically squeaked, "no!"

"All right then," she responded. "I was hopin' you would say that." She put down the knife, much to his relief, before tying the strap around his "tenderloin" and yanking it tight.

64

He squealed like a girl who just got a diamond for her birthday. "Get comf'table now, it's gonna be a long night." She pushed him and he fell backward onto the dirt floor of the cabin with a thud, still bound tightly to the chair. "An' if you make another sound, I'm gonna cut that snake off and throw it on the coals. An' make you eat it. You hear me?" she yelled. He made a high pitched sound that served as "yes!" "Alright, then," she said, before floating away.

She didn't sleep soundly but it was a more restful night and much different than it would have been had things gone according to his plan. Big Mama Rue was the best root doctor around, and had told Martha Jane precisely which poisonous plants to choose, how much to use, and how long the effects would last. "Don't kill'im," she had said, matter-of-factly. "Just give'm enough to keep'im still and spooked out, then let'im go in the mornin' after you scare the devil outta him. I promise you, he won't be back."

She followed the hoodoo woman's advice and it worked flawlessly. Martha Jane got up a few times during the night to torment him, and loosen the tourniquet around his sore private parts. She didn't want to permanently injure him – she just wanted the experience to be unforgettably painful. At one point she pulled the shirt away from his body and cut it into strips while humming some morose melody. He would have turned white with fear if he could have. She knew no one would bother them because everyone on the plantation knew why he was there, and wouldn't dare to interfere.

He realized this, too. No help was coming for him and his limbs were bound tightly to the chair. The next day would be easy for her because the overseer and others would naturally assume that she would be recovering from a night of barbaric and painful sex, and they would not expect to see her. In fact, it would look suspicious if she went back to the fields in the morning as if nothing had occurred.

Goliath was still fading in and out of the netherworld from the monkshood and other toxins he had ingested as night began to draw to a close with the approach of dawn. But they would be wearing off soon, so Martha Jane was up at first light, ready to let go of her big fish. She still had one more act before her performance was complete.

She put more charcoal dust around her eyes and mussed up her hair and sprinkled it with ashes to make herself look even more deranged. As he opened his eyes, she was standing over him with the knife. He whined because he believed the end was nigh, which is precisely what she wanted him to think. Because, when she opened the trap, she wanted him to run for his life and never look back.

Trussed up like a turkey for Sunday dinner, Goliath now looked like a once swaggering cock whose bright feathers had all been plucked. He had the hang-dog look of a mutt whose master was swinging from the gibbet. As she leaned down with the knife, he closed his eyes as if preparing for the worst, making a sound like a guitar string that was sprung from being stretched to the breaking point. Now he was fervently mumbling some multisyllabic litany of past wrongs for which he was now seeking forgiveness. Once again, she pulled the tourniquet around his loins tight. Too terrified to pass out, he emitted a long, low sound like a muted trumpet and his eyes nearly popped out of their sockets. When she swung the knife down with surprising force, cutting the ropes that bound his useless legs, he squealed like a piglet. Suddenly realizing he had not been castrated, he gazed at her with a mixture of confusion, gratitude, and fear - thinking it was a cruel ruse.

With her knee bearing her full weight upon his chest, she held the knife over his face and spat out her warning with venom.

"If you ever come back here, I'll cut you into a hundred pieces and feed you to the hogs! An' I'll throw the rest of your bones into the swamp with the duppys! An' everybody'll think you just ran away."

He nodded a thousand promises and pardons with a gurgling sound through the dirty, wet rag in his mouth. "Now git the hell outta here!" she shrieked. He emitted a series of panicked staccato protests and then a long, high-pitched whine as she raised the knife high over her head. He slammed his eyes shut and winced as she brought the knife down in a powerful arc that slashed through the ropes holding his useless limbs. Pushing off from his chest, she sprang up and stood back, raising the knife in readiness in case he attacked.

Goliath moved as if he had been struck by lightning. Gasping for air and scuttling around on his back like a giant beetle trying to turn over, his impotent arms were finally able to feebly push himself up onto wobbly legs. The pain from his groin, wrenched by the merciless tourniquet, was excruciating. Some unearthly sound gushed from his lips, ejecting the tainted rag from his mouth with a spray of spit. He then flew out the door as if his manhood was on fire, clutching himself to keep his pants from falling down, and foaming at the mouth as he ran up the path wailing like a siren.

She never saw Goliath again. And somehow, word got around that the biggest, baddest, buck in the county was last seen fleeing her cabin like the Devil was chasing him. Martha Jane was still a breeding woman, and she still had to have babies – but other women now gave her a measure of respect. On her next visit to her sister-mother, Big Mama Rue, the two women laughed about the encounter all evening over dandelion wine. In 1855, when Martha Jane was 15 years old, she gave birth to a baby boy she named George Washington Parham.

CHAPTER 10

Squire Ridley

Life passed by at Boonie Doon more according to the seasons than by the years. The plantation continued to prosper and grow under the watchful eye of Colonel Ridley, and it ran as smooth and steady as a waterwheel. Uncle Robert and Big Mama Rue had grown older and grayer while Brother Daniel had grown from old to ancient. Despite the years, the poor nutrition of their slave diet, and their lot in life, they seemed surprisingly as strong of body and clear of mind as they did the day Cornelius was born. Black Turtle's long braids were now the color of old silver and Uncle Robert said he was going to start calling him "Gray Turtle."

Being a bit younger than her husband, Two Moon's hair was still as dark as raven's wings, but now had silver strands interwoven. Their son, Little Horse, had married a smart, hard-working Chickahominy woman from eastern Virginia named Shenandoah, which meant "daughter of the stars," who was as beautiful as her name implied. The enmity between the Virginia tribes had subsided years ago, hastened in part by the dominion of ever increasing numbers of whites buying, stealing, fencing, and farming the land. Coming in like a rip tide, they pushed the few tribes that were still left onto small reservations. However, Black Turtle couldn't have been more pleased to have a daughter-in-law descended from a warrior race.

Even Big Man's hair was now dappled gray, and he was still following Uncle Robert around like a giant shadow. All these long years he had never spoken a word but his natural personality was as pleasant as a morning in spring, and he never lost his avuncular love for Cornelius. Uncle Robert had been allowed to retire from the fields

68

and now mostly tended his garden, often spending the evenings on Mama Rue's porch, which pleased her greatly.

"Henry, Lula's boy" – as he was always called, because there was more than one "Henry" on the plantation – and the eponymous "Black Bobby" (so-called because his skin was black and there was more than one "Bobby" at Buckhorn) had replaced Uncle Robert as co-foremen of the work crews. They were intelligent, strong, likeable young men, who often sought Uncle Robert's advice whenever there was a difficult logistical problem in the field or forest to be resolved. And they all smiled whenever they saw Cornelius driving by atop Colonel Ridley's carriage. The redhead would doff his hat in respect for the people of the little village that had raised him.

Cornelius had obviously grown since the days when Big Man had to lean down to hold his hand, but he was still not much taller than a jockey. However, one thing that never changed was his circumspect outlook on life and his place on the plantation. He had the same sunny disposition he was born with, and had become a handsome young man. Since he had grown up among the horses and seemed to have a personal knowledge and understanding of each one, the Colonel appointed him carriage driver when Tiberius was too old to continue. However, that wasn't the only reason. Colonel Ridley valued the boy's quick mind and respectful manner. And his keen memory of every major, minor, and back country road insured that he was never lost. It was this geographic knowledge that was most rare for a slave, because the average slave seldom traveled more than five miles from home during the course of an entire lifetime.

Slave holders deliberately kept their "property" ignorant – particularly of the geographic region – because that limited a slave's ability to successfully escape, since most simply didn't know where to run. For Cornelius to be permitted – and trusted – to travel on his own with the modern day equivalent of an expensive limousine around the tri-county region and often beyond was rare, indeed. Ironically, it would precisely be this geographic knowledge that would enable his flight to freedom one day.

Slave or not, as with his sister Rosa, his looks couldn't help but attest that he was a son of the Ridleys. All things considered, he was a suitable choice for a carriage driver, which in some ways made him emblematic of them. As members of the landed gentry in antebellum Virginia, the Ridleys often entertained important visitors on a variety of social, political, and business occasions. For these special events, Cornelius was outfitted with proper livery, and he made a dashing sight. This splendid uniform prompted the old folks to admiringly call him, "Squire Ridley" - because, as in the days of old, he was like the shield bearer for a noble house. It was on just such a trip to Fortsville Plantation that Martha Jane first caught his eye.

Though they were nearly the same age, and had grown up barely 20 miles apart, their lives had been on vastly different trajectories. But even asteroids on different orbits occasionally collide. Although she had visited Big Mama Rue at Buckhorn a few times, she had never seen Cornelius before. Perhaps because on Sundays, he was often at Rock Spring visiting Rosa and Uncle Wilson. However, on this cool, clear morning in the late 1850s, he had arrived at Fortsville like a country zephyr uplifting her spirits. She stood behind Mrs. Mason, straining to get a better look at him without being obvious. One word entered her mind when she spied him - *beautiful.*

The team of horses sauntered up slowly so as not to raise dust. The driver was obviously an experienced one despite his youthfulness. He sat upright and proper in his seat as if he was in church, and wore a cardinal colored shadbelly riding coat with tan lapels that appeared to be leather, although she couldn't be sure from where she was standing. He also wore a tan waistcoat vest underneath with the letter "R" embossed onto it, which made it look like a badge.

A short tan top hat and tall brown leather boots completed the outfit. He doffed his hat respectfully before the carriage came to a complete stop, after which he applied the brake. Romulus, Judge Mason's slave, held the bridle as the driver jumped to the ground and deferentially greeted the hosts. "Judge Mason, sir; Madam Mason: I am Cornelius and my master, Colonel Ridley, desires the pleasure of your company this fine day." The Masons were thoroughly impressed.

Many years later, Martha Jane would tell her granddaughter, "when my eyes fell upon him, I knew he was the one for me." Cornelius was the most amazing creature Martha Jane had ever seen – and like no one else she had ever met. Sure, she had seen men in uniform before – but never a slave and never one so elegant and well-mannered as this one. He reminded her of the little toy soldiers, brightly painted, that young Master Lewis Mason had played with when he was a boy. She silently reprimanded herself for gawking like a fool at this strange visitor, and she noticed her heart beating rapidly, while Cornelius discretely noticed her, too. She helped Romulus load the overnight bags, after he had loaded a small keg of brandy onto the boot in the rear, while Cornelius skillfully assisted Judge Mason and his wife Ann onto the carriage.

Cornelius sprung into the driver's seat, unlocked the brake, and carefully turned the carriage around in front of Lewis Mason and the little group of slaves waving good-bye. He tipped his hat once again and Martha Jane was certain his smile was meant just for her. "I'll be along later in the day, Father," Lewis called after them. A festive occasion was planned at Bonnie Doon that night, featuring a rousing performance by the Virginia Minstrels – who would be stylish in black face, and singing some of their most popular songs, with a dance to be held afterward. In the future, Martha Jane would always try her best to be about whenever Cornelius came to Fortsville to ferry visitors back and forth. She vowed that somehow, some way, some day they would be together – somewhere, very far away.

CHAPTER 11

Blackface and Barbecue

By late in the afternoon the barbecue pits behind the old mansion at Bonnie Doon were glowing red-hot with hardwood coals – oak for heat and pecan for flavor. Serving as pit boss, Uncle Robert issued orders like he was conducting a military campaign, but he didn't need to shout, because when Uncle Robert spoke, everyone listened. The house cooks normally supervised the preparations but on special occasions, the old man commanded the barbecue pits.

There was nothing Colonel Ridley liked more than the barbecue sauce concocted by Big Mama Rue. It was a recipe that included tomatoes, molasses, brown sugar, cider vinegar, coffee, juniper berries, and a few secret herbs and spices that she swore she would never divulge even under the threat of torture. As they often did over the years, Uncle Robert and Mama Rue – who once seemed like polar opposites – found increasing comfort in each other's company. Whenever she got a little too familiar with him, he'd warn her that "I'm no young buck anymore, Rue."

And she would respond coyly, "An' you ain't no old plow horse, neither – you still got a few more miles left in you, Robert." Each had finally been able to put aside the profound pain in their respective lives and create a companionship as warm as a handmade quilt. Whatever they did together was usually for the benefit of all. So, he supervised the men and she directed the women, with both insisting on order, speed, neatness, and attention to detail.

According to the Colonel's wishes, the slaves had slaughtered a couple of fat calves, two or three large hogs, and a gaggle of plump chickens. A trespassing deer shot for eating tender shoots of newly sprouted corn rounded out the larder. Nobody roasted venison like Uncle Robert. There were root vegetables, sweet potatoes, spring peas and green onions, biscuits and butter, red velvet cake and rhubarb pie, cool root beer that had been stored in the spring house, and sassafras tea sweetened with honey, with a sprig of fresh mint adorning every glass. For the guests there was beer and wine. But special guests would be treated to brandy and cigars later in the library.

The arrivals began to pour in, conveyed by carriages that were parked behind the barn after discharging their passengers. The Ridleys received them warmly and their young driver, looking resplendent in his uniform, helped to set the tone for their guests' arrival. The most welcome visitor of all for Cornelius was his sister Rosa, who had accompanied Robert Ridley's widow, Mrs. Ann Eliza Blunt Ridley, to the party as her maidservant. His heart leaped when he saw Rosa and she took his hand as she descended the carriage steps after her mistress.

Cornelius was frequently sent on errands to fetch guests or deliver goods and messages among the five Ridley plantations, in addition to those of their friends, business associates, and relatives – like the Mason's Fortsville plantation, or Ann's parents' home at Elm Yard in Greensville County. Thus, Cornelius and Rosa were kept increasingly apart and busy with their respective duties. However, if Cornelius seemed the quintessential herald of this noble house, Rosa made a most elegant lady-in-waiting.

Older than Cornelius by two or three years, she had grown tall and willowy, with chestnut hair flowing from under her bonnet, adorning her shoulders. Her skin was a soft *café-au-lait*, her lips the color of rosebuds, with eyes that sparkled like serpentine gemstones declaring Ridley descent. Much like Cornelius' innate ability to put

74

others at ease, Rosa's contralto voice was as soothing and mellifluous as a clarinet.

She was of marriageable age but had escaped the fate that had befallen Martha Jane. Although not to the same extent as her brother, Rosa was allowed a certain leniency and privilege as a child of the clan. Though no promises had been made, all assumed that she and Cornelius would follow in the footsteps of Brother Daniel and his sister Aunt Jo, who had been valued for their handsomeness, interpersonal skills, and personalities as well as the admiration it engendered from other planters for the patrician Ridleys. Because, the siblings provided proof that despite the necessary evils of slavery, the institution was not limited to brutal beatings and breeding - as northern abolitionists preferred to portray it. This gave these refined members of southern gentry a healthy measure self-deception that they were actually lifting up the most promising of these lowly creatures to a higher level self-actualization and personhood - blackface comedy tonight, notwithstanding.

Although the Virginia Minstrels would bring musicians with them, on such occasions, Colonel Ridley often wanted to hear the music of a few of his talented slaves as well. "Sailor" played the fiddle, which he had learned from Brother Daniel; and "Banjo Joe" needed no introduction, though his name was sometimes shortened to "Jo-Jo." There was a tan-colored lass with long black braids and a silky voice who sometimes sang with them. And "Po' Boy" pounded a drum made from an old wooden bucket - the bottom of which had been removed, and a piece of cow hide stretched tightly across the top. But the drum was strictly regulated and primarily used when entertaining the Colonel and his guests. Southerners refused to let slaves use drums freely for fear they would foment sedition through cryptic messages.

On special occasions, the Colonel allowed the slaves to play the drum a bit when making music down in the Quarters but that was the only time the drum was ever heard there. A lanky fellow called "Long John" was adept with the Jew's harp. His long legs also made him quite a stepper, and so were his young sons who must have had real names but were always called "Hambone" and "June Bug." The youngsters delighted folks down in the Quarters with their "high steppin" – each one trying to outdo the other, and sometimes, the Colonel would call for the boys to perform for his guests, as well.

A cadre of neatly dressed slaves served the guests seated at long rows of tables outside. It was a perfect spring evening with a gentle breeze, and since clouds of hungry mosquitoes hadn't yet hatched in the swamp, Colonel Ridley decided to host this portion of the party outdoors. It would also make for less mess inside his stately old Virginia home. Besides, a country barbecue always tasted better outdoors. After the feast, guests could rinse their hands in mint-infused water and retire indoors for entertainment and dancing.

Evening fell gently and the lavender sky was sprinkled with tiny twinkling stars that grew brighter as the night wore on. The popping hardwood coals fed by animal fat crackled and hissed, shooting sparks skyward, only to reach their zenith and drift slowly down, glowing like fireflies. The plantation was a beehive of activity with platters of food coming and going, and pitchers being passed down the length of the long rows of tables.

Torches were lit, the guests grew happy, and guards were let down by the overwhelming ambiance of good food and drink. The slaves executed their duties flawlessly, with a ready smile and respectful nod of the head in the event their eyes accidently met those of a guest. The trio of bondsmen played their instruments at just the right volume so as to not interfere with conversation, but their music

76

still encouraged lighthearted toe-tapping. A convoy of carcasses and containers moved methodically up from some other part of the farm; trash and bones traversed the return route for disposal. The slave labor was a symphony of movement, coordination, ebb and flow.

As the sky grew dark and when the guests had feasted their fill, Colonel Ridley cordially invited everyone inside as the musicians for the Virginia Minstrels could be heard tuning their instruments. Tonight, his guests would be treated to the songs of Daniel Emmett, Stephen Foster, and Thomas "Daddy" Rice. The Minstrels, painted in blackface, would step and dance and engage in tomfoolery just like "coons on de ole plantation, good Lawd," as one performer promised. There was nothing the blacks could do about these insults but hide their contempt behind obligatory smiles, or pretend not to see.

Inside, the show was getting started; while outside, the army of chefs and servers now moved at double-time to clean up the remains of the banquet so they could have a little time to enjoy the music before heading off to bed back down in the Quarters. Not a cup had been dropped, not a dish had been broken, and not a single guest had voiced a complaint. Quite the contrary – they marveled at the culinary skills of the Ridley slaves and their level of preparedness, organization, and execution that perilously challenged their beliefs about the capability of black people's brains. The service would not have been better at the best restaurant in Richmond. A few of the gentlemen flipped a coin to a server here and there, and a couple of the ladies made a point to compliment Big Mama Rue and Uncle Robert personally.

Before heading inside, Colonel Ridley gave a grateful wink to his two gray-haired field commanders, which signified that ample leftovers would be sent down to the Quarters tonight, and so would a keg of root beer that hadn't been emptied. If the night ended as well as

77

it began, he might allow them a full day off next Saturday, instead of just the customary half-day. This was a significant gathering for him, and far from just a social event. For, late into the night over brandy and cigars, he and other prominent business, political, and military leaders would discuss their growing concerns about the gathering storm that threatened to tear the nation asunder.

"Light Horse Harry" Lee's son, Robert E., was expected to be among them; and so was Colonel Ridley's teenaged nephew, Robert Ridley, Jr. – son of the Colonel's late brother. This young future warrior would earn noteworthy acclaim as a cadet at the esteemed Virginia Military Institute, who along with 240 others, would fight valiantly at the Battle of New Market in the Shenandoah Valley Campaign, where they would suffer heavy losses while capturing a battery of Federal artillery.[vii] Robert E. Lee's military career, however, would earn him mythic status in Southern history.

The Minstrels were in full swing now and the crowd was loving it. They were on a tour of Virginia and had already performed before packed theaters in Richmond and Petersburg. After this private party, their next show was in Norfolk. The enthusiastic hand clapping and foot stomping, punctuated by an occasional "Rebel yell" could be heard far afield through the open windows that rattled as if an earthquake was underway.

The guests held their sides as they responded with deep belly-laughs at the comic contortions of the bobbing heads, wiggling white gloves, and the exaggerated mouths of the bug-eyed black-faced performers. Song after song regaled the audience. Stephen Foster's *Camptown Races*, Dan Emmett's *Blue Tail Fly* and *Ol' Dan Tucker*, and *The Old Oaken Bucket* by Samuel Woodward and G.F Kiallmark, were clearly popular with the crowd. But when the band kicked off *Turkey in the Straw*, Mrs. Ridley feared her French chandelier would

78

fall and shatter from the pulsing vibrations of heavy boots pounding the floor.

Outside under the stars and ringed by torches, the blacks were having a party of their own a short distance behind the big house. They had made a small platform by using the tops of two makeshift wooden tables placed tightly together on the ground. Dancers were taking their turns struttin' and steppin', surrounded by dozens of perfectly-timed pairs of clapping brown hands. During the brief intermission, one of the Minstrels stepped outside to catch a breath of fresh air and run his neckerchief under the pump at the horse trough to soak it in cool water to daub the back of his neck. Before he could ask, Hambone magically appeared like a genie with a clean towel draped over his left arm and a cup of cold well water in his right hand. The performer was pleasantly surprised.

"Suh," said Hambone with well-hidden sarcasm sounding like utmost respect, while appropriately looking down at the ground; "you is a mighty fine dancer. Mighty fine, suh!" The man took the towel and sopped up the sweat from around his neck, careful not to smudge his brightly painted white lips or the black greasepaint on his face. With a patronizing smile he replied, "you keep practicin' boy, and maybe one day you'll learn a step or two." Hambone replied graciously, "thank you suh, good evenin' to you suh," as the man strode away. When his brother June Bug walked up, Hambone rolled his eyes and said, "Come'on June Bug, let's show'em how to do it."

They ran back behind the house and alighted on the little wooden platform like finches, with fellow slaves urging them on with rousing music of their own. Not only did the boys accurately mimic the white dancers they had spied through an open window, their step-dancing was far more fluid and syncopated.

After playing the Jew's harp, their daddy Long John took over. His legs were so pliant it appeared as if they had no bones. With Sailor raging on the fiddle and Jo-Jo's blistering banjo, Po' Boy thumped the drum to complete the ever-increasing speed and intensity of the rhythm. When Long John's two sons rejoined him to finish the jig, black and brown faces broke into beautiful smiles and their laughter brought them heartfelt, if momentary, pride and joy. Even a few of the white guests who had ventured outside to cool off – like the widow Ann Ridley, accompanied by her servant Rosa – joined in the applause, before retreating inside for the second half of the Virginia Minstrels' performance.

The evening rendered artistic representations of two different cultures sharing the same space. The white men danced with perfect timing, but their bodies were rigid and less fluid in their movements, and they stomped their feet as if they were angry with the floor. But when the blacks danced, it seemed more like a celebration of the freedom of physical movement and a syncopation of rhythm that had muscle and sinew working outside the customary boundaries of time and limitations of joints. Their happy feet stroked and polished the makeshift wooden platform instead of punishing it.

The two distinct groups of musicians also played differently. The whites performed with perfect pitch and timing, precisely as the music was written, but it had a utilitarian feel to it. By contrast, the black banjo and fiddle players sometimes suspended certain chords, or would bend certain notes, pushing the string upward instead of traditionally holding it in place; allowing their music a level of freedom from the confines of convention that they themselves could never enjoy. At times, one stringed instrument would pause in mid-chorus to allow the other to complete its musical phrase.

This displayed a certain "cat and mouse" or contrapuntal playfulness between them; but both always managed to return to their respective parts on time by the end of the bar. Sometimes a white musician would scrutinize Sailor's fingering, baffled by his improvisation. Frustrated by his inability to follow the fiddler's logic or technique, the white musician would turn away in disgust declaring, "that nigra don't know how to play proper music." But Sailor explained the difference in style by comparing the way a white cook might fix collard greens versus the way Big Mama Rue made them: "same greens, jus' different seasonin'."

Toward the end of the minstrel show, the frantic pace slowed for two sentimental standards. When the entertainers launched into Stephen Foster's *Old Folks at Home* (commonly referred to as *Swanee River*) it provoked much silent eye-rolling among the crowd out back.

"I sure wish dey'd try pickin' a hunnerd yards o' cotton, an' see how bad dey wanna go home," someone sneered in a stage whisper. Perhaps it was the closeness of room, or the effects of the abundant alcohol that had been imbibed, but the nostalgia that some of the guests felt during the performance of *Old Black Joe,* that provoked many a misty eye and longing looks between spouses and sweethearts who lovingly held hands and envisioned an imaginary South that was beloved, even by their adoring slaves.

How deeply they cherished the fictional protagonist of the ballad stood in stark contrast when juxtaposed with the reality of the lives of the blacks they considered little more than beasts of burden, who labored from dawn until dusk to make this Southern incarnation of the Roman Empire possible. This was a mythical homeland that would exist in the imaginations of some whites for a dozen decades to come.

The final number was Dan Emmett's extraordinarily popular *I Wish I Was in Dixie* - reportedly a favorite of even President Lincoln - which was slowly becoming the standard of increasingly militant Southerners, bringing the crowd to its feet. The audience inside the house clapped, cheered, and whistled for a full ten minutes or more afterward. Standing outside by the hitching post alone, Cornelius felt a vague and inscrutable unease, as if he could hear the moody rumblings of a storm still miles away.

The slaves cleared away the last of the banquet tables and made certain the area was pristine. Supervised by Big Mama Rue, the leftover victuals were carried in a procession back to the Quarters on tired but happy shoulders with torch bearers lighting the way, bringing to mind a safari on the savannahs of Africa. Like the caboose at the end of a train, Big Man proudly pushed a wheelbarrow carrying the promised keg of root beer, with a rare grin from ear to ear, humming a melody known only to him. Uncle Robert and the field hands made certain the charcoals from the barbecue pits were covered and out for good, posing no threat to the barn or the big house. Since Colonel Ridley was already engaged in discussion, Mrs. Ridley came out to dismiss the servants for the night.

Cornelius and a few of the stable hands methodically helped most of the guests onto their horses and carriages, offering them deferential good-byes and sending them on their way. He and Rosa shared a few private moments together and vowed to try to see each other more often before saying good-bye. She had been told that Colonel Ridley wanted to see her soon, and she hoped that meant that she would be brought back to Bonnie Doon, and closer to Cornelius.

Led by the Colonel, a dozen or more gentlemen withdrew to the library for brandy and cigars, political strategy and sedition.

"Thank the Lord tomorrow is Sunday," Cornelius thought to himself. He wouldn't be called to drive the Masons back home until after supper at Noon. As he trudged back to his cabin next to the stables, he recalled the details of a very long day, culminating with the gift of seeing his sister again. However, the image that remained foremost in his mind was the striking, dusky young woman with the high cheekbones of a West African princess he had caught a glimpse of when he arrived at Fortsville. There was yet another storm brewing – but this one was in his heart. And he would make certain he would see her again.

CHAPTER 12

Day the Sun turned Blue

One night on the front porch of Mama Rue's cabin, Cornelius asked Uncle Robert about what happened the night General Nat came to Bonnie Doon. Slaves were strictly forbidden to talk about the Insurrection and would be severely punished if caught doing so. He had asked Uncle Robert before but the old man had always parried the inquiry without responding, because he had wanted to wait until Cornelius was older, so he would fully understand the complex reply. But on this particular night when Cornelius asked him, Uncle Robert looked up at the stars, took a long pull on his pipe, thoughtfully exhaled a puff of blue smoke, and with sad eyes that betrayed this was a painfully vulnerable moment, he slowly unfolded the tale.

"That happen in 18 and 31 – eight years 'fore you was born, son. I 'member that night. Fact is, I'll never be able to forget it, that's for darn sure. Wish I could. It was like the Devil was loose in the land." He paused for a moment trying to determine how best to begin.

"Nat was a peculiar man, unlike anyone else 'round here. Thought'a himself a prophet. Maybe God did talk to him – I don't know. But he wuddn't no stranger to me. I known'im fo' years. We was 'bout the same age. Mr. Ben Turner owned him – an' his grandmama – Old Bridgit. She were from Africa; was a princess, I think, come from mighty proud people – fierce, warrior people – live far across the sea."

He sighed wearily before resuming the memory. "There was a e-clipse o' the sun that winter. I seen'em before. Jus' Nature workin'; it jus' happens sometimes. You see, the sky is like God's pocket watch. Lot goin' on up there. An' everything has its season, the Bible say.

84

"Well, one day that summer," his voice grew quiet, "the sun turned blue in the sky. Darndest thing I ever did see. Don't know why it happen. Never seen that before nor since. Nat said it was a sign for him to start a holy war. Him an' his men was comin' 'round all the farms tryin' to rally the slaves to join their 'rebellion.' But the whites called it an 'insurrection.' Mighty big difference in meanin'.

"By God it was a fearsome sight - some had blood on'em already - an' lookin' for more. Some had hatchets, others had knives, clubs. A couple was carryin' sickles. Nat was ridin' a horse - he had a sword. A few of 'em had guns. But they didn't wanna use'm - 'cause'a da noise. They wanted to kill, quiet like. They wassa grim lookin' bunch - like they was ready'ta murder anybody stood in their way. It scared me, son. It scared me real bad." He looked into the young man's eyes as if pleading for help. Cornelius had never seen fear before in Uncle Robert's face.

"Felt like the whole world was comin' to an end. Like it was Judgment Day. How you prepare for somethin' like that? Or know what to do? Ain't nobody ever seen nothin' like that happen before 'round here. Sure, I'd risk my life if it was worth it; but I ain't gonna *throw* it away. If we'd joined'em, we'd been swingin' on the gibbet, too.

"An' for what rebellion? What freedom? An' go where? Ain't many of us know the roads 'roun' here or been far from home like you, son. What about our old folk? How they gonna get there? Who gonna carry'em? Who gonna feed'em? Mr. Nat didn't think about that. No sir, he didn't. I tole'im, 'you wanna start a war to free all the slaves, I understands that. We all wanna be free. But there's a whole lotta chil'ren an' ole folks who can't go on the warpath with you.'"

He again lowered his voice. "Now, you lissen careful to what I'm sayin' here, son. I ain't sayin' Nat was a bad *man*. I'm sayin' he had

85

a bad *plan*. Had that fire in his eyes like John Brown. But there wasn't no possible chance o' winnin'. What Nat have? Couple dozen men, maybe a little more - one horse, few muskets, no maps? Hell," he paused, turning his head momentarily to spit a little piece of tobacco from his mouth, "he couldn't even whup the *paddyrollers* with that little bitty 'army,' let alone the Southampton Militia, with all their soldiers, guns, an' horses. 'Specially, up ag'inst a milit'ry man like yo' pappy? His posse jus' *call* Nat a 'General' - but he weren't no soldier. Heck, yo' pappy was a Major then - a *real* Major - just like his pappy, an' his pappy before him. Soldierin's in the Ridley blood. An' there wuddn't no Union Army to go run off to then, like there is now. Southampton Militia was the *only* army 'round' these parts then.

"'Course, it all ended pretty quick - by your pappy an' the militia. Nat hid out in the swamp a month or two, a'fore they caught'im. Had a quick trial down the Court House in Jerusalem. I was surprised they give'im a trial at all," he said bemusedly. "You know how angry white people can get. After the trial they hung his head from a tree out there on the big road," he said, pointing with his pipe stem. "So everybody can see." His voice began wavering now.

"But first, they took off all his skin, an' cut'im up in quarters - some say, while he was still alive. I wouldn't doubt it. The white people had blood lust somethin' terrible, then. An' there's a whole lotta paddyrollers 'round here got tobacco pouches made from Nat's skin - like some kinda trophy." Cornelius swallowed hard, trying to repress his gag reflex. "Thass true. There some *real* evil devils 'round here who should have'ta reap what they sew.

"Ever'body was afraid to say a word. Even Black Turtle an' his people made theyselves scarce for a while 'cause they didn't wanna get caught up in all that fury. Anybody black, brown, or red was fair game for lynchin'. Didn't matter who. It was just'a excuse to murder a whole lotta innocent black folk - like the *two hunnerd* other slaves who didn't have *nothin'* to do with Nat, who they hung for 'good measure.' 'To setta 'xample for us, so we don't forget,' they said!" he declared ardently and teary-eyed. "Forget? How anybody ever gonna forget somethin' like that?"

"Then later on, some was whisperin' that we was cowards - that the Ridley slaves was all cowards. An' there weren't no white people sayin' it, neither. It were black folk. Our *own* people," he said thumping his chest. "They could point a finger at me, but nunna them joined up with Gen'l Nat, either. Somma them known me twenny year or more!" He looked at Cornelius in bewilderment. "Other slaves, who ain't got no power. People jus' like us, who know what we go through, day after day, year after year," he said, perplexed. Anger smoldered in his eyes. "'Course, didn't nobody say nothin' to my face - jus' behind my back. But I heard it all the same." He paused to puff on his pipe, bolstering himself so he could finish the tragedy.

"Well, they can *all* go to Hell, far as I'm concerned." Pointing his pipe stem at Cornelius, he said, "First of all, there wuddn't no possible way a gettin' outta that hornet's nest alive. Ev'ry slave know he can die any time, jus' fo' lookin' at a white man the wrong way, or God forbid, some white *woman*. We know our life hang by a thread slimmer than spider silk. Fear is our constant companion.

"By God, inna lotta ways, I'm dead already. Been dead a long time! Lost my wife and my boys years ago." Cornelius' face was full of questions - he had never heard Uncle Robert talk about his family. So, the old man explained, "We was slaves in Carolina, down on the Cape Fear River. Overseer dragged my wife off one night. She knew what was comin' - he'd been watchin' her a long time. I tried to stop it. But they whipped me good. *Real* good. Sold her off to one farm an'

87

our boys to another. She went out an' hung herself. That broke my heart," he said, with his voice cracking, followed by a long pause.

"After that, to keep me from causin' any more trouble, they had me sold to some slave traders who turned around an' sold me North to the Ridleys at a profit. But before they took me away, I got me some revenge, yes sir, I got me some revenge." His eyes flashed heat lightning.

"They had me tied up in a shack all by myself, with the slave traders comin' for me in the mornin'. After it got good an' dark when nobody was around, I licked my wrists 'til they was slippery wet, slipped my bonds, went down to the river an' got me a candy stick." Seeing the confusion on Cornelius' face, Uncle Robert explained.

"Candy stick is what we call a coral snake. Got red, black, and yella stripes. Rue knows. She seen'em down in South Carolina where she come from." Arms akimbo, Mama Rue nodded in silent assent. "Awful lotta snakes down there boy," Uncle Robert continued, "an when you in the fields all day, you gotta learn'em right quick or you die. Down there they say look at the stripes on'em. 'Red touch yella - kill a fella. Red touch black - friend o' Jack.' That's how you tell'em apart from a kingsnake. They look alike, but the kingsnake is harmless. A candy stick's got more poison than a cottonmouth or a water moccasin and they don't make no rattle to warn you, neither."

I snuck over to the overseer's cabin in the darkness, like the Grim Reaper. I know he comin' back late an' drunk with whiskey an' hate after hurtin' some other poor young gal. So, I put that snake in his bed, pulled the blanket up real tight so it couldn't move none - an' I smacked it couple times, make it real mad. Then I slipped back to my shack and put the ropes back on me, 'cause gettin' sold off the next day was my ticket outta there. An' they was takin' me in the right

88

direction, too - farther north - closer to the Mason-Dixon line. Maybe from there, who knows what I could do?

"After he stumbled back to his cabin and jump in that bed, I heard him screamin' 'bloody murder' in the middle of the night - an' I knew that candy stick got'em. An' got'im good. Wuddn't nothin' nobody could do - doctor's too far away. An' the doctor couldn't help him, no-how. Poison work too fast. They say he suffered somethin' terrible in that bed with that poison burnin' through'im like hellfire, 'til he finally died at dawn. Guess he thought dyin' was a blessin' - 'cause it was a long, hard death. Nobody ever suspected me - nobody, 'cept the overseer - 'cause I was tied up when they checked on me. But dead men tell no tales," he said ominously, with quiet satisfaction.

"Never did see my boys again - heard they both died. Don't even know where, 'xactly." He looked up at Cornelius. "So, what I got to look forward to in life 'cept this," he said with the hands raised, palms up, like a supplicant. "What slave don't wanna be free?" he asked, in a strained whisper, thick with emotion. "What slave don't dream o' freedom every night? White like you or black like me - who don't wanna be free?" he asked, with a tinge of anger in his voice and in his stare. "Ain't nobody *wanna* be a slave. Least nobody I know."

He was visibly shaken now. "I might be a slave here," he said, tapping the arm of his rocking chair, symbolizing the plantation. "But I ain't no slave here" - he tapped his temple with his right forefinger. "Or here," he said, pointing to his heart.

"So, I ain't sayin' I never wanted to kill no cracker," he confessed with a conspiratorial look. "Plenty o' times I did. An' once, I did do it - for what was done to me and mine, sure 'nuf. An' I ain't sorry 'bout it, neither - I'm jus' sorry I couldn't kill'im twice. They's a few bad ones 'round these parts could use some whippin' or killin'," he

89

said in a low and menacing tone. "Give'm a taste of they own medicine. They'd deserve it, too. An' I ain't the only one feels that way," he said, looking around cautiously. "It ain't no crime to beat a slave to death, rape a black woman, kill a black baby. No suh! They can do want they wants with their 'property.' But an 'eye for an eye' the Bible says." Cornelius was wide-eyed at this rare glimpse into Uncle Robert's past.

"But the time Nat come to Buckhorn, the price o' freedom was high that night, son. Yes suh. Mighty high!" He rocked once or twice in his chair, staring into the past, then stopped and looked Cornelius directly in the eyes again. "Too steep for me, Cornelius. Lord have mercy. I knowed a lotta them white chil'ren all they lives! Hell, I help raise somma them. So, how I'm s'posed to grab them by the throat, an' look into them little eyes filled with tears and fear - as they askin' me, why I'm killin' them? 'Why, Uncle Robert, why's you doin' this to me?' - beggin' for they lives - his eyes wide and voice choked with emotion. He shook his head. "I couldn't. That'd haunt me the rest of my life.

"Somma them Ridley young'uns, I taught'em how to fish. Spent hours with'em, jus' like I done with you. They talk to me all about they lives, an' I give'm advice. An' they *lissen* to me - more'n they lissen to they own pappy. When they was li'l pups, settin' on my knee, they called me 'Uncle Robert.' An' they meant it! *They* didn't make me no slave! That weren't *their* fault what happen to me before they was born. An' they can't escape it, neither. They's slaves, too, in a way. Slaves to this way of life.

"But they can't love me *and* slavery at the same time - an' that's what I'm tryin' to teach'em - widdout sayin' it, mind you, 'cause I can't say it aloud. But I want'em to see my face in the face of every other slave they see. I want'em to look at us as *people* - not jus' like animals or property. 'Cause God made *us* too, jus' like He made *them*.

90

"I love somma them chil'ren like they was my own. In some ways, maybe they is - by bond if not by blood. Somma our women folk like Rue here, took care of a lotta them ol' white people. Cleaned'em, bathed'em, doctored'em, fed'em - when they was too sick to feed theyselves. Somma our girls nursed a lotta them white babies, because they own mommas didn't have no milk to give'm. Sometimes, a white baby and a colored baby be nursed from the same breast, an' then play together as chil'ren. They didn't know no different 'til they got bigger an' growed up some. You know - you played with'em 'round here when you was little. Then the white chile go off to school, an' the colored stay in the Quarters. Like a fork in the road, they go separate ways in life. They remember how it was, but they can't turn the clock back. Like it or not, right or wrong, that's jus' the way it be," he said, sounding somber and circumspect.

"What about you, Cornelius? Could you kill your pappy, Colonel Ridley? He don't *say* he your pappy, but he been pretty good to you, son. I truly believe he loved your momma, God rest her soul," he said solemnly, looking up toward Heaven.

"Maybe he didn't show it right, an' maybe he couldn't. But mos' folks 'round here don't hold it ag'inst you, that you his son. He treat you pretty good by my way'a reckonin.' An' he should. You a good son! But jus' 'cause he own you, that make it right for you to murder him in his bed?" Pausing, he added: "Gets complicated, don't it?" Cornelius could only nod sadly in agreement.

"Life ain't black an' white - an' neither is most people. It's a whole lotta shades in between. Sometime, a shackle ain't jus' the kind you see. Sometime, there's another kind that binds people together, no matter who they are. Them heavy chains is jus' makin' us black folk more determined to be free. But for the white folks, slavery like a

91

chain around their necks draggin'em down. One day a storm's gonna come with fire an' sword, an' a army bigger than Pharoah's gonna put slavery down, set us free. Wish Nat could'a lived to see it," he mused.

"I can't do the kinda evil these white men do. I gotta answer for my sins come Judgment Day! I jus' couldn't kill no white chil'ren, or some feeble ol' white woman who soils herself; or some young white lady with babies, scared to death. That's who got killed mostly, you know," he said with disdain. "Women an' chil'ren, hacked to death. Chopped up in pieces, an' slaughtered like hogs." His pursed lips were trembling as he was on the verge of tears.

His voice rose with anger. "So, I don't give a good goddamn *who* thinks I'm a coward 'cause the rest of us here, an' over at Master Robert's at Rock Spring - like your Uncle Wilson - defended these houses and protected our white people. An' if the white people wanna think we was just bein' good nigras, then go ahead an' let'em think that! But we also did it to try to save somma our own people, 'cause we knew what was comin' next. We jus' couldn't save the 200 innocent ones who didn't rise up in rebellion, but still got hanged anyway." He was silent for long moment. "Like I said, they weren't no strangers to us. They was folks we knew, friends we had, people we loved."

The tracks of his tears on his brown weather-beaten cheeks glistened in the moonlight as he rocked gently in his chair, trying to regain his composure. His temples were pounding. He took a long pull on his pipe, exhaling blue smoke and staring someplace deep inside where he had made a tenuous peace with himself long ago, for the choices he made that hot summer night. He then continued his story.

"I ain't one of Colonel Ridley's runnin' dogs, an' he know that. But he didn't forgit what somma us did that night, neither. So, he put me in charge of the work gangs; let me help our people out a little bit here an' there. He ask me my opinion sometime – jus' like wit Rue." She nodded silently. "He don't always agree, but he *lissen* to us, an' he take our word same as a white man's. Now, that *means* somethin' 'round here. An' sometime, it can mean the diff'rence 'tween life an' death. Thass a fact, son. Now, is that all I want? No! But it's all I got.

"*Nobody* should never have'ta live the life of a slave, from cradle to grave. From the moment you start thumpin' in yo' momma's belly, you already a slave. I had'ta make a choice that night, best I could. There wasn't no 'good' choice. Somma us saw things diff'rently from Nat, an' not jus' 'cause we was 'afraid.' Hell, we live every single day of our lives in fear. Doin' all that killin' wasn't gonna set us free."

He looked into Cornelius' eyes imploringly and the trauma that still haunted him, like an ice pick pierced Cornelius to the bone. "We had to make them little coffins for the children, an' dig all them graves – for their people *and* ours. We had to bathe the bodies of our people an' lay them in their graves. I can't never sweep that outta my mind." He continued rocking slowly in his chair, with watery eyes, envisioning phantoms Cornelius could not see. "So, now you knows why I never wanna talk about it before, son," he said gravely. "'Cause life can be so god-damn ugly sometimes." He wiped his eyes with the cuff of his sleeve, sniffed quietly, and tried to clear his throat.

Uncle Robert would say nothing more the rest of the night. Cornelius deeply regretted causing the old man he loved to relive so much pain. And it was one of those rare times when Mama Rue stood silent, with tears in her eyes. But her heart ached for Robert.

CHAPTER 13

What the right hand giveth...

Cornelius looked forward to his trips to Fortsville, each time trying to seek out Martha Jane. As time wore on, he came to understand her lot on the plantation, but that didn't diminish his growing love for her. He could discern the goodness and decency in her face as well as the pain in her eyes for what she endured. Although he would soon be of marriageable age, his options were limited. White women were out of the question, and there were few mulattos like him among the local female slave populations, because the masters always wanted them to serve as concubines. Any who weren't, could easily be sold at great profit - especially to planters or prominent businessmen in New Orleans - to be wives, mistresses, or prostitutes in high class brothels that served an upscale clientele. At any rate, they would fit easily into that multiracial society, perhaps eventually being absorbed by the *gens de couleur libre* - slave descendants of French gentry who became "free people of color" - where they would have much more mobility than in the rigid social strata of Virginia.

However, the color of one's skin was of no concern to him because he knew, like the duties demanded by their masters, slaves had no say about either, and that each color was an accident of birth. One's color, stature, mental or physical capacities determined how a slave would be used on a plantation. They were all a part of a community of slaves who, had they been given a choice, would have chosen any other life but this one. What mattered to him more was how he treated others and how they treated him in return. Brother Daniel had taught him the Golden Rule, and Cornelius was determined to live by it.

Although he had many weighty responsibilities, Cornelius was also given many privileges by his Master, which he neither asked for nor expected. Indeed, this may have accounted in part for their fondness of him, and why they considered him an asset and not a liability. Deep down, he hoped his connection to the Ridleys and his loyalty and devotion to them would result in some modest reward, such as allowing him to marry Martha Jane and deliver her from her particularly repugnant brand of bondage. Perhaps he could find a way to earn a little money each year until he could save up enough to buy their freedom, and he began doing so on his time off.

As spring turned to summer their courtship bloomed and they periodically found ways of spending a little time together. A few times a year she was able to get to Bonnie Doon to stay over on Saturday nights at Big Mama Rue's, where he was always welcome to visit her. And they conducted themselves with a formality and properness their elders admired, giving credence that these young people were indeed in love and one day should be allowed to marry.

One fine Saturday afternoon, the following year, they found themselves standing before Brother Daniel, surrounded by two dozen or more other slaves, behind the big house at Bonnie Doon with Colonel and Mrs. Ridley as the guests of honor. At the back of the little crowd were Black Turtle and his wife Two Moons, their son Little Horse, and his wife Shenandoah cradling their baby in her arms. Cornelius wore a clean white shirt with long sleeves, open at the neck, with his tan riding pants and tall leather boots. Martha Jane wore a simple calico frock tied at the waist with a ribbon, and a delicate pattern encircling the shoulders and the hem below that had been hand-printed on using pokeberry dye. In her hair she wore a garland of spring flowers that had been woven together, and on her feet were a pair of wedding moccasins Two Moons had made for her.

With Brother Daniel officiating, Uncle Robert and Mama Rue stood by as parents of both the bride and groom, since Martha Jane's father had passed on last year and her mother was in poor health. Looking radiant, Cornelius' sister Rosa stood next to Martha Jane. His Uncle Wilson stood beside Cornelius and immediately behind them was Big Man with his child-like grin, softly humming his happy tune, towering above them all and holding the wedding broom that resembled a fly swatter in his huge hands.

After earnest entreaties to the Lord, and prayers for their prosperity and happiness, Brother Daniel pronounced them man and wife. The couple looked up at Colonel and Mrs. Ridley who nodded approvingly, and the bridal couple shared a glorious kiss. Hambone and June Bug – each wearing an old brown derby that was slightly too big for them – held a broom length-wise just an inch or two above the ground. When the couple locked arms and jumped the broom, a rousing cheer was raised and Sailor began to fiddle. Banjo Joe joined in as Long John started playing his Jew's harp, and Po'Boy beat a light and festive rhythm on the drum. The dancing boys locked elbows, swirled around once and began doing the Cakewalk.

The Colonel had permitted a few tables to be set up for the celebratory supper and willingly contributed some meat for the occasion, while the guests brought the rest of the victuals from their gardens. At the insistence of Mrs. Ridley, the Colonel also donated a bottle of local brandy and a small keg of root beer. After all, it was a wedding. They congratulated the happy couple and after toasting to their health, appropriately retired inside. After supper, the guests immaculately cleaned the area, and the party moved down to the Quarters to continue the celebration. Half a deer, compliments of Little Horse, was roasting on spit waiting for them.

CHAPTER 14

Nobody Knows the Troubles I've Seen[viii]

The comet showers appeared particularly bright and frequently that spring. Each month brought them anew and the newlyweds often noticed them in the early hours before dawn as they were separately preparing for the day's work. They viewed the falling stars as a sign of celebration and good things to come, but Big Mama Rue didn't quite see it that way. She feared they were a bad omen for everyone involved, because the bones had told her so. After their initial bliss, the couple found it difficult to enjoy their marriage.

Slave marriages had no legal standing and did not affect one's duties whatsoever. For the owners, it was a harmless piece of legal fiction that, like a placebo, made their slaves feel a little better about life. Their property did not change hands or change locations. For them, life went on with business as usual. Cornelius knew better than to ask for any special dispensation, because he held such a hope as a once in a lifetime appeal, that he would reserve for some dire emergency.

Martha Jane's old master - Judge Mason had died last October. It was now the spring of 1860, and his son Lewis was desperately trying to manage two foundering plantations. Cornelius made no pleas to his own master to bring his new wife to Bonnie Doon, because he knew full well that Colonel Ridley would never interfere in the business affairs of another planter when it came to managing his slaves. Besides, the Colonel was preoccupied with frequent visitors coming and going, who wanted to solicit the opinions and advice of the richest man in Southampton County. Cornelius often overheard fragments of conversations revealing serious growing differences between northern and southern political leaders.

As head of the Southampton Militia, the Colonel frequently had local officers visiting him, but the rank of the soldiers arriving lately grew increasingly higher, and he now often directed Cornelius to drive him to Petersburg or Richmond on urgent business. There was tension in the air, as the Virginians began building battlements and defenses, using slave and conscripted labor, around the two cities. Cornelius was ever vigilant for signs of danger, and he was saving his "ace in the hole" request based on his years of dedicated service to the Ridleys for just an occasion.

Although Cornelius symbolically walked with one foot in each of two worlds, one of the few white men he completely trusted was the kindly Quaker, Samuel Darlington, who operated a country store near Capron, not four miles away. He had grown to like this man over the years and had known him since he rode on the buckboard wagon as a helper for old Tiberius, when they came to pick up sugar, coffee or other essentials not produced on the plantation. Cornelius had been just a boy then, but he nonetheless had a keen aptitude for sizing up people that never failed him. He began to consider this ability a God-given talent, and for good reason.

Whenever Cornelius arrived at the store, he enjoyed talking with the affable old man who treated him like an equal and took a genuine interest in his intellectual growth and development. Darlington immediately recognized that Cornelius had a bright mind and would have loved to have taught him how to read. Aside from being strictly against the law - which didn't bother him one whit, because he believed God's Law was higher than man's law - he knew it would jeopardize the young man if they were ever caught.

But he schooled Cornelius informally every chance he got, by talking about wide-ranging subjects like weather patterns, the political climate, and the towns and roads beyond the region. It was this talk of geography that assisted Cornelius on his travels. During these conversations, the old Quaker would speak of other *Friends*, as he called them, and the locations of their homes and Meetinghouses. Cornelius assumed this was in case his wagon ever broke down or his horse pulled up lame, he would know where to seek help. Darlington never made a point to declare otherwise. The young driver soaked up this information like a parched field, thirsty for rain.

In the course of his duties, Cornelius had driven as far north as Richmond, and as far east as Norfolk on urgent business that was never explained to him, knowing better than to ever ask. Despite his quizzical nature, Cornelius never felt like he had to completely understand everything, which sometimes saved him a great deal of frustration. He took it on faith that most things had a purpose or a reason he would later decipher or that would eventually be made clear to him. Meanwhile, his mind stored a library of secretly accumulated knowledge and he wanted it kept that way. He never fully understood the Quaker's kindness, but he instinctively knew him to be a good and decent man who loved the Lord, his land, and his family; and who quietly abhorred slavery.

When Cornelius stopped at Fortsville one evening on his way back from Petersburg, the look on Martha Jane's face hit him like a load of buckshot. He tied up the horse and they hurried to her cabin so she could tell him the news he didn't want to hear. Most of the slaves were to be sold off soon, including her mother, her brother Andison and his daughter Sarah. Sarah's mother had already been shipped west to the Mason plantation in Mississippi. Andison and his daughter would be sold to a planter in Northampton County, across

99

the North Carolina state line. He was big and strong and would fetch a good price. The planter had a young daughter who needed a companion, so Sarah would go as part of the deal. If Martha Jane's mother ever recovered, she would be sold to someone nearby as companion for an elderly white woman for a marginal price. At the moment, she was of little value on the plantation and simply one more mouth to feed.

The Masons would keep Martha Jane and one other breeder and perhaps a dozen children who wouldn't fetch much right now, but were also not costly to maintain for the time being. In a few years their value would increase and they would be shopped around or auctioned off to slave traders. She had overheard the young master saying "the war is coming - maybe not this year, but surely the next." He was urgently trying to consolidate the family businesses, diminish their debts, and maximize their assets. Holding her hands, Cornelius waited for the worst of it like the bite of a bullwhip.

"I have to start breedin' again. It's the only reason they keepin' me here. An' they know I won't run 'cause you over at Bonnie Doon." She began to cry. The brief respite she had been given had more to do with the periodic fluctuations of finances at Fortsville than any consideration or kindness on the part of her new owner, as enlightened as he was. Despite his bright mind and sunny disposition, given his diminutive size, Cornelius was not suitable to serve as a breeding man. No master would have been interested in having him sire any children, who would likely be similarly small in stature.

Despondent, Martha continued, "I'm ashamed to have been with so many men. I always felt nobody loved me 'til I met you. I was hopin' things would be different now that you and I're married. I don't know what you want with a woman like me." With a sinking heart, he said, "We're all slaves here, darlin'. And we have'ta do what

100

we're told. You didn't choose that. It was forced on you. You're a good, strong, beautiful woman - inside and out." Hot tears rolled down his cheeks. For the first time in his life he felt a murderous rage.

"Those men don't mean nothin' to me, Cornelius. They never had my heart. It never was what I wanted. I hate it. When I think o' them and then I think o' you, I cry somethin' fierce. I hate myself for what they make me do. If you don't want me no more, I understand. You need a proper wife you don't have to share with nobody."

With a voice thick with emotion, she continued: "But you the only man I ever loved. From the first time my eyes fell upon you, I knew you was the one for me. And every night I prayed that somehow, we would be together someday, free." He held her tight, "we will darlin,' I promise you one day we will." They lingered, sharing a few more stolen moments.

It was dinner time now and he had to get back on the road. The ride home to Bonnie Doon would still take another two hours - an hour and a half if he hurried, but it had been a long ride for horse and rider, and he didn't want to drive it too hard. He had just enough daylight to make it back to Bonnie Doon before curfew. He had never been stopped by the county militia or the paddyrollers, but since Colonel Ridley was head of militia, it wouldn't be good if his driver was caught after curfew without a pass. They wouldn't detain him since he was the Colonel's property and heading home; but they would report it, and he didn't want to add any more tension to an already tense household. He should have thought to ask for his pass. With all that had been on his mind lately, he couldn't afford to become careless. Not now.

He got back just as darkness fell, careful to bring the horse from a full gallop, to a canter, to a walk as he turned down the long road to Bonnie Doon. Colonel Ridley was pacing the porch slowly, deep in thought, and didn't notice his rider moving quietly toward the barn. Cornelius led the horse to the stables, where he removed the bridle and saddle and brushed the horse down after the long ride. He gave it a long drink of water from a bucket, then some oats and hay, patting it lovingly before exiting the stables and closing the door behind him. When he arrived at his cabin, he noticed a feather stuck in the door, which was a sign from Big Mama Rue that meant she wanted to see him - right away.

He was too tired to wash the road dust off his face, and he trudged down to the Quarters anyway to see the woman he revered as a grandmother. It wasn't very late, and Uncle Robert was on the porch next to her, both sitting in rough-hewn rocking chairs smoking their pipes and talking casually. "I been powerful worried 'bout you, boy" she said as he approached. "Evenin' Mama, evenin' Uncle Robert," he replied wearily.

"Dem bones' been talkin' bout you" she said warily. Too tired to question the efficacy of "the bones," he rolled his eyes at the comment and plaintively appealed to Uncle Robert with just two words: "Uncle Robert?"

The old man shook his head gently from side to side to signal his mutual skepticism of divination. "I know, boy, I 'gree wit'chu, but Rue's always right - at least mos' of the time," he said wryly. "But this about real people, an' not about haunts this time. Come sit on down here an' lissen to'er son." He patted Cornelius on the shoulder as he sat down by the old man's feet.

Though he lacked formal education, Cornelius didn't share most of the beliefs in the supernatural that many other slaves had. He had traveled much further and more widely than any other slave on the plantation. He had seen the ocean, been to cities, and met people from many distant places. And he had certainly spent a great deal of time on the roads at night.

Big Mama Rue was an extraordinary root doctor and psychologist, with the ability to cure people of many physical and emotional ailments. But Cornelius also knew that belief was a powerful force in people. What someone *believed* to be true - could often be more compelling than what was *actually* true. Personally, he believed in God and angels but he had never seen a ghost, nor did he want to. Come to think of it, he had never seen God or angels either, for that matter, and he didn't know what the difference was between a ghost and an angel, anyway. However, he knew good people who believed they had seen such things. So he accepted the possibility that perhaps he was simply not gifted in that way, and that there were some things greater and more mysterious than he could understand.

"I rolled da bones three time las' night," Mama Rue continued. "One for you, one for Martha Jane, one for Rosa. He raised his head slowly as she now had his attention. "What'd the bones say, Mama?" he asked, with obvious fatigue in his voice. She replied resignedly - "they tell me what I already know; or at least what I *think* I know."

As respectfully as he could muster at this hour, yet tinged with frustration, he asked: "Then why you need them bones, Mama?" She frowned and scolded him: "Now, don't you be sassin' my bones, boy." Too tired to object, he apologized with a wave of his hand.

"I'm sorry Mama, but I had a long day, and a bad one, too. I didn't mean to sass your old bones," he said sheepishly.

Mama Rue's voice softened with understanding. "I know, Cornelius. I know what be goin' on over dere at Fortsville. It's bad, but Martha Jane ain't the one I'm worried 'bout." He straightened up.

"Well, you sure don't have to worry about me," he insisted. "I'm not worried 'bout you right now, son, I'm worried 'bout Rosa," she replied tenderly. He turned toward her with the question written on his face: "Why?"

For once, Big Mama Rue was at a loss for words. "I don't know, 'xactly." He interrupted before she could continue. "But I thought you said you already knew." He shot a glance at Uncle Robert, who shrugged his shoulders, and with his pipe in his mouth, held up his empty palms indicating that he didn't have the answer, either. The surrogate grandmother tried to explain.

"These is dangerous times. Saw another fallin' star las' night. They been troublin' me somthin' fearful, Cornelius. Been a long time since I seen so many - not since Gen'ral Nat and the Rebellion, before you was born. But I knew you comin' even then, 'cause the ole bones tole me," she recalled with maternal pride.

He responded with a look of mild impatience, silently urging her to continue. "So when I rolled da bones three times las' night, they say you gonna be free, and one day soon." Cornelius looked hopeful but still puzzled. "Next time I roll, the bones say your bride gonna be free, too - but not so soon. An' some time'll pass that'll separate you two." Concern crept into his expression as he held his hand out to ask his next question silently. Bolstering her courage, she said: "But trouble for Rosa comin' real soon. She goin' far away, never comin' back," reluctantly adding, "you never see her again, baby."

Cornelius looked at her in astonishment. He leapt up with a start and blurted out, "Why Mama why? Nobody has said a word

104

about Rosa 'round the Ridleys. An' she told me herself they're bringin' her back to Bonnie Doon," he insisted.

"She comin' back to Bonnie Doon, sure enough," Rue replied, "but not to stay. She goin' away. But she don't know it." He looked quizzically at Uncle Robert who appeared as perplexed as he was. Cornelius was startled and annoyed now. "How can I go to the Colonel and tell him some old bones told me he's sellin' Rosa?" Anguished, Mama Rue clasped her hands together pleading, "you can't son, you can't. 'Cause he don't know about it yet, either."

"What?!" he declared, flabbergasted. "'Cause it ain't happen yet," Mama Rue admitted. Cornelius rubbed his forehead as if trying to erase the thought. "Then how do I stop somethin' the Colonel don't know about and hasn't even happened yet?" he asked impatiently.

Mama Rue was equally frustrated as she responded. "I don't know, son, I don't know. Rollin' the bones ain't like talkin' to people. They don't give a lotta details! *I* gotta do the 'terpretation!" She immediately regretted the unintentional sting of her words and was touched by his crestfallen face. "Look, son, let's talk more inside about our plan for you. Uncle Robert'll keep watch out here."

The two went inside and sat at her little table, and she continued: "You gonna walk away to freedom." Cornelius was completely stumped. "What? How am I gonna just walk away?" he implored. "Ain't nobody gonna see you. You gonna be invisible," she replied. He stood up in protest, calling out: "Uncle Robert?" But the old man responded calmly over his shoulder, "I know, boy, it sound crazy to me, too, at first. But jus' lissen to her. Please. Jus' lissen."

Big Mama Rue continued. "Your path is easier because the Quaker, Mr. Darlington, gonna help you." Cornelius looked at her, bemused. "How do you know him?" he asked.

105

Rue responded matter-of-factly, "I been livin' 'round these parts a long time, boy; you ain't the only one who knows a lotta people." They talked late into the night, making three sets of detailed plans – one for Cornelius, one for Martha Jane, and one for Rosa.

≈

Rosa returned to Bonnie Doon and it was wonderful to see her there again. She brightened up the old manse like the sunflowers adorning every corner. When she opened the door to visitors, tastefully attired, with the grand staircase behind her, she appeared to be the epitome of elegant Southern womanhood. Had she been born in another country or in another time, she could have passed for a princess or the wife of some foreign potentate. She set a tone of refinement and decorum that visitors to Bonnie Doon relished, and was the perfect matching bookend for the dapper young liveryman who ferried the most prominent guests about on all official occasions for the patrician Ridleys.

Like the fine china and ornate carpets, Rosa was viewed as an alluring ornament by the gentlemen who arrived to meet with Colonel Ridley on increasingly urgent affairs of state or business. These meetings grew more frequent after Abraham Lincoln won the nomination as the Republicans' presidential candidate in May of 1860. In addition, the rising tides of federalism and abolition were reversing the political gains achieved by powerful Southerners under the sympathetic, conservative President James Buchanan from Pennsylvania. It was also possible that Lincoln would win the Presidency in November, after which some firebrands proclaimed that "all Hell would break loose." No mistake about it, war was coming as

106

surely as the army of cicadas every summer. Secession was not just in the air – it was a foregone conclusion.

Mama Rue warned Cornelius, "you gonna have'ta leave soon, and take Rosa with you if you can. But you gotta be north of the Mason-Dixon Line 'fore the war start. Time is slippin' by like water through a sieve." But he wasn't ready to leave yet. The plans were in place but he hadn't had a chance to speak with Rosa about them.

As welcome as she was at Bonnie Doon, Rosa also presented a dilemma for the Ridleys – the same kind that had vexed Cornelius. She was beautiful but not physically strong enough to be a breeding woman. These were leaner and less leisurely times, and not optimal for a pack of hungry little half-breeds running around. The war was coming and the Ridleys needed no new mouths to feed – especially, house slaves. Like the Masons, other prominent planters were hastily diversifying their investments, liquidating liabilities, and seeking ways to protect their fortunes by keeping it out of Yankee hands. Some were transferring funds to banks in the Deep South. Others chose colonial banks in Bermuda, Jamaica, or the West Indies. For a few, nothing but old, pedigreed firms in England would suffice.

Although France and England had abolished slavery years earlier, they were still sympathetic to the Southern cause, in part, because its burgeoning cotton industry enriched European markets. On plantations across the South, property of all types was being itemized and assessed. Many decisions were being made but more were on hold – including the futures of Cornelius, Rosa, and Martha Jane, none of whom wanted to get swept up in the misfortunes of war.

While some abolitionists held a simplistic view that war would end slavery and preserve the Union by bringing rebellious Southerners back under control, most people knew – especially those

107

around Bonnie Doon – that war would lead to destruction, chaos, and loss. Because, the fighting would be fierce and far-ranging, and almost entirely in the South. Late-night conversations in the library, now serving as the "War Room," indicated the only hope for prominent planters was for the South to secede and form a confederacy of states that could maintain strong economic and diplomatic ties of their own to sympathetic European nations.

However, the focus of the war would have to be on States' Rights and principles of self-government, and not become a moral referendum on slavery. Many Southerners knew that the days of slavery were numbered among the community of nations, but now was not the time to eliminate this essential institution. It would have to be done slowly and methodically, to give the planters and politicians time to redesign their regional economies, and develop effective control mechanisms for four million illiterate and dependent black people. After all, who would feed, clothe, house, and take care of them? They could certainly not fend for themselves, the whites reasoned.

Adding to the angst Cornelius was suffering was the fact that Martha Jane was pregnant with another child who was not his own. He had to get away with Rosa and see that Martha Jane and her children also escaped. How would she be able to manage that now that she was with child? In six months, travel would be virtually impossible for her. He had to make final preparations, for time was growing short, and he wondered how could he possibly make plans with Rosa – even though she was residing in the big house – when he was kept traveling, constantly.

CHAPTER 15

Gentleman from New Orleans

A few weeks later, the Colonel directed Cornelius to meet a visitor arriving by ship at Norfolk. The person would take the train to Franklin City, and Cornelius would drive the carriage to pick him up there. Wearing his standard black and tan livery - not the fancy outfit used on special occasions - Cornelius met the traveler at the appointed time, collected his bags, and loaded them onto the carriage.

The gentlemen needed no help climbing on but appreciated the offer. It was obvious by his clothing and his bearing that he was a man of means and well educated. He had sailed to Norfolk, around the tip of Florida, from New Orleans - which was his home. But he was not a planter, politician, or soldier like Colonel Ridley. He was a young banker and appeared to be quite successful at it, with the grand name of Monsieur Antoine Daniel Marie-Andrée de Beaurainville. A few foreigners, mostly Englishmen and planters from the West Indies had visited Bonnie Doon over the years, but that did not occur often. This man was unique, however, and though he never revealed it, Cornelius was intrigued by him and uncharacteristically curious about the nature of his business.

The passenger spoke perfect English but with a French accent - actually, more Creole than continental French. He was reserved and had an egalitarian air about him that was absent in other Southerners Cornelius normally interacted with. The rigid boundaries between slave and free seemed less important to this man, and he was more interested in the climate, crops, and countryside than demonstrating his white superiority over servants. They kept the conversation light, and since the traveler didn't raise the topic of politics, neither did

Cornelius - nor would it have been his place to do so. However, de Beaurainville was impressed with the young driver's intelligence and affability, and asked if Cornelius had any Creole ancestry because their complexions were not noticeably different. "I am mulatto," Cornelius said. "I am Creole," replied his passenger, "I understand," he added with a smile. "We are not so different, you and I."

There was an easiness between them that was nonexistent between Cornelius and other associates of the Colonel. None were ever rude toward him, and a few even appeared to be fond of him, albeit paternalistically. But this one appeared to accept him as a fellow member of the fraternity of man. Had they met at another time or place they might well have become friends.

During the ride to Bonnie Doon, each man developed an unspoken admiration for the other. Although he knew the gentleman was exhausted from the long trip, Cornelius perceived a deep melancholia about his passenger, and his innate ability to put others at ease worked its magic with this man as well. Bit by bit, layer by layer, as if peeling back the petals of a chrysanthemum, the Creole offered a glimpse into his world.

In a mellifluous baritone voice he began: "My father was a French naval officer assigned to the Caribbean; and after his term of meritorious service, was appointed to a diplomatic post in Martinique, where he met and married a French Creole woman from an old island family who happened to be a cousin of Joséphine de Beauharnais (the driver did not recognize this name, but assumed she was a woman of some importance, giving the name a deferential nod) and later, I was born. For a time we lived on Montserrat, but my father wanted a less provincial and more cosmopolitan environment in which to raise me, so when I was still a young boy, we moved to America and settled in New Orleans."

At this point he removed a flask from his waistcoat and took a sip or two of excellent French brandy. "Here my friend," he said offering it to the driver, "please join me, I do not wish to drink alone." Cornelius tactfully declined the astonishing offer, knowing full well that he could not drink from the same vessel as a white man, but the passenger was cordially insistent. "Please, you're an excellent driver, and it will fortify you" - conspiratorially adding - "of course I will not tell your master. Frankly, I find your company quite refreshing." The offer had more to do with sharing than with drinking; and sensing it would be impolite to reject this symbolic and remarkable offer, Cornelius reluctantly accepted. After taking a sip, he deferentially wiped the mouth of the bottle with his clean kerchief, and passed it back as the Creole continued his tale.

"My father was very successful in business, and sent me off to Paris for a proper education. We never owned a plantation like your master; instead, we have always been in banking and shipping. My father's contacts in the French Navy and colonial government were of immense value. And with my help, or so he says, we built one of the most successful banking and brokerage firms in *le Vieux Carré - the French Quarter*, as they say in English. Our brokerage firm is *de Beaurainville et Fils* - 'and son.' We have a large home in the Garden District, and an estate on the Gulf Coast we call, *Montreuil-sur-Mer* - after the town in northern France where my father was born." Pausing to gently massage his tired eyes before continuing his story, he was exhausted but talking kept him from sinking into gloominess.

"Everything was going very well, or so it seemed. I met and married a beautiful woman who was one of the *gens de couleur - free people of color* - a bit like you my friend, except, free." Cornelius was puzzled and uncharacteristically asked a question. "You married her? They let you do that down there?" The Creole smiled and took

111

another sip of brandy. *"Certainement, mon ami,"* he replied. "Things are very different there, compared to your Virginia. Yes, we have slavery, but even that is different there. Not that it is easy nor merciful, but in many ways the slaves have more freedoms there. And often, a wealthy man will sire children by his slave mistress..." The driver broke in - "that happens here too," he said, immediately regretting the interruption.

"Yes," the Creole continued, taking no offense to the comparison. "But there, the children are often well taken care of, and sometimes sent to Europe, as I was, for a proper education. And when they return, their father gives them land or money and they are freed. I know that is not the custom here." Cornelius could not believe his ears. "No sir, it's not like that at all here," he said pensively.

"That," the Creole responded, "is very harsh and uncivilized. Slavery was a stain on the soul of France, as well. And how the slaves were mistreated in Haiti was an affront to the Almighty. And He punished the French planters there dearly for it. My family has servants at home, but no slaves. Many others do, however. Yet at least for some, there is a way to escape slavery there - like my wife's family did." Cornelius did not know what to say. This epiphany rendered him speechless and now *he* was beginning to feel a bit melancholy himself. "Well," he said trying to sound cheerful, "I wish both of you much happiness, Monsieur de Beaurainville."

The Creole was touched by Cornelius' genuineness. He sighed and continued, "I don't usually talk so much with *un étranger* - a stranger. Perhaps it is the brandy and this fresh country air. In fact, for the past several months I have not spoken much at all. But there is something familiar about you - as if we have met before. We call this feeling, *déjà vu*. In fact, you could easily be my wife's brother.

112

Cornelius, was equally touched – "Why, thank you kindly, sir. I feel honored. I'm sure your wife is a wonderful woman." The Creole looked away as he took another sip. Like a levee, the wind held back the tears behind his eyes. The brandy and conversation made him feel warm – not intoxicated – but relaxed. He had felt very lonely on this trip, and this bright and interesting young slave had more humanity and decency than anyone else he had met thus far. He remembered that sharing can help to lighten one's burden and ease one's pain.

"Yes, she was very beautiful – but she died suddenly, and very recently." Cornelius instinctively winced. "I'm so sorry, sir, I'm terribly sorry. I never meant to..." he stammered.

But the Creole interrupted: *"C'est ne pas necessaire, mon ami"* – no apologies are necessary, my friend. How could you possibly know? You are a good man, Cornelius, and I hope one day that Fate smiles upon you and sets you free. There is something about you that makes one feel at ease. And I have felt little comfort since I left New Orleans. My father had planned to send another, but I insisted on coming – I needed to get away for a while." The passenger drifted off for several minutes into quiet reverie, and the driver perceptively allowed de Beaurainville a measure of privacy to let the wave of personal grief to wash over and roll past him.

The gentleman from New Orleans seldom showed his feelings and was resolutely stoic during times of great difficulty. These were skills he had learned during his fencing lessons and pistol practice at the academy in Paris. Yet he had always been inherently optimistic about life's challenges. But the loss of the woman he loved made his heart sink into a chasm of despair. Indeed, it pained those closest to him to see their good friend and kinsman suffering so.

During the first weeks after her passing, he was inconsolable. Nothing could free him from his prison of pain - neither strong drink, nor music, nor the brilliant beauty of the trees and subtropical flowers that had burst into bloom that Louisiana spring. His eyes were open but he was blind to it all. He felt anesthetized and watched himself go through the motions of living. Everything they had loved and shared, painfully reminded him of her. It was inescapable.

He had to look away whenever he rode past the park where they first kissed and he ached when hearing the echoes of her words or seeing shadows of her smile in his head afterward. He couldn't bear to see the flowers or hear the songs of which she had been so fond. In moments of supreme solitude in his once happy home, his sobbing sometimes burst forth so suddenly that it startled him, and he fought to catch his breath as hot tears streamed down his cheeks. He was wary and withdrawn in public. At times, when riding in his carriage, he would erupt into tears without warning, and cover his mouth with one hand to hide his grief from passers-by. His tinted Parisian glasses obscured the anguish in his eyes; and he wore them constantly, claiming that his eyes were weak and bothered by the sun. But it was just a useful ruse.

He loved nearly everything about her. Her French ancestry was as obvious as her pale blue eyes that sparkled in sharp contrast against hair as dark as night, accented by the faintest of freckles on her face. Her olive skin was smooth and fair and glowed when kissed by the sun - or by him. Her body adored the touch of his hand, and when he did, it set off a silent explosion within each of them. As soul mates, they felt a primal recognition as if their love had been a recurrence from previous lifetimes.

She loved it when he walked up behind her and held her tight in his arms, kissing her neck gently. This was a love unlike any other.

114

Yet there had not been time to say goodbye. Looking at the portrait of her smiling brightly, gave him deep pangs of pain. It had taken them far too long to find each other in life and now she was gone forever. With much regret, he could have abided her falling out of love with him. But the thought of never seeing or speaking with her again was unbearable.

After an initial outpouring of condolences, incrementally and almost imperceptibly, people slowly retreated from him - as if her death was somehow communicable. Or perhaps it made them question their own fates or the longevity of their own loves or lives. For the first time in his life he lived in fear. Certainly, he had felt fear before - such as during a battering storm at sea, but he had never let fear rule him or change the course of his life. Now he felt like an emotional invalid, abandoned in an abyss of loneliness.

Long walks in the rain transformed him into a soggy spirit that slowly merged into the mist. He frightened people who unexpectedly encountered him under lonely street lamps casting amber cones of light. Yet he never noticed. His somnambulant eyes stared straight ahead, searching for something he could not see - no matter how much his heart ached for it.

He had taken it for granted that he and Evangeline would grow old together, because time stood still whenever they were together. Now, he felt like the last man on Earth. The gravity that had held his life together, that made the universe make sense, was now gone. That gravity was now dead. And so was love. He woke up every morning bereft of hope - as shattered and incomplete as the pieces of the mirror laying broken on the bedroom floor.

He would never experience that kind of love and affection again - nor did he want to. The mere possibility of it was terrifying to him. All of the platitudes about finding love again someday that well-meaning friends and family members dubiously promised him rang hollow. Yes, he would go on, but the love of his life was gone.

Those around him began to worry that he was spending too much time alone. His warm and sunny disposition grew cloudy and somber. He roamed aimlessly around his house, speaking to her as if she was in the room, asking her over and over: "Why did you leave me?" He raged at God and everything else he held sacred for allowing this tragedy to happen. He could not sleep at night nor bear the memories of happier times. These gave him no comfort. Indeed, he was fearful of waking from a dream and seeing her spirit entering the room, which would only serve as evidence of his melancholy madness. Yet, he also longed to see her one last time.

Every aspect of his being changed as he was slowly consumed by the wrath inside of him. The once dapper scion of a prominent banking house frequently forgot to shave and bathe, his clothes always appeared wrinkled. He refused to look in the mirror for fear of the mask of desolation he might see staring back at him.

He haunted the gaming establishments in the French Quarter at night, often waiting until midnight to slip out of the house, then spend the next several hours drinking and gambling until the sun came up, before retreating to the darkness of his rooms where the shades were always drawn, day or night. Once he heard the soft singing of the early birds of morning, it was safe to sleep - because he would be too exhausted to dream. Some of the neighbors whispered that he might be a *loup garou* - a werewolf; and perhaps he'd been bitten on the night of the full moon. In old, mysterious New Orleans one could never be too sure, nor too careful, when considering such a serious claim. And Antoine did nothing to dispel the rumor because it was a useful piece of fiction that helped keep people away from him.

116

The handsome, sophisticated young banker became mercurial, wild-eyed, surly, and quarrelsome at times; engaging in shouting matches and flashes of rage. At other times, he'd spend some days in total silence. Antoine never roamed the streets at night without his Philadelphia Derringer in his vest pocket, for the power it packed as well as its ornate beauty. It was a gentleman's gun. After all, de Beaurainville considered himself a French colonial gentleman – not some barbarous pirate like La Fitte, who hid out in the bayous of Barataria. And unlike the pirate, he would carry no common hogleg about for sapping salty dogs around amidships on the high seas.

Darkness consumed him, and during a late-night game of Faro in an upscale sporting house in the French Quarter, he ceremoniously slapped another gambler in the face with his lambskin gloves, after the lout made an ill-considered jest about de Beaurainville's late wife.

The pair met for a sunrise duel in a narrow alley between the marble tombs of St. Louis Cemetery No. 1, on Basin Street. The sharp report of the pistols startled the sleepy pigeons from their roosts atop the stately mausoleums and into frantic flight. His opponent collapsed instantly – as though he had dropped through a hole in the ground. Antoine was left standing, too numb with absinthe to realize he had been shot in the chest – with a silver bullet, no less. Word seemed to be spreading he was indeed otherworldly. After all, he was known to frequent the home of Marie Laveau – the Voodoo Queen of New Orleans. His opponent also survived, and promptly left town.

After considerable discussion, the surgeons decided to let the bullet rest where it was, since it had missed his heart yet was too close and too great a risk to remove. Ironically, the silver provided a stroke of luck – evidence of voodoo some would say – because unlike lead, the silver would not poison him. The wound seldom bothered him anyway - except at times when it was about to rain.

A flask of absinthe became his constant cure for everything - good or ill - and succeeded in keeping him in a perpetual fog. It was strong enough to ease the pain *around* his heart, but not the one *in* his heart. In his descent into purgatory, he began to frequent opium dens near the slave market at the Port of New Orleans - losing track of time, days, consciousness, identity, self, and life.

On one dark night of the soul, as the bell at St. Louis Cathedral on *rue de Chartres* on Jackson Square was striking three past the witching hour, he found himself hovering like a phantom atop a levee on the Mississippi just a few blocks away, staring blindly at something lurking deep beneath the dark water, calling him to come. It was never officially determined whether he actually jumped or simply fell, but he later awoke in a hospital bed among hushed voices and a bustle of activity around him. He thought he had drowned and that he would finally see Evangeline again, but he wept when he realized that he had merely returned to a world of suffering.

When he was with her, laughing or holding hands, he believed that nothing evil could assail him. Life had meaning and purpose, and hope as expansive and shimmering as great Lake Ponchartrain. And despite all the troubles of an imperfect world, the love they had shared lifted his spirits and grounded his soul. He looked forward to watching their grandchildren grow like Bougainvillea in the garden. However, all that ended the night that she, and the baby she was carrying, died - and he could not imagine life without her. He had never felt more despondent or alone. And the only thing he could feel at this very moment in time was the wind on his face.

118

Cornelius pretended not to hear the sniffling behind him and turned his face to the wind, as his heart began to ache to for reasons not entirely dissimilar. He could not help being touched by the outpouring of this kind stranger's sadness. "Prince or slave - any man can suffer," he thought; and began softly humming a spiritual to comfort them both, which brought the young widower out of the past and back to the carriage.

"Don't worry, my friend, we will play our roles when we arrive at your master's home. But I wish to say again that I do not like the brutality of slavery - especially for you. In France, we say: '*Liberté, égalité, fraternité,* which, in English means 'liberty, equality, fraternity.'" The two shared a smile and another sip of brandy, and both were buoyed up by this moment of camaraderie.

By the time they arrived at Bonnie Doon, his legs were stiff after the long journey from Norfolk, so Cornelius helped the gentleman down from the coach and unloaded his bags while the Colonel greeted his honored guest. "*Bienvenue, Antoine!* Welcome to Bonnie Doon. It is wonderful to see you." He gave his guest a warm handshake. "*Bonjour, mon Colonel!* And it is wonderful to be here," de Beaurainville replied. Cornelius handed the gentleman's luggage to a house servant, and greeted the Colonel with a tip of his hat and a formal, "Colonel, sir!"

Cornelius asked his passenger: "Will there be anything else, sir?" De Beaurainville replied with a wink and said, "No, that will be all driver. Marvelous job," and flipped Cornelius a coin. Cornelius caught the coin in mid-air and with a curt nod of the head replied: "At your service, sir."

As Colonel Ridley and his guest entered the house, Antoine remarked: "excellent driver, Colonel. Not a bump or a bounce the

119

entire ride. Good with the horses, too." His host replied, "Yes, good man, Cornelius - worth his weight in gold. Now," as he gave his guest a friendly pat on the back, "how is your father?" he asked. Antoine replied, "He is well Colonel - thank you very much. He sends his warmest regards and gratitude that you have allowed us this opportunity to be of assistance to you."

The men were greeted by a butler who took the visitor's hat and overcoat. De Beaurainville remembered to resist the urge to say "thank you." He was still in the South, but this was a far different society than the cosmopolitan one he was accustomed to in New Orleans. After returning from hanging up the visitor's hat and coat, the Colonel spoke to the butler - an elderly black man with gray hair, and a slender build, dressed in black tails and starched white shirt, with a black bow tie and impeccable manners. "Hector, show the gentleman to the water closet so he may refresh himself." Hector nodded respectfully; "Certainly sir," he said. Motioning the way for the visitor, he said: "This way, sir," and led him down a hallway.

The Creole emerged from the hallway a few minutes later, visibly refreshed. Hector led him to the living room where the Colonel and Mrs. Ridley were waiting. "Oh Antoine," Mrs. Ridley exclaimed, as she grasped her guest's hands in a warm greeting. "My how you've grown since the last time I saw you. You are one handsome young man!" Antoine blushed and chuckled at the compliment. "Ah, Madame Ridley, you are too kind - and as lovely as ever," he said - giving the back of her hand a light kiss, in response to her offer. "*Enchanté*," he said gallantly, adding: "it has been far too long since you have graced our humble home in New Orleans."

"Yes, a charming city, and much too long since we've visited there," she replied, giving her husband a mock frown. "Always, our

120

home is your home, Madame," Antoine assured her with a respectful nod, "and my parents would be delighted to see you again."

"Well," said Mrs. Ridley, "I will let you gentlemen conduct your business, as my husband tells me you are on a very strict schedule." Antoine agreed, "Yes, Madame, that is unfortunately true. I wish I could stay longer, but perhaps next time." Mrs. Ridley was gracious. "I understand completely, Antoine. These are difficult times for us all."

"*Oui*, Madame, *c'est vrai*," he replied with nod." As she walked to the door she said, "Rosamonde will bring in refreshments shortly." Closing the French doors behind her, Antoine said, "Thank you Madame Ridley, that is very kind of you." She smiled radiantly, in response.

The men sat down in large upholstered chairs, angled toward one another, with a small shiny table of black walnut between them. De Beaurainville took in the room with a sweeping glance. It was elegant and well appointed, full of polished furniture, tapestries, paintings, and sparking crystal. An impressive mirror hung over the fireplace mantle above two crossed swords. Colonel Ridley spoke first. "Well, thank you again, Antoine, for traveling so far on this urgent matter. I know you are fully aware of the critical state of affairs and what that portends."

"*Oui*, Colonel." Antoine nodded affirmatively. "We have gathered from your dispatches that should Lincoln win the presidency in November, within six months the Southern states will secede from the Union and surely war will break out." The host concurred, "Precisely. And we know the North will have no choice but to bring the war to us in the South, attempting to defeat us militarily as well as economically. And that is where you come in."

There was a delicate knock at the door. Colonel Ridley looked up from his guest and said: "Come in." Antoine took advantage of the momentary interruption to look at his pocket watch for the first time since he had arrived at Bonnie Doon, trying to assess how long he had been traveling. When he heard a luxurious feminine voice, he involuntarily searched for its source.

"Colonel Ridley, sir?" It was Rosamonde - standing in the middle of the French doors that had just been opened by Hector, holding a silver tray with a carafe of French wine, glasses, and food.

Antoine slowly rose to his feet, propelled by a power that was not his own, as the heavy pocket watch slipped from his hand and dropped to the floor. As if seeing a mirage he whispered, "*Sacré bleu,*" to no one in particular. He could not believe his eyes, and he winced from a sudden pang from the muscles constricting around the wound in his chest.

Perhaps it was the melancholia, the lack of sleep, or the long voyage followed by the considerable carriage ride - or perhaps all of these together - but he had certainly not had enough brandy to make himself hallucinate. He looked confused and rubbed his right temple as the words "*Mon Dieu*" unintentionally escaped his lips as if they had been spoken by someone else. With his tired eyes and the light behind her, this woman looked astonishingly like his late wife. What took only seconds seemed like a very long moment; and he was transfixed, riveted on her face when the muffled words being spoken suddenly became clear, and he heard Colonel Ridley speaking his name. The spell was broken but the dazed look etched on his face remained.

"Rosa, this is our honored guest, Monsieur Antoine de Beaurainville, of New Orleans." Her smile was beatific and she

122

curtsied after carefully setting down the tray. The Colonel then turned to his guest. "Antoine, this is Rosamonde - everyone but Mrs. Ridley calls her, *Rosa.*" Antoine instinctively held out his hand. She quickly glanced at the Colonel who saw the look on the beleaguered young man's face and nodded approval while stifling a smile. Her hand was smooth and delicate, soft and warm. Still marveling at the exquisite touch of her hand, he impulsively kissed it, murmuring: "*Enchanté.*"

She was bewildered and slightly distressed as she withdrew her hand, stammering, "Thank you, sir. It is a pleasure to meet you, sir. Welcome to Bonnie Doon." Now blushing with embarrassment, she turned and nodded to Colonel Ridley and hurried out of the room, closing the French doors deftly behind her. Antoine stared at the doors replaying her exit in his mind.

Smiling, Colonel Ridley broke the silence. "Antoine, are you all right? You look like you've seen a ghost, son." Slightly flustered, he answered sheepishly, "Perhaps I have, sir." Then as he sat down, he added: "Colonel, *who* was that extraordinary woman?" His host poured them each a glass of wine from the carafe, and lowering his voice explained briefly. "Her mother was a mistress of mine many years ago, when I was overwhelmed by the ardor of youth. I was quite fond of her, actually" - he admitted in a surprisingly detached voice.

"Sir, she is *astonishingly* beautiful. For a moment...I was a bit surprised...because she so resembles my late wife Evangeline - I was quite fond of her, too," he recalled tenderly. The two men shared a knowing smile that belied sadness. "Yes, I am so very sorry about the loss of your wife and child. Your father wrote me." Sipping his wine and having regained his composure now, Antoine politely probed the subject a little deeper. "Who is she? Is she married, does she have children, a suitor, someone she is promised to, perhaps?"

123

"No," Colonel Ridley replied, "no family except her brother Cornelius - your driver today - and an older uncle on another one of our estates." Antoine made the connection as the epiphany dawned on his face. "Of course," he said. "Good man, Cornelius - very bright."

"Yes," the Colonel concurred, "Cornelius is indispensable to me. Especially in these times, when there are so many pressing affairs of state. I have always treated him well, so he is quite dependable and trustworthy. He often carries important dispatches for me."

"But given these times," Antoine asked, "wouldn't telegraph be faster?" The Colonel smiled sagely, "Yes, faster but not as secure. Anyone can connect to a telegraph line, anywhere for miles along the road. There are Union spies here in Virginia, just as we have ours in the North. When I give Cornelius a dispatch, only three hands touch it - mine, his, and the recipient. Cornelius cannot read, so he does not know the content of my messages. It's very safe."

Antoine had to know for certain. Like a chess player, he made a strategic move. "And his sister, Rosa...?" Ready to return to the business at hand, the Colonel answered, "She has no children, and though she is of marriageable age, she is not promised to anyone - at least, not yet. But there are many who would like to have her."

"*Certainement*," Antoine replied. "But let us complete our business first, and if you would like to discuss Rosa further, I will be happy to do so," the Colonel said kindly. Accepting the proper parry and the constraints of social convention, Antoine graciously agreed.

As if struck by a bolt from the sky, there was suddenly a smoldering in his heart he thought was long dead and buried with his wife and unborn child. His mind was racing with possibilities as if calculating a complex return on investments with a bewildering number of variables. He was weighing the possibilities of Rosa's future

124

here, versus how well she could live in New Orleans - with *him*, and alternately feeling joy and panic at the prospect. Pangs of guilt shot through his reverie like rays of sunlight piercing a cloud. The words he had spoken earlier to Cornelius now seemed hollow as they echoed quietly in his head - *liberté, égalité, fraternité.* His family did not own slaves, he had told the young coachman. The clarity of his thoughts was rapier sharp and considerably cruel. At once, he felt an agony and an ecstasy as if touched by a benevolent God. Each side of his brain was ardently debating the other.

One side labored on with Colonel Ridley, while the other simultaneously argued *l'affaires du coeur* (the affairs of the heart) in this moral conflict. Risk. Chance. Fate. Serendipity. Love. Longing. Joy. Despair. Hopelessness. Hope. The past. The future. The present. And this very moment in time. "There are no coincidences," he had decided long ago. The same thoughts raced circuitously in his mind like horses on a merry-go-round, desperately seeking a solution.

The gentlemen continued their lengthy discussion over lunch. In summation, Antoine explained... "As you say, Colonel, should the Southern states secede from the Union, Richmond could serve as the capitol of the Confederacy. And if the North invades, as you suspect, it may be necessary to move the new capitol farther South - somewhere distant with navigable waters to the Gulf - such as Vicksburg, or Mobile, perhaps. England and France are indeed sympathetic, but the issue of slavery complicates these matters greatly," which struck a self-effacing and critical chord within him.

"It is possible they may await the apparent outcome of the war before officially recognizing the Confederacy. But regardless of what happens, we believe your investments will be safer abroad than in the continental United States. It is always best to find shelter *before* the storm as my father often said during his years in the French navy.

125

If the South is victorious - which, given the caliber of its military leadership we believe it will be - there will still be serious economic repercussions, because the loss of major agricultural revenues and interstate commerce will be a decisive blow the North. And Wall Street banks and investment houses may not willingly honor their financial obligations to prominent Southern landowners like you."

"And you suggest?" the Colonel inquired. The young banker replied, "We suggest you transfer some of your assets abroad. There are a number of old and established national banks in England, Scotland, and Sweden. But given international relations and treaties, you may prefer the private banking industry - for example, in Italy or Switzerland - if you have corporate connections in those countries." Ridley nodded negatively, indicating he did not.

"Therefore, my father and I recommend the *de Rothschild Frères* who provide international banking from the continent to the Caribbean. We also suggest a new, aggressive and very successful bank in France - *Crédit Agricole*, which opened this year, founded by some of my father's business partners. Their policies are specifically designed to provide funding for agriculturalists like yourself, because they realize the sun and the seasons often have as great an impact on agricultural finances as do deadlines dictated by the calendar. With this bank, you would become a charter member who would be entitled to the best interest rates in the world. In diversifying your portfolio, you will employ two new firms - one old and established, where your financial growth would be conservative but quite stable; and the other, a young but impressive firm where your risks may be slightly higher, but so will your dividends. And of course, you would still have local assets in Petersburg and Richmond to provide you with more immediate liquidity. Should the North prosper as a result of the war, your French banking firms could surreptitiously invest some of your

126

funds in lucrative and influential American firms such as those owned by Northern tycoons like William Rockefeller or J. S. Morgan. This will give you a decided advantage given the mercurial economic nature of war. We believe this is the most beneficial and financially prudent plan for your family," he ended with panache.

Visibly pleased, the Colonel exclaimed, "Well done, lad! Very well done, indeed! You have done your research, and have not disappointed me." Pleased at this response, Antoine replied, "Thank you, sir. This is also the plan for our own money. We would suggest nothing less for friends and associates as old and dear as you."

The men stood up, shook hands, and sealed the deal with a toast of brandy. "That settles it, then," said Colonel Ridley. "I'll review the legal documents tonight. Tomorrow, we shall take the train to my banker's office in Petersburg to file the necessary papers, complete the transfer of funds, and have them issue you bearer bonds. My solicitor is also in Petersburg, and I will have him meet us at the bank. You can take the train directly back to Norfolk for an earlier ship home, as 'time and tide wait for no man.' And right now, time is of the essence." The Colonel noticed the disappointment on the younger man's face.

"Don't worry, son," he added. "We'll discuss Rosa after dinner this evening." Antoine beamed. "You and your father have always been loyal to me - and extremely beneficial. I am sure we can come to some mutual agreement about her. Now, you've had a long day and a very long trip, my young friend. Hector will show you to your rooms where you can rest. Mrs. Ridley, Roberta, Eliza, and I will meet you for dinner at seven. My nephew William will be joining us. Bright young fellow - a cadet at the Virginia Military Institute. I am certain you will like him."

Antoine occasionally caught glimpses of Rosa during dinner. She did not eat with them, but she did serve some of the courses. Although she tried her best to avert her eyes - according to convention - she could not resist stealing glances at him, and on the few occasions when their eyes met, he smiled at her. She was flattered and bemused, because he did not look at her the way other men did - like she was an exotic object of great yet base desire. This frightened her, making her wonder why he was so intently interested in her.

She did not want to leave her brother, her uncle, or Bonnie Doon. Yet, this Frenchman did not have the greedy eyes of a slave trader; and beyond the obvious sadness, there was a look of authenticity and wonderment in his eyes. Rosa could see this man had a heart and a soul but the encounter was still unsettling for her.

Antoine made a point of briefly thanking her at the end of the meal - which he knew somewhat overstepped the bounds of local tradition. However, he could also surmise from the sedate yet perceptible fondness the Colonel and Mrs. Ridley held for this young woman, that she was no ordinary house slave. After responding with a few gracious words and a curtsey, she flew from the room like a pheasant flushed from the brush. Amused, the Colonel noted that Antoine's French chivalry extended even to house servants.

After dinner, before speaking with Antoine about Rosa, the Colonel and his nephew first needed to discuss some private matters, so Mrs. Ridley and their daughters took their guest out on the veranda to enjoy a mint julep and the evening breeze. It had been years since the Ridleys had visited New Orleans and they peppered their patient guest with questions about his family, the latest fashions, and French Quarter society. After dutifully answering all inquiries, he briefly mentioned the similarity between Rosa and his late wife.

128

Mrs. Ridley knew of his heartbreak, and pondered that Rosa might be the perfect remedy for him. As a young Southern belle, Mrs. Margaret Ann Bynum Jordan Ridley, had had her share of suitors, and she knew a good man when she saw one. She did not believe in miscegenation, but she also knew the French to be a different people; and that New Orleans was far more a European and cosmopolitan city than any American one, where foreign culture, customs, and mores ruled society.

Still a beauty at age 40, Margaret Ann had long dark hair and eyes as black as onyx. She was intelligent, self-assured, and had a mind of her own. Like many Southerners, she had deeply mixed and troubled attitudes about slavery. She knew the entire Southern economy and the bountiful and elegant lifestyle hers and other planters' families enjoyed were dependent upon slaves, and though she would never admit it to a living soul, there was also a part of herself that she secretly despised because of this hypocrisy.

She considered a caste system ensconced by brutality less a privilege and more of a moral weakness on the part of people who deemed themselves so superior to blacks. Yet at the same time, whites were inextricably linked to and dependent upon them. She knew that fellow Virginian, Thomas Jefferson, had said that among his earliest childhood memories was of him being carried on a pillow by a slave riding on horseback, while traveling between his family's estates. As did Jefferson, she wondered how to let go of a wolf one is holding by the ears. She knew whites were vastly outnumbered by slaves, and that freedom – which was inevitable someday – would likely be fraught with conflict, danger, and bloodshed, as the approaching war promised.

Although she didn't hold abolitionist views, she nevertheless thought it wrong to abuse slaves; particularly, women and children.

She was a cultured and religious woman who abhorred the so-called "privilege" many white men had become accustomed to, in forcing their attention on any female slave they fancied, at the drop of a hat. With finely tuned ears she had heard the whispered gossip of coarser companions who had it on good authority if not from personal experience, that the converse of *what is good for the goose is good for the gander* was true. Though it was not discussed in polite society, she was well aware that mulatto children sometimes had white mothers.

She could understand how resentful some might feel, but she thought it wrong for planters' wives to mistreat their husband's slave mistresses who had no say in the matter – and if given a choice, would have probably declined the generous "offer" to be a concubine. She knew Cornelius and Rosa were the "issue" of her husband, and originally that angered and vexed her to no end, but since their mother died leaving two small children, she harbored a secret sympathy for them and others like them, whether born out of love or lust, who seemed never to find a proper place in either race.

Half-breeds, like Cornelius, were rarely able to find a mulatto mate because wealthy white men always took the mulatto women for themselves. Therefore, she found it cruel to create a breed of ugly ducklings – not that Cornelius and Rosa were physically unattractive. No, they were quite handsome, and bright, actually. But they were not accepted in Southern white society, and never would be.

Quietly over the years, and behind the scenes, she prodded her proud husband a little at a time, to provide a better life for his issue. She could no more bring herself to refer to them as his "children," any more than the other slaves he owned and who labored long in the fields. That was one reason she maneuvered to have Rosa returned to Bonnie Doon – so she would not end up as the unwilling bed mate of some selfish man who might eventually sell her or her children

130

without any more consideration or attachment than a serviceable horse or wagon.

Mrs. Ridley knew that life in New Orleans held infinitely more promise, hope, and possibilities for a young mulatto like Rosa than Tidewater Virginia ever could. This young Frenchman wasn't simply looking for a slave or concubine - he was looking for a wife to replace the one he loved and lost. And if he did marry her, which was a distinct possibility given the way he was obviously smitten with her tonight, Rosa might eventually gain her freedom, and likely that of her children who could enter adult life with an education, proper means; and, equally important, without the stigma of "the mark of Ham."

The problem would be splitting up Cornelius and Rosa, and that would be extremely painful for both of them. Mrs. Ridley believed that she had done all she could do to help Cornelius. He would never be accepted in white society, but he had been properly raised, had a good vocation, and had even gained a measure of esteem among the Colonel's close friends and associates.

Indeed, he was certainly well thought of by other slaves on the plantation, but like Brother Daniel, for whom she also felt some affection, Cornelius was destined to live out his life here on this plantation, and probably without a wife he could *exclusively* call his own. Perhaps if this union worked out, she might find a way to convince her husband to allow the young banker to eventually purchase Cornelius as well, as Antoine very much wanted to do. But she knew this would be extremely difficult for the time being because Cornelius was her husband's most trusted courier.

She was genuinely fond of Cornelius, but there was little more she could do for him at the present time. However, she *could* help Rosa to have a better life – a far freer and less parochial one than she could ever have at Bonnie Doon. And with the way things were going and the likelihood of war, this might be Rosa's best and only opportunity to escape a life of perpetual servitude. Consequently, Mrs. Ridley resolved that she would support her husband's decision to sell Rosa to the love-struck lonely Frenchman from New Orleans. But they would have to find a way to speak with Cornelius to help him understand, although she doubted he ever would. There was no one in the world he loved more than Rosa. Perhaps after the war, there would be some way for them to see each other again. Still, Mrs. Ridley felt badly about the pain this would cause Cornelius. However, she also felt this was the best decision for all concerned. Considering the circumstances, she was willing to commit what she believed was a lesser wrong for a greater good.

"What else could I do about this?" she wondered. This whole style of living, based on slavery, was wrong. Slavery itself was wrong. It was evil. But this was their lot in life at this time. To do nothing, and watch Rosa follow in the doomed footsteps of her late mother, seemed the greater evil. For Mrs. Ridley, this was a choice between a lesser of two evils, because she could not bear being guilty of inaction.

CHAPTER 16

Prodigal Son

Colonel Ridley and the gentleman from New Orleans stood on the platform of the Norfolk & Petersburg Railroad station, saying their good-byes. Each man thought he had reaped the better part of the bargain. The Colonel was relieved that he was able to move a large portion of his wealth out of harm's way, should hordes of thieving Yankees overrun his homeland. The younger man was overjoyed to find a reason for living again. Like many creoles from the Crescent City, he accepted that there were powerful and influential forces which could neither be seen nor comprehended. He was not a firm believer in voodoo but he had learned early on not to ridicule it. When he was on a sailing ship, he seldom saw sharks in the ocean, but he respected that they were there. The words of his old housekeeper, Nanna Navarre, who had raised him from childhood, came to mind.

As he was leaving his mansion in the Garden District, her parting words to him had been: "When you lose something, you cannot always find it where you are. It is not like the story in the Bible about the woman who lost a piece of silver, and swept her house to find it. Sometimes, one must go far away to find what you have lost. Even then, you must not seek it. It must find *you*." Overwhelmed by grief, he hadn't paid much attention to her advice because it seemed inscrutable and contradictory. But when he returned home, he would lift that little prophetess up off her feet, give her a nearly smothering hug, and swing her around with joy. She had been right.

Unbeknownst to him, negotiations regarding Rosa had been conducted late into the night between the Colonel and his wife.

Colonel Ridley would leave it to his wife to tell the girl, as this was not a typical fiduciary affair for him and more a matter of the heart, better left to women – but he would tell Cornelius, himself. As a military man, he had little interest in the convoluted details of domesticity. Once he made a decision it was done and it was meant to be followed. He, too, had been wondering of late what to do with Rosa. He felt little obligation to her as his daughter, because legally, she was not. Yet he did feel affection for her and she reminded him greatly of her mother, for whom he did have a depth of feeling he would never dare to divulge. A number of his associates had persistently expressed interest in Rosa and she was becoming a distraction to his business and political affairs during these troubled times.

This decision was in the best interests of all concerned because she would be removed from the scene, ceasing all competition among his associates. As a parting gift to this remarkable young man to whom he was not only indebted, but for whom he also felt a certain fondness, the Colonel would see to it that Rosa would be waiting at the gangplank for Antoine when the ship set sail on the morning tide. However, he would have someone other than Cornelius deliver her. Since his nephew William was returning to school, he would ask William to take Rosa to Norfolk by train, and from there, he could take the train back to the Virginia Military Institute.

The gentlemen shook hands one last time as passengers began to board. "You will speak to Cornelius?," Antoine reminded Colonel Ridley. "Yes," the Colonel replied reflexively. Each man silently vowed to see the other after the coming war. A porter carried Antoine's luggage onto the train, and he followed with the valise full of bearer bonds handcuffed to his wrist. As the locomotive slowly pulled away, he tipped his hat to the Colonel. The Colonel responded with a wink and a sanguine smile. He would have loved to have been

134

there at the boarding dock in Norfolk, to see Antoine's face when William escorted Rosamonde up the gangplank to meet him.

≈

The time for final preparations had come for Cornelius. He met once more with Mama Rue and Uncle Robert. Brother Daniel was also there to give his blessing. It was the third week of August, and the Perseids meteor shower had put on a brilliant display the week before, which may have been charming for lovers, but it alarmed Mama Rue like a cock crowing at dawn.

"Cornelius, it's time to leave, now, son. I don't want you to go. But you can't wait no longer. You gotta obey the stars," she pleaded. Brother Daniel agreed. "War's comin' son. An' so is winter. It's gonna take you three, mebbe four weeks of walkin' to get to the Quakers in Pennsylvania - dependin' on weather." The third member of the triumvirate of elders, Uncle Robert, pulled the corncob pipe from his mouth and spoke next.

"You gotta figure 'bout 20, or 25 miles a day, mebbe a little more. I know that don't sound like too much - 'cause you could do more. But you gotta go easy - can't look like you runnin'. The Lord blessed you with white skin, so you won't raise no suspicion, long as you takes your time and look like you know where yer goin'."

Cornelius nodded affirmatively. "Plus, I'll have Rosa with me, so we won't be able to go much faster than that," he responded. But he was met with dead silence, and he searched the three troubled faces for a full accounting. "What?" he asked in growing concern as Big Mama Rue struggled to find the words.

135

"She gone, son," Mama Rue said gently. Cornelius exploded. "How - when - where'd she go? Why didn't you tell me?" The pain in his voice was palpable as he begged the three elders for an explanation. "We didn't know, son," Uncle Robert said in his typically avuncular tone. "We just found out ourselves."

Cornelius' eyes welled up, as did all the others'. "When? Where?" he pleaded. Uncle Robert continued, "Black Bobby had one of the work crews down by the train station in Franklin yesterday, workin' on a section of rail fence some cows knocked down. He saw Rosa and the Colonel's nephew at the station, boardin' the train to Norfolk. He wasn't forcin' her, but he say she look real sad - like she didn't wanna go."

Anger roiled up in Cornelius and his face and neck flushed red. "So that's why he sent me on that wild goose chase to Emporia yesterday! He knew it would keep me on the road all day." He instinctively got ready to storm off but Mama Rue and Brother Daniel held him back.

"No," insisted Mama Rue - "you can't go rushin' off in anger! That'll ruin everything we planned for so long. First thing you need to do is finish goin' over your plans with us. Next, you better slip over to Fortsville to see your wife and say a proper goodbye. You may not see her for a while."

"But what about Rosa?" Cornelius demanded. Brother Daniel responded, "She in God's hands now, son. An' maybe in less danger than you are. Sister Sara said she was in the kitchen up the big house, an' heard somebody say Rosa was goin' to New Orleans with that creole man who came to see Colonel Ridley. We love her jus' as much as we love you. But right now, you gotta make sure everything is

136

planned down to the minute, 'cause, one wrong move and all is lost. We come too far now - we been waitin' years for this chance for you."

"Everything and everyone is dependin' on you now, Cornelius," Uncle Robert added firmly, looking at the other two gray-haired elders to concur. "Best thing you can do to help your sister - and your wife - is to get free. Once you do that, you can work on the rest of it. An' we'll try to find out more about where they sent Rosa."

"He's right, honey," said Mama Rue. "You know the three of us love you both like you was our own. We watched over you an' Rosa since the day you was born. You got a chance here, Cornelius - you got a *real* chance. Not like us. The only way we gonna leave this ole plantation is if you carry us away in your heart," she said, her voice cracking. Cornelius had rarely seen her cry. He had known this woman all his life, and she always seemed as tough as tree bark. She - and these two men - had forever been his guardians, mentors, protectors, parents, and family. The reality of leaving them, along with Rosa and Martha Jane, stuck in his heart like an icicle.

He didn't want to go, and couldn't bear the thought of leaving his family - his wife, his friends, his giant protector Big Man, and Uncle Wilson. However, Brother Daniel convinced him that "you have to go, because you're the only one who can make it. You're one in 300 at Bonnie Doon, and by getting free you will free us too, in a way. Someday, when things settle down, and the war is over, maybe you can come back for us, and we will welcome you home like the Prodigal Son," Brother Daniel prophesied. For, he *was* their son. He was *truly* their son. "Sure, your momma birthed you, but God called her home and delivered you into our hands - just like baby Moses in the Bible. You are our Moses and you have to find the Promised Land for us. Only *you* can carry our hopes and dreams of a better life to come - not in the next world - but in this one."

137

"We ain't goin' nowhere, boy," Uncle Robert said, struggling to smile. "We be here when you come back for us afta the war."

They went over his plans in detail, reminding him of minor points he had confused or forgotten. On Saturday afternoon, he would come to Mama Rue's and pick up his ruck sack. It would have his supplies – his boots, a compass, some clothes, matches, medicine, a few clean strips of cloth to use as bandages, a folding straight razor, a bar of soap, a piece of flint, a hunting knife with a steel blade, a tin cup and plate, and a few utensils – and finally, an old inexpensive pocket watch. It had taken the elders years to acquire all of these things through bartering, saving, and scavenging. They had pooled their resources and kept them well hidden for just such an occasion.

Little Horse would meet him here and bring an extra horse. They would make their way to Darlington's Store. Little Horse would buy his supplies and use the mare as a pack horse to haul his packages home. Mr. Darlington would explain the rest of the plan to Cornelius.

This was a plot that had been slowly evolving over the years, without Cornelius ever knowing of it. Each of the three elders had originally considered escaping themselves at some point in their lives. What began as wishful thinking when Cornelius was still a boy grew over the course of many late-night discussions on Mama Rue's porch, when they realized his intelligence and potential. No one was better suited or had a better chance than Cornelius, because he had two invaluable assets that no other young runaway being tracked by dogs in the swamp could ever have. Cornelius had a map in his mind that stretched for more than 100 miles – twenty times farther than the average slave at Bonnie Doon had ever traveled.

The other thing of value that no other slave on the plantation had was his straight red hair, green eyes, and skin pale enough to pass

138

for white. Added to this arsenal of advantages, was that it was public knowledge that he was permitted to travel far and freely alone. As long as his behavior appeared normal, none would ever risk incurring the wrath of Colonel Ridley - head of the Southampton Militia, local judge, and the richest man in the county - by interfering with the business this authorized representative was presumably conducting on the Colonel's behalf.

There were only a few more pieces to the puzzle to complete. One: even with these superior advantages, he still needed the help of the Quaker farmers and businessmen, and free blacks who served as conductors on the Underground Railroad. He had long had a friend and guide in Samuel Darlington, who had prayed for years for an opportunity to help this child of bondage escape to the North. Two: he would need to appear invisible - as just another white journeyman on his way to work on a farm or at a local mill. And three: he would need to get clear of the Colonel's sphere of influence as quickly as possible. Leaving Saturday afternoon would give him a 36-hour head start before he was missed on Monday morning. God willing, he would be well on his way by then. With Rosa unfortunately no longer in the picture, his chances of success were ironically enhanced.

But first he had to quietly say his good-byes, and he would not be able to say them all in person to those he loved and admired. That would cause unnecessary risk. Although he didn't believe anyone would deliberately betray him, he could not take the chance of some innocent comment or youthful indiscretion by a child who only meant well and who would miss him. He would let his three loving elders say his goodbyes for him to most of the folks at Bonnie Doon. His first farewell would be to Martha Jane. The three elders had planned for her, too.

With her brother and their three children, collectively, they could not leave until after the war began and the Yankees invaded. If they could reach the Union lines, they just might be free if they were not returned to their master. Commandeering "contraband of war" would be an easy way for the North to impoverish the South and decrease its supply of free labor that was beginning to be used to build fortifications against the threatening North. Their journey would be long and arduous, perhaps taking years before they were reunited. However, when they were finally reunited, they would all be free.

Cornelius and Martha Jane had said their good-byes long before, so there was really not much more to say. They spent most of the brief time they had left holding each other tightly, as lovers do, trying to memorize the feeling of warmth, oneness, and love. He hugged her one last time in the doorway of her cabin. Her son George was five or six years old now, and long and lanky as a split rail. He would be a tall man someday. He was swarthy and his hair was straight and black as a horse's tail, and could easily have been a Nottoway, a Spaniard, or Portuguese. He was fiercely protective of his mother and quite fond of Cornelius - who hugged him as well. The baby in Martha Jane's belly was just beginning to grow. As he said his final farewell, he reminded her of Big Mama Rue's words: "No matter how long, someday, deliverance will come. It *will* come."

CHAPTER 17

Go Down Moses[ix]

He should have never done it. It could have ruined everything - but Cornelius couldn't help himself. He was polishing the saddles inside the barn when Colonel Ridley approached him. The doors to the barn were open wide to let in sunlight and fresh air. As Mrs. Ridley gazed out the windows of the house, she could see the Colonel giving Cornelius orders about one thing or another. However, Cornelius couldn't hear the words because his head was pounding from the pressure of hot blood racing toward his brain.

Mrs. Ridley had asked her husband to speak to Cornelius beforehand about Rosa, but more pressing issues were on his mind and he had forgotten to do it. He had urgent business - a military conclave in Lexington, at the Virginia Military Institute, with the commanders of all of the county militias in Virginia. He would do so later, he told her. War was coming sooner than anyone expected and the Confederate Army was in the process of being organized. She knew what might happen when he spoke to Cornelius, and putting it off would only make it more difficult. Mrs. Ridley knew that selling Rosa would break Cornelius' heart. But it was also an opportunity for Rosa to have a chance for a better life, she reasoned, which helped her justify it to herself. She had wanted her husband to promptly tell Cornelius, even if it was after the fact.

She knew that slaves could now only be freed by being manumitted in the Last Will and Testament of the owner, or by a special act of the state legislature. And none of Virginia's state senators and representatives were in a willing mood to do that on the eve of war. By selling Rosa to Antoine, the Creole could free her in

141

New Orleans as he wished without permission from anyone. For Mrs. Ridley, it was a "Hobson's Choice" - which is really no choice at all.

Cornelius suddenly blurted out - "Why did you sell her, sir?" The Colonel was taken aback. "What did you say, boy?" he demanded. "Why did you sell my sister," Cornelius snapped back with fury flashing in his eyes. "How dare you take that tone with me," the Colonel bellowed. "Goddammit boy, you forget yourself and your place!" Mrs. Ridley watched the argument escalate from the rear of the house. She didn't want to intervene, but she could see that it wasn't much of an argument. Her husband was excoriating the young man with a torrent of vitriol. It resembled a thrashing.

Cornelius was seething with anger, yet keeping his eyes riveted to the ground and his arms pressed against his sides like any other slave undergoing a beating, for fear of what his uncontrolled rage might allow him to do. It was the ultimate act of self-restraint and loyalty - a Herculean effort to resist the Oedipal urge to kill his father. As her husband's voice grew louder, she could more clearly distinguish what he was saying through the open window. When she heard something about selling him off or sending him to work in the fields, she marched out of the house and toward them. When the Colonel raised his hand to strike Cornelius, she screamed.

"Thomas! Don't you dare strike that boy!" Colonel Ridley whirled around in shock. "Damnation Maggie, don't you interfere in my business," he yelled - but she ignored him and barked back. He was stunned by her audacity. "This *is* my business! This boy is no obstinate field slave. He is the most loyal person to you on this plantation, other than me!" The Colonel staggered backward a step. Something suddenly snapped inside her. Perhaps it was a lifetime of trying to ignore the injustice and hypocrisy of slavery. For the first time in her life, this well-mannered, conservative, conventional,

142

refined woman of genteel Southern society was out of control. She would later regret her words and never speak of this incident again, but for the moment, The Furies had taken possession of her.

"*You* brought him into this world!" Ridley tried to object but she would have none of it, and continued her blistering attack. "Do you think I'm a fool? Didn't you think I noticed you sneaking off to her cabin at night when I was pregnant with Leonidas?" Colonel Ridley winced as though he had been struck by a pistol shot. With a mixture of angst and anger he cried out in pain, "For God's sake, don't speak his name here!"

But she sprang at Ridley like a panther, with a ferocity he had never seen before. "I'm not one of your slaves, Thomas! I can say whatever I damn well please! I helped you build this plantation. I gave birth to your children - all except for Cornelius and Rosa!" Their names pierced him like arrows, and her wavering voice could be heard nearly half a mile away.

"You and your *ilk* - all fine Southern gentlemen," she said mockingly. "All you ever want to do is make money, make war, and make more slaves... At first I hated these children, and I hated you for making them. Why do you think I never rejected or mistreated them, like another wife would? Because their mother died due to a difficult childbirth - she died after giving birth to your children. She died because of you! They never had a mother or a father. Oh, they had a *Master* all right - but never a *father!*"

Ridley crumpled from the blow, but she continued the assault mercilessly. "Look at him, Thomas! Look at him!" she demanded. "He even looks like a Ridley! And why wouldn't he? He's not your 'issue' as you so callously call him. God in Heaven thinks he's your son, and so does every man in the County. And Cornelius is the best son you could have ever had. He's your only son, now! Even your soldiers are fond of him. Had he been born white, instead of *almost white*, he could have gone to the Institute and become a cavalry officer like you, and your father before you. He is a smart, kind, decent young man who has accepted his lot in life, never asking you for anything. Not one damned thing! Never a special favor or a gift his entire life! All he has ever wanted is to serve you faithfully, and he has - more so than anyone, except for me. Only the Lord knows why! Now, when he asks you one thing - just one thing - why we sold the only sister he loves more than anyone in the world, you threaten to beat him!" Cornelius was dumbfounded and immobilized.

Her quaking voice began to lower but it held just as much mettle. "You should have told him, Thomas, liked I asked you. You should have talked to him to make him understand. He's not one of your field hands - he's a smart young man; he's different and he has feelings. He loves her! If you had talked with him, and explained to him that Rosamonde could have a better life this way - and that maybe this was the *only* way - he would have listened.

"You should have told Cornelius how people like him and Rosamonde can have a more normal life in New Orleans, and not just be born and die a slave like their mother did on this farm!" A sound of frustration punctuated her final sentence like a coda. Depleted by her litany, she turned away in anguish, embarrassment, and disgust - hurrying away to the sound of rustling taffeta and tears.

The Colonel struggled for breath as if he was having a heart attack. Cornelius, shaken by what had just happened, was holding the sides of his head as if it greatly pained him. Colonel Ridley turned back toward him, feebly holding up his hand as if trying to explain.

144

"I...I..." he began, grasping to find elusive words; but he couldn't. He turned around and trudged slowly back to the big house, staggering like a man who had just been thrown from his horse.

CHAPTER 18

Steal away[x]

Cornelius dropped down onto the wooden stool just inside the doors of the barn in a state of shock. He couldn't believe what he had just seen and heard. He had never heard Mrs. Ridley say so much, and he had certainly never seen her so angry; but in many ways it was a validation of nearly everything he had thought and felt his entire life. He often asked himself why he was so dedicated to the Colonel. And he wondered about his mother - who she was, where she came from, and how her life had been. Except for Rosa, he felt like he had materialized on this plantation with no connection to the past.

"Rosa...poor Rosa," he mourned. He never even had a chance to say good-bye. He did have those he thought of as family in Buckhorn Quarters, and there was Uncle Wilson - but Rosa was his only sibiling. Losing her left a hole in his heart that would never heal. "I just pray she finds happiness and freedom," he thought. "There's no turning back. I absolutely have to leave, now," he told himself.

Going through the motions without thinking about what he was doing, he finished polishing the saddles and put them away - making sure the bridle gear was in order. Though it would be nearly impossible, he had to follow his normal routine. He groomed, watered, and fed the horses, and as noon approached, he said one last good-bye to the chestnut mare he loved so much, and who loved him in return. Next, he collected a few things from his cabin next to the barn - he didn't need much because most of what he was taking with him was already secreted at Big Mama Rue's.

146

Over the past few weeks, whenever he visited her, he would take one or two items with him, so that when he was finally ready to leave, he wouldn't be seen carrying a bundle of clothes. The stable boys would come by soon to bring the horses out to the exercise yard so they could clean out their stalls and put fresh hay and straw in them. Cornelius took a quick glance around at the place where he had spent so many years, committing it to memory before heading down to Big Mama Rue's where the elders would be waiting for him.

He walked down the path to her cabin as if he was carrying the weight of the world on his shoulders. The three elders were waiting at the cabin and Little Horse had just arrived. They said their farewells with a minimum of words, because it was too painful to say much more. Over the past few weeks, they had already done this many times, because they knew this separation would have to be kept brief. They told him that by leaving, and finding freedom, he was freeing them all. It would give them hope that one day, they too would be free.

"You will tell everyone I said good-bye?" he asked poignantly. "Especially Hambone and June Bug. And my Uncle Wilson, over at Rock Spring?" They nodded silently. "I feel like I'm runnin' out on Big Man. I wish he was here so I could tell him in person."

As if he had just spoken the secret words that freed a genie from a magic lamp, Big Man appeared, coming down the path behind Mrs. Ridley, who was headed directly toward them with a determined step. She was dressed in her riding outfit and appeared to be visibly upset. Mama Rue gasped. Everyone rose to their feet, and Uncle Robert exclaimed "what in the Hell..." to no one in particular. Mistress Ridley had rarely been down to the Quarters, and she didn't look happy. The behemoth behind her was carrying the old

147

blunderbuss from the carriage Cornelius always drove, with a leather pouch of shells hanging from a cord around his shoulder.

"What is she...how did she...Big Man?" - Brother Daniel couldn't complete a single sentence. All they could think was that Cornelius would be held here at gunpoint by the misguided giant until a couple of militia men arrived to put him in a cell in the basement of Bonnie Doon. Still mounted on his horse, Little Horse narrowed his eyes as if he was taking aim at the pair. The rest of the group stood dumbfounded.

Mrs. Ridley broke the silence as she came to an abrupt halt. "You all look like you've just seen a ghost," she said, smoothing her jacket and patting her hair, trying to restrain the errant curls that had popped out of place during her strenuous walk. "I suppose I do look a fright," she admitted, feeling obviously flustered.

"Afternoon, Missus Ridley," each of the elders stammered, but she cut them off with a wave of her hand. "I didn't come down here to meddle in your affairs," she said testily. "After what happened this morning, I know you have to leave now, Cornelius - and I think it is in your best interests to do so."

Cornelius began to explain but she stopped him by holding up her hand. "I don't want to know about your plans, and I hope you've planned well," she warned. "But here is some money to help you on your journey," she said, pushing a small pouch filled with coins toward him.

Cornelius was baffled. "Mistress Ridley, I can't take..." But she cut him off again in mid-sentence. "Now, don't argue with me, Cornelius," she said forcefully. "You take this, now. God only knows what is going to happen to you, and you will need all the help you can

148

get. It's not a gift - it's just, consider it back wages if you must. You have earned it, and then some."

He saw the futility in disagreeing with her - and the truth of her words. "Thank you, ma'am," he said as he put the pouch in his pocket. "Big Man," she said curtly; then turned quickly and took the blunderbuss from Big Man and shoved the gun into Cornelius' hands.

"You take this, too. You have a long road ahead you - no matter where you're going. The roads aren't safe at night. And the way things are going, they won't be much safer during the day. There are hillbillies and highwaymen all the way from here to Washington, and you need to protect yourself. Besides, you're the only one who knows how to shoot the silly old thing."

Big Man then took the bag of shells off his shoulder and handed it to her while she spoke to Cornelius. After handing him the gun, she gave Cornelius the bag of shells. "I know I can be a pretty cold fish sometimes," she said unapologetically. "But I truly am quite fond of you, Cornelius - and I deeply regret the way things worked out. You're a fine young man and you deserve a better life. You all do," she said as she scanned the faces of the elders. "May God bless you and Rosamonde - she was dear to me, too. I pray He finds a way to reunite you two someday." Her voice cracked momentarily with emotion but she took a deep breath, regaining her strained composure.

"Now, Colonel Ridley has left for Lexington and will be gone for three days. You have three days to get as far away as you can. I wish I could have done more. Good-bye Cornelius," she said brusquely. She gave him a quick, awkward hug and walked several steps away to wait for Big Man to escort her back up to the mansion. Like a big brown bear, he slowly ambled up to Cornelius, took a small colorful river stone that was smooth and polished out of his pocket, and looked at Big Mama Rue, wanting her to speak on his behalf.

She said: "Big Man wanna give you this. It's a present." He looked at Cornelius and nodded slightly, then looked at Mama Rue again for her to continue. "He found it the day you was born, and he kep' it ever since. It's the most special thing he has; but he wanna give it to you, so you remember him." Big Man placed the stone in Cornelius' hand, and Cornelius marveled at the gift, deeply touched. Then, with his large and beefy palms, the giant enclosed Cornelius' smaller hand within his own, squeezing it gently. Big Man looked deep into Cornelius' eyes, and conveyed the lifelong love and devotion he had felt since the day he had first cradled his little friend in his massive arms. But Cornelius couldn't have been more baffled.

Looking to Mama Rue for answers, Cornelius asked in disbelief: "How did you know all that? He really say all that to you?" Mama Rue sighed patiently, shaking her head with the hint of a smile. "Now, Cornelius, you know Big Man can't talk," she insisted, with her hands on her hips.

"Then how did you know what he wanted to say?" he asked with exasperation. "You seen Big Man talk with his hands sometime. But mostly, he talks with his eyes, Cornelius - he talks with his eyes," she said tenderly. Big Man nodded gently.

As Big Man gave Cornelius a bear hug, a low guttural sound welled up in his throat through damaged vocal chords as he struggled to say, "Cor-neel-yus." It sounded more like a growl than a word, but everyone was thunderstruck. It was the only time anyone had ever heard Big Man speak. As he stepped back from Cornelius, he tried his best to smile his little smile as enormous tears rolled down his brown cheeks. "I love you, Big Man," Cornelius said softly. With that, the
150

giant nodded again then turned and walked away, lumbering up the path behind Mrs. Ridley on their way back to the big house.

"By God," said Brother Daniel, "I've seen two miracles today – Mistress Ridley down here in the Quarters, and Big Man speak. I got no doubt now, Cornelius, that you are gonna make it to the Promised Land. "

"'Cause that surely was a sign from God," Mama Rue testified. Uncle Robert uttered a reverential "Amen!" Even Little House nodded "yes" in amazement. Because, no one could argue the signs.

"You gotta go now, son. Not a minute to waste," said Mama Rue. "I love you all," Cornelius responded. With tears in her eyes, the tough old, Obeah woman replied: "See, boy? I told you that no matter how long it takes, one day, deliverance will come; yes indeedy, deliverance *will* come."

Cornelius put the shells in his saddle bag and slid the gun through the saddle straps. Grabbing the reins and the saddle horn, he put his foot in the stirrup and climbed onto the horse that Little Horse had brought for him. Uncle Robert hoisted his ruck sack up to him. "Jus' follow the *Drinking Gourd*, Cornelius - jus' follow the *Drinking Gourd*," he said, motioning up at the sky. Cornelius leaned down, kissed Mama Rue on her wet cheek, and shook hands with Uncle Robert and Brother Daniel. He tipped his hat to them one last time, and rode off with Little Horse without saying another word.

CHAPTER 19

Follow the Drinking Gourd[xi]

The riders arrived at Darlington's General Store before mid-afternoon, and the old Quaker was expecting them. They were welcomed inside and after an hour of conversation, Mrs. Darlington had an early supper waiting on the table for them.

Darlington had developed the escape plan over the years, hoping he would live to see the day when he could set Cornelius on the road north to freedom. The old Quaker was a conductor on the Underground Road, or Underground Railroad as some called it, and he was part of a constellation of connections that served as tributaries for the small stream of escaping slaves flowing north. His closest collaborators were amongst his fellow members of old Blackwater Quaker Meeting, not far away, but there were also free and enslaved blacks, abolitionists, sympathetic Southerners, and many others including children - most of whom he did not know.

Although he had the entire plan laid out in his mind, he only shared part of it with Cornelius. It wasn't from lack of trust in the bright young man - it was simply Darlington's strategy. That way, if Cornelius unfortunately got caught, he could not divulge much information about the secretive shadow organization. Darlington did explain how each conductor would guide him to the next stop, and he shared with him the names of some Quakers in Pennsylvania, so he would know he was in the right hands once he got there.

Since Darlington was now up in age, Little Horse would accompany Cornelius on the first leg of the trip, 20 miles northeast to the farm of a compatriot named Taliaferro - pronounced, "Tolliver," in the regional Tidewater dialect - who lived near Wakefield, Virginia. Little Horse would then return home with his horses, avoiding the main roads, confident he could get back by dawn.

The general idea was to make a wide berth around Petersburg by traveling to Wakefield, then to Surry, and cross the James River by night, landing at Jamestown. From Jamestown, Cornelius would continue on to Williamsburg, and cross the York River at night, landing at Gloucester Court House near Powhatan's Chimney above Gloucester Point. Gloucester County was a fortuitous choice because Cornelius looked like many of the free people of color there; and race relations were not as tense as they were in other parts of the South.

Once he passed Richmond, he would make his way first northwest toward Fredericksburg, and then take an easterly course along the Potomac River, skirting Washington - which still had plenty of Southern sympathizers - toward Towson, Maryland, where there was a strong community of free blacks. He would then continue in a northeasterly arc, following the Baltimore and Jerusalem Turnpike, until he reached the village of Darlington where he would cross over the Susquehanna River below the Conowingo Falls.

Once he crossed into Pennsylvania, he would be in the realm of ardently abolitionist Quakers. There he would continue following Baltimore Pike through Oxford, Kennett Square, Darlington Valley, and eventually to Media, where local Friends would care for him. Hopefully, Martha Jane would be able to join him there in due time.

During supper, the Darlingtons shared their advice with Cornelius. The important thing, Darlington said, was to act like he belonged wherever he was, and to show a confident demeanor. "Remember," the old Quaker said, "you have a decided advantage over other runaways - you look white." Cornelius smiled because he

153

remembered when Mama Rue first told him he would be invisible. He now fully appreciated the wisdom of her prescient words.

As dusk approached, the young men prepared their horses and Mrs. Darlington packed each one a bag of food for their journey. When it was dark enough to see the first fireflies twinkle brightly, Darlington and Cornelius said their goodbyes. The old Quaker was surprisingly sentimental. He had watched Cornelius grow from a toddler to a fine young man, and it grieved him to now part company. He knew he might never see Cornelius again, and if he did, it would take years. However, he assured Cornelius he would keep in touch with his elders at Buckhorn, and help them whenever he could.

"May God watch over thee, son. Like your elders told you, just follow the Drinking Gourd, north, Cornelius. Just follow the Drinking Gourd," he said. The sojourners then set off on their journey.

CHAPTER 20

Garden of Eden

In early October 1862, nearly 400 miles away in Fayette County in southwestern Pennsylvania, a young couple was slowly making their way up along a deer trail carpeted with leaves, to the top of a high hill. The woods were thick with hickory, elm, sassafras, tulip poplar, sugar maple, and a variety of pine trees. The two shadowy figures were occasionally illuminated by shafts of golden light piercing the dense leafy canopy.

"Where're we goin', Solomon?" the young woman asked, nearly out of breath. "Over the Alleghenies?" He turned around and looked at her with love in his eyes. He smiled in response, extending his hand to help her over a large, muscular tree root clinging tenaciously to the steep slope. She was no dainty maiden, and she loved hiking among these hills as much as he did. Her people were hardy, and she was one of the fastest runners in town.

"No, honey, just up to that outcrop of rock. We used to call that 'Indian Rock,' when my brothers Willie and Jacob and I climbed up here as kids." In a few moments they had reached the plateau, nestled just below the top of the ridge. Here was a cozy little clearing covered with moss, roomy enough to pitch a large tent. He held her hand again as she found a comfortable place to sit against the back of the alcove. Rising, he surveyed the land below like the liege of a realm. To the east, the forest grew thicker and more impenetrable. To the west, the hills sloped down toward broad meadows and the Monongahela River just beyond.

Her sunny disposition returned as she caught her breath, and she smiled at him as he stood, hands on hips, savoring the view. Shading his eyes with his left hand and pointing with his right, he said: "over there is Cornel's farm. Shading her eyes she replied, "I see it. You're a real nature boy, Solomon. A farmer, a mountain man..."

"And I love to fish," he interrupted. "We used to go fishin' for trout all the time at Dunlap's Lake. Or when we felt real frisky, we'd walk to the Monongehela, down by Nemacolin." She was impressed. "That must be ten miles," she exclaimed. "More like twelve," he replied with a haughty grin.

"Or sometimes, we'd hike over to Fort Necessity and Jumonville Glen where General George Washington fought the battle that started the French and Indian War. And other times, we'd head south down to Negro Mountain, on the county line. We loved to roam through the caves down there and around here, too. Lot of 'em 'round these parts."

"You're lucky you didn't get lost down one of those tunnels. Or get eaten by the trolls who live under the mountain," she teased.

"This is beautiful country, Mary. When God wanted to make the Garden of Eden, He must've thought Pennsylvania would be one mighty fine place to put it." She nodded silently because it was hard to argue the point.

"My people've been in these parts a long, long time. Since my Grandfather Isaac's time," he said proudly. "Sometimes my father would take us huntin' for deer, wild geese, ducks, turkey, rabbit, or pheasant. And my grandfather told me that when he was a young man, there were still some forest buffalo around."

156

"Buffalo?" she asked in amazement. "Yes, buffalo. But they were all hunted out about 50 years ago," he replied. She, in turn, responded: "But what about black bears?"

"We never hunted or ate bear. Don't rightly know why. Papa and Grandpa didn't believe in huntin' them, an' said there was somethin' special about bears. Grandfather Isaac called them 'Makwah'." She repeated the word slowly: "Makwah?" she asked.

"That's the Indian word for bear," Solomon replied. My grandfather said we have to share the woods with them, because it's their home, too. They don't bother us and we don't bother them. We give each other the space we need." She nodded thoughtfully.

He pointed to the farm in the valley and continued, "After we get married next week, we'll have our own farm some day and raise a family. And I'll take our sons huntin' and fishin' and teach'em to love the mountains and the rivers and valleys. I love these hills and woods, and trees that reach up tall like a church steeple." She looked at him accusingly.

Smiling sheepishly, he shrugged his shoulders and continued, "I know I'm not a regular church go-er." She concurred, nodding authoritatively like a judge. "But when I'm out here, in the woods, I feel like I'm in church, and I can look up to a patch of blue sky and talk directly to God. And I can hear His voice, too." She looked at him quizzically, now.

"Not in words, mind you," he explained, "but in the wind in the trees, and the songs of the birds; the way the water splashes over rocks in a stream; in the little faces of the flowers; or the way the crickets sing and the jar flies (cicadas) call out to each other on summer nights, and in the color of the autumn leaves. The buzzin' of

157

the bees and the crickets singin' remind me of a church choir." He was so earnest and adorable she just had to kiss him.

"You Cliffords must have some Mingo in you," she said, smiling. He returned her smile with one of his own. "So, is this where you bring all your little country gals?" Mary asked, as she looked around, feigning jealousy. He turned and looked solemnly into her eyes, as if he was swearing an oath.

"There's no other girls, Mary - just you. This," looking around proudly, "is a special place. I've done a lotta thinkin' about my life up here. This place is a big part of me. It's in my blood and in my soul. And so are you," he punctuated with a kiss. "But you do hav'ta watch out for timber rattlers 'round here, though," he said with false concern. "Really?" she gasped, clutching his arm and pulling closer to him. "Maybe - you can't be too careful," he feigned ominously. As they basked in the warmth of each other's arms, a pair of hawks circled high overhead like guardian angels.

They sat and talked until the middle of that Indian summer afternoon, with crickets and birds chirping throughout the green-wood, before deciding to begin the climb back down before the sun fell too far behind the trees, throwing deep shadows across the circuitous path which would hamper their walking. Though it was still late summer, the air in the highlands was cool because fall arrives earlier there. As they made their descent, a gentle gust of wind breezed up and shook loose the first of the autumn leaves, showering the soon-to-be newlyweds with giant flakes of orange and amber, chestnut and gold.

≈

Bethany Baptist was a little old white clapboard church with a tiny steeple in the middle of a clearing not far from town. Dressed in his Sunday best, Solomon sat silently in the front pew alone. It was actually his only black suit, but he took meticulous care of it, and had purchased a freshly starched shirt and collar just for the occasion. He didn't expect many people to come, but he got there early anyway and slipped inside unseen. With his head in his hands, leaning forward with elbows resting on knees, he closed his eyes and listened to the quiet. He rubbed his eyes slowly as if washing his face in the dark, trying to ease the pain in his forehead. He loved the silence, and remembered that the Quakers he knew said they can hear God's voice in the silence. Since he had been a boy, roaming the deep woods, he had understood precisely what they meant.

The coolness of the room and the dim light weren't helping to ease the pain. "People'll think I had too much to drink last night," he thought to himself. In fact, he hadn't had nearly enough to drink to calm his nerves. He hadn't been able to sleep because of the parade of memories passing through his mind. So, he got up just before dawn, lit a candle, and standing inside the small circle of light, got dressed. He then sat on the edge of the bed collecting his thoughts, and as the gray light of dawn gave the curtains a ghostly glow, he stood up, blew out the candle and walked stolidly toward the door like a man on his way to a funeral. This was one church service he wasn't going to be late for - Mary would not have liked that.

He didn't turn around when he heard the church doors open behind him with a flash of morning light and a gust of fresh air, making the room seem even darker when the doors closed again. The footsteps coming toward him were soft as a person walking on eggshells, trying not to break them. Solomon's thoughts drifted aimlessly until he felt a strong hand on his shoulder. He knew the owner of that hand, and he whispered, "Hello Pastor Henry."

"She looks beautiful," the pastor said, gazing down at the young woman laid out in the wooden casket facing the front pew. "Um hum," Solomon replied absently.

"It's time to start the service, son. The others are here." Solomon gave the same two-grunt reply as the pastor patted him on the shoulder once more and walked back up to aisle to open the church doors.

Solomon watched the process unfold from emotionally afar. He felt numb and barely heard the hymns, the singing, or the sermon. He watched silently as the parishioners filed past the casket to pay their final respects to Mary, his wife of six months. They would then turn and shake his hand or offer words of sympathy, and he nodded as if he understood but he really couldn't decipher what they were saying. Their words seemed muffled and his field of vision, like a fish eye lens, was confined to the parameters of the casket. He was lost in a maze of thoughts.

At some point the service ended, the pall bearers strode up, closed the casket and solemnly carried it out. Someone, his father Jacob perhaps, grasped his arm, helped him to his feet and escorted him out. His brothers and sisters gathered around him. The casket was loaded onto a mule-drawn cart and slowly led away. As he walked behind the cart all he could see was glimpses of Mary's face. Sometimes smiling, sometimes in pain. He never really understood what happened, because it had all happened so quickly. He could see she was sick and getting worse. The local country doctor was a good medical man, but he couldn't diagnose the problem.

"Septicemia - blood poisoning" the city doctor, Dr. Harvey, had diagnosed. The able and highly respected physician had come nearly 50 miles all the way from Pittsburgh. He said the infection had raced through her entire system. Made her breathe too fast, made her heart give out. Solomon didn't understand, and life would never be the same without her. This changed him in the most profound ways.

Solomon had thought a lot about life, and love, before Mary died, but he had rarely meditated on death. The Cliffords were a large mulatto family who had been free people of color stretching at least as far back as the American Revolution. There were many siblings, cousins, aunts and uncles, and children. They were a tenacious bunch who lived long and multiplied. He had occasionally seen death before - perhaps a cousin here or a neighbor there, but mostly just a few older people. He had expected that his grandparents and other elders would die. He had known them all his life and had watched them grow older year by year. He had been prepared for that. But a young person like Mary dying so suddenly? He had rarely seen that before. He hadn't been prepared for something like this. It was an unrelenting and searing pain, like a smoldering coal fire glowing red and hot; inescapable, inextinguishable, all-consuming, unbearable.

Growing up along the old frontier in western Pennsylvania with its verdant fields and forests, densely covered mountains, mighty rivers and sparkling streams, and air so sweet and fresh one could almost taste it, was intoxicating to the senses. Digging his hands into the rich brown soil, nurtured by the warm sun and cool rains made corn and other crops nearly burst from the ground. These things could only make one think of life, but he couldn't be a farmer any more. He had lost his faith in life, and in the hope of a future that now looked solemn, empty, and bleak. All he could look forward to

161

now was growing old alone. Maybe he'd move to Pittsburgh, into the city, where he could lose himself and try to start a new life. He knew for certain that his life had to change. And it would change dramatically, much sooner than he thought.

CHAPTER 21

Fraternity of Friends

Cornelius had traveled far – farther than he had ever traveled before, beyond the boundaries of his known world. Although the odyssey had been perilous and overcast with constant worry, it had also been disquietingly peaceful. He was a sojourner on the road to freedom, and had entrusted his faith in the kindness of strangers who profited not at all by keeping him safe. To the contrary, they risked a great deal by abetting in the theft of his father's property and would have profited them far more had they turned him in to the nearest magistrate for sizeable reward. Unlike Diogenes in ancient times, Cornelius needed no lamp to seek an honest man on this journey. In fact, thus far he had met *only* honest men and women whose courage and kindness seemed embedded in their children. Many were Quakers, some were not. Some were black, some were brown, and others white – farmers, tradesmen, craftsmen, and bondsmen. Common but courageous people.

He was delivered from one "conductor" to another and welcomed in home after home. It was nothing like the midnight escapes fraught with fear and danger, often being chased by hounds through woods and swamps that he knew other runaways had to endure. He kept waiting for the bottom of this bucket of wonder to drop out but, miraculously, it never did.

Though he had walked nearly the entire way, he was often treated to a hot meal at night. He usually slept in a bed, not under the stars or on a pile of straw in a cold, dank barn like just another farm animal. He was always addressed as "Mr. Smith" or "Mr. Jones" or occasionally referred to as "our passenger" or "our guest." He was never questioned and conversations were always kept light – often revolving around the weather, crops, or the care of horses. The children of his hosts warmed to him quickly and were often saddened to see him go, as he headed to the next stop on this "underground road." He appeared to be just another proper white journeyman traveling to find the company of friends, and not the slave son of one of Virginia's wealthiest and most powerful planters.

At night he dreamed of Bonnie Doon and the loved ones he left behind. He longed to see his sister Rosa again, and to hold Martha Jane in his arms. Or, to smell the smoke with a hint of dried cherries from Uncle Robert's pipe and see the peaceful look in Mama Rue's eyes as they sat on her makeshift porch talking quietly under a starry sky serenaded by crickets and cicadas, with Brother Daniel playing softly on his fiddle. He dearly missed his gentle giant Big Man, and his wide-ranging travels with Little Horse around the county down back-country roads.

However, he pushed these thoughts to the back of his mind during the day and only let them seep forth in the final moments before falling asleep at night so no one would see the mist they brought to his eyes. Sometimes before he drifted off, he could hear Mama Rue's deep, rich voice saying: "One day, deliverance will come. No matter how long it takes, one day deliverance will come." And finally, today was that day.

As Cornelius crossed over the great Susquehanna by rowboat in an early morning mist, he thought of the Jordan River he had heard about in the Bible stories Brother Daniel recounted long ago. Mason and Dixon's Line that separated the North from the South seemed like the border of the land of Canaan. This part of Chester

County was a hotbed of anti-slavery activity, and a number of escape routes passed through this very region.

He arrived in Kennett Square - a place of farms, fields, and trees - at the home of Bartholomew and Rebecca Fussell, members of the Religious Society of Friends, better known as "Quakers." Nearly a century earlier, Cornelius' white great-grandfather - Major Thomas Ridley, I - had fought at the Battle of Brandywine, not far from there, with the 10th Virginia Regiment. Now Cornelius was fighting his own battle for freedom with the help of strangers who feared the Lord more than they feared the law.

Cornelius had met many kind and caring people on his sojourn, but this was not just another stop on the Underground Railroad - it felt more like a homecoming. And he was surprised by the number of people sharing the noon day supper with him. Besides his hosts, there were other members of Longwood Progressive Meeting whose homes also served as stops on the Underground, like Isaac and Dinah Mendenhall, John and Hannah Cox, and a stout gray-haired Quaker with kindly eyes named Thomas Garrett, who had moved from Upper Darby Township in Delaware County, Pennsylvania, to Wilmington, Delaware, so he could help even more slaves escape from bondage.

Garrett, a scourge of the pro-slavery forces, had twice been fined his entire life savings by the court in Wilmington, for aiding and abetting runaways; but he considered this merely a fee paid for a license to do more. Garrett was one third of a remarkable triumvirate that included William Still - sometimes referred to as the "Father of the Underground Railroad" - and the legendary Harriet Tubman, a former runaway slave herself.

Still and the distinguished Octavius V. Catto - a teacher at the Institute for Colored Youth, which years later would be renamed *Cheyney University* - had traveled from Philadelphia together for this impromptu meeting. Though Cornelius could have never foreseen it, 60 years later he, Catto, and Still would all be buried just 30 yards from one other in the John Brown Section of Eden Cemetery on Springfield Road in Collingdale, roughly 25 miles away.

Other Friends who were there to welcome him to Pennsylvania included feisty and fearless Graceanna Lewis, and Isaac and Elizabeth Smedley Yarnall - all three of whom were members of Providence Monthly Meeting in nearby Media. The Yarnalls would take Cornelius home with them that evening where he would live for the next few years as he established a new life for himself while waiting for Martha Jane and her children to make their escape North.

Like Thomas Garrett, these quiet Quakers lived their faith. They were Christian soldiers - though some might reject that notion, because Quakers generally eschewed titles and formalities. Friends had often fought in wars - including the great William Penn, the founder of Pennsylvania - who had fought for the English army in Ireland to subdue Irish rebels in 1666.

Some 20 years after this meeting at the Fussell's farm, yet another Quaker soldier from nearby West Chester would be born in 1881, who would make an indelible impact on American history. Major General Smedley Darlington Butler of the United States Marine Corps would become known as "The Fighting Quaker" and the most highly decorated Marine in U.S. history when he died in Newtown Square, Pennsylvania, in 1940.

Quakers are a politically and theologically diverse sect. Most feel they should not receive recognition or accolades for acting upon moral obligations. They consider such their religious duty. The group gathered here were activists who put not only their money and property, but also their personal freedom at great risk. Although Pennsylvania was a "free" state, the Federal Fugitive Slave Act of 1850 was still in full force, and any person - black or white - who assisted or harbored a runaway slave could be arrested on the spot, imprisoned for six months and fined $1,000 (worth roughly $25,000 in 2014). Yet many Quakers believed there was a higher law put forth by God which they were bound to obey.

A short time later, a small, wiry black woman called Harriet Tubman slipped into the house unnoticed. Cornelius had heard her name mentioned in heated conversations in the South. He knew the Southerners greatly disdained her and had put a bounty on her head for stealing slaves, but he had also heard slaves speak of her in hushed and revered tones as the "Moses" of her people. Araminta Harriet Ross - the name Tubman had been born under - was brilliant, resourceful, courageous, and cunning. She also carried a pistol which she used to threaten the life of any runaway who began to have second thoughts about escaping. Tubman had returned to the South many times to guide dozens of slaves north to freedom - including members of her own family. She would serve as a scout, nurse, and spy for the Union army. But for all her battle-hardened exterior and world weariness, it was easy for anyone to see that she and Garrett held a special fondness for one another. They couldn't have been more different in background or appearance, but spiritually, they were connected.

When greeting each other, Tubman said to Thomas Garrett: "I will need five dollars to buy shoes for some of my 'passengers'."

Garrett feigned surprised. "And how does thee know I have five dollars, Harriet?" he responded.

"The Lord told me and sent me here to get it" she said with certainty. The Quaker laughed heartily and replied, "Well, I cannot argue with thee. I will give thee the five dollars." Harriet beamed as if she had just won an arm-wrestling match.

The Friends of Light, as Quakers sometimes referred to themselves, began their gathering in worshipful silence. After the silence was broken, the members of the group spoke to one another in a spirit of fraternity and equality, with no distinction in status between men and women or blacks and whites. Much to his relief, Cornelius was not the focus of an interrogation, but many were keenly interested in his life and experience because his was unique among slaves – given his ability to travel widely and exposure to many critical conversations of prominent planters and politicians in the South. He was an anomaly, even for a group as diverse as this one.

Some were surprised to learn of the complexities of convoluted master-slave relationships. From considerable geographic and cultural distance, many in the north assumed that all of "the peculiar institution" was as they had read in the 19th century's best-selling work – Harriet Beecher Stowe's *Uncle Tom's Cabin,* published in 1852. Many, including President Abraham Lincoln reportedly believed this compelling work may have been a contributing factor in precipitating the Civil War.[xii]

The relationships, and sometimes the affection they engendered, greatly complicated the institution of slavery. As Cornelius admitted, he had been treated well. None of this was meant an apology for slavery, for which there was no moral excuse,

168

but it did vex the Quaker concept that everyone – even slave owners – must have a spark of the Divine within them, whether they chose to follow it or not.

William Still had interviewed hundreds of runaways to glean information about their personal lives and the conditions under which they had escaped. During one such interview he discovered his own brother who had been left behind by his parents in slavery. Others at the table had also collectively helped dozens of slaves make their way North, sometimes as far as Canada. Seldom, if ever, had the Quakers gathered at the Fussell's farm that day, met a slave who was as white in appearance as any one of them. It was unfathomable to these learned and spiritual people how any slave owner could buy or sell a member of his own family – sometimes his own child.   They believed slavery to be an abomination before God, and the sexual exploitation of slave women was deemed a sin particularly worthy of eternal damnation.

Cornelius was moved not only by the group's extraordinary kindness and acceptance, but also by the courage of their convictions – traits he had seen in Mr. Darlington in Southampton County. Cornelius was not subordinate among these chosen people – they considered him their equal. They in turn admired his intelligence, sensitivity, humanity, and gentle manners. Someone asked him: "Mr. Ridley, do you consider yourself to be white or Negro?" His sage reply was: "I go for both." They viewed this progressive response not as the perspective of a man who was trapped between two worlds, but rather a citizen of both. Though their hearts were saddened by the fact that this earnest young man had been born into a life of bondage and raised without knowing his mother, they were also gladdened that one more child of God was now free.

Of particular interest to Cornelius was Mrs. Tubman, who had been born a slave in Dorchester County, Maryland, roughly 130 miles away. He felt a deep sadness for the harsh treatment she received at the hands of brutal masters – something he was fortunate not to have endured, and for which at times he felt guilty. He greatly admired her wisdom, astonishing bravery, and apparently special relationship with God, who forever seemed to watch over her and speak to her in visions or "sleeping spells," she called them. She was miraculous to him and he knew Big Mama Rue would have loved to have met this strong, kindred spirit.

He was also impressed with William Still, whose parents had also lived as slaves in Eastern Maryland. Still's father had purchased his own freedom, but his mother was forced to escape, being recaptured the first time. Although her second attempt to flee with two daughters was successful, she had to leave two sons behind who were sold to a plantation in Mississippi, much like Cornelius' beloved sister Rosa was sent to Louisiana.

Cornelius also greatly admired the remarkable *renaissance* man, Octavius V. Catto, whose father had been a slave in South Carolina. Catto was not only a staunch abolitionist and activist, but he was also a teacher and athlete, breaking racial barriers as a talented baseball player and cricketer in Philadelphia.

By late afternoon the gathering had drawn to a close, and most had started on their long journeys home. Still and Catto wanted to get back to Philadelphia by nightfall, and Garrett was returning to Wilmington. Tubman never said where she was headed next and by mutual agreement no one ever asked her. She knew where she was going and so did the Lord, and that was all who needed to know. The business of procuring freedom for slaves, as well as their respective spiritual leadings, brought members of this group together periodically. Therefore, they did not bid each other farewell, they simply said, "until then."

A few Friends who lived nearby remained for a little while to celebrate their gathering in song. And they began with the traditional hymn *Brethren We Have Met Together*, with their voices rising nobly, as a recessional for those who were departing.

As he walked to the Yarnall's carriage with them, Cornelius instinctively proceeded toward the driver's side, but Isaac touched him lightly on the shoulder and smiled, saying: "thank you Cornelius, but I am happy to drive thee." Slightly embarrassed, as some habits die hard, Cornelius returned the smile and replied: "thank you, sir."

Isaac grasped his hand in friendship and looked into his eyes. "You have much to learn about your new life, friend. The first is that you need not call anyone of us 'sir' - we are all equals as you have seen. You must call us by our given names." His wife Elizabeth and Graceanna smiled warmly and nodded in agreement. Cornelius shook Isaac's hand and fumbling for words said: "yes, sir...I mean, yes Isaac. Yes, I will. And bless you all for your kindness."

"You are welcome, Cornelius," said Graceanna. "As you have blessed us with your presence." Isaac and Cornelius helped the women onto the carriage, then climbed aboard themselves. Isaac wheeled the carriage about, waved to his hosts and headed east down the road toward the Baltimore turnpike.

CHAPTER 22

War Drums

Thirteen moons had passed since Cornelius had gone, but his elders knew he was safe because along with the cooler breezes of autumn, word had reached them through old man Darlington that one of his best Smithfield hams had arrived safely, much to the delight of fellow Quakers, in the North. Only once since then, had they received a similarly cryptic message that recipients in the North hoped for the day when another such delivery would be possible.

However, another long year had dragged on after that. Big Mama Rue continued to monitor the celestial signs in the night sky. It was during the Ides of July 1862 - over a year since Virginia and ten other states had seceded from the Union - that she perceived urgent cause for alarm, never having seen a comet so bright nor a tail so long, fearing it might belong to Lucifer himself. She didn't have to witness bloody battles or hear the evil laughter of the cannon - she could feel the disturbance to God's dominion over the world moving slowly but steadily toward Bonnie Doon like a rumbling deep inside the earth. In tortured dreams she saw the gates of Hell opening and a torrent of blood pour out leaving fields of broken bodies in its wake.

Mama Rue was speaking fervently, as Martha Jane listened intently. "Child, the war is comin' and the Federals comin' with it. Yankee gunboats're on the Blackwater River near Franklin. We hear the big guns in the distance at night. Sound like war drums callin' soldiers to their deaths. But the Blackwater's too narrow and twisted for the Yankee boats to get by, and the Rebs is fightin' somethin' fierce tryin' to block their way. The war is comin' to us - and you gotta

172

be ready to flee when the time is right. Won't be another chance, now." Rue paused to take a pull on her corncob pipe. Uncle Robert, sitting in the chair next to them nodded his head approvingly. It was Saturday evening, and Mama Rue had sent for Martha Jane who had brought her baby, Rachel Ann, with her. She had left her son George with her brother Andison back at Fortsville.

"But how am I goin' to get 30 miles from Fortsville to Franklin, past the Rebs, with two children?" she asked. "Won't have to," Uncle Robert noted. Martha Jane was perplexed, but Rue continued.

"Thass right, daughter. You won't have to. Boats fly fast on water – this is jus' the beginnin'. Takes soldiers longer to march on foot. But sooner or later, the Union army'll be here. It's gonna take'm a while 'cause they gotta come in force. Can't win the war from way up north – they gotta bring the war down here to the south. When they do, you and your brother and your children make your way to the Union lines and they'll take you in. You be free, then."

"They won't send us back?" Martha Jane asked, worried and surprised. Uncle Robert shook his head back and forth slowly to indicate "no, don't think so."

"Runaways is 'contraband' now – spoils o' war," said Rue. Slaves worth big money – you know that. If the army frees the slaves, it's like takin' money from their masters. All without firin' a shot."

"Really?" Martha Jane persisted. "Thass right," Rue assured her. "Firs', they did send'em right back. But then, some Yankee general said, 'no, keep'em – that's worse for the Rebs and better for us.' And somma the slaves wanna join up with the Union to fight for 'em. Lotta runaways ready to do that now." Martha sat back in amazement.

173

"She's right," Uncle Robert chimed in. "Rue always right about dese things. That's why I stopped arguin' wit' her years ago. She know what she's talkin' about - so you listen to her, girl. And God willin', you see Cornelius ag'in someday soon." Martha Jane was stunned, her mind racing faster than her words. Her eyes darted about as if struggling to follow a honeybee in flight, trying to fully grasp the miraculous possibilities. She tried to speak but her tongue couldn't catch up with her thoughts. Looking down at her baby, Martha Jane's eyes welled up with tears. Rue rubbed her shoulder gently.

"I know chile, sometimes somethin' good's as fearful as somethin' bad. But you got some time to get ready - this ain't gonna happen today or tomorrow. But we have to make plans now, so that when the day comes, you be ready." Martha Jane nodded as a tear ran down her cheek.

"Now...you talk with your brother, and next Saturday, you send him to me and you stay home with the babies so we can talk with him. All our people on the farms around the county be talkin', so we'll know when the Yankees're comin'. Dependin' on which way they come and where they're headed, they might be as close as fifteen or twenty miles. Remember: the picket line's always a few miles to the side of the main body of soldiers, so all you have to do is cross the picket line. That's only one night's walkin' for you. It's hard miles, for sure. But in another year or so your boy George'll be eight or nine and he can race that far. You'll have to carry the two little ones in a sack or a wallet. But all you gotta do is get to the picket lines, and you're free."

The young mother was speechless and could only respond with more tears. She looked up with a question in her eyes. "I know what you're thinkin', chile. But we too old to go with you you," Uncle Robert confessed. "Our runnin' days long gone now, daughter.
174

You take us with you in your heart," he added. Martha Jane struggled greatly just to say, "all right."

Mama Rue continued. "Now, if you plan it good and time it right, you can make it. You only travelin' one night, and fast. You won't need to carry much food or water. Jus' a little somethin' to give you all strength. A blanket or two that you can roll up and sling over your arms with a piece of rope in case it gets cold. I can give you something to make the babies sleepy. But you gotta travel fast and light. Once you make it to the Yankees, they'll take you in and give you food, water, and shelter. And if you're lucky, they'll send you on to a refugee camp where maybe you can find some Quakers to help you further north." She paused to emphasize one final point.

"But the mos' important thing, is you can't say a word to nobody. *Nobody!* Just go about your business like the war don't matter. Can't take nobody else with you no-how, You'll have your hands full as it is. Let anybody who's thinkin' of runnin' make they own plans. I know that sounds hard, but that's the way it's got to be."

Uncle Robert took the pipe from his mouth. "Thass the most important part, darlin' - don't breathe a word to nobody. You don't know *who* you can really trust these days. Somebody catch wind o' this, an' let it slip out from bein' careless, or tell your master to gain favor, he might sell you down to Mississippi where you'll never come back," he said sternly. Martha Jane replied, "I promise."

Uncle Robert continued..."And maybe when the war's over, you and my boy come back here and see ol' Robert and Ruth. You be like the prodigal son and daughter." Martha Jane stood up with her infant in her arms, walked over and kissed the two gray-haired saints.

175

CHAPTER 23

Bounty Man

In the summer of 1863, Josephus "Sēphus" Walker, a big, burly man with close-cropped gray hair adorning the sides of his head like silver laurels encircling a smooth brown dome of scalp, was the owner of a barber shop on a busy street in Uniontown – the county seat of Fayette County in Pennsylvania.

In his younger years he had been a stevedore, loading and unloading heavy cargo along the docks at the confluence of the Allegheny, Ohio, and Monongahela rivers at Pittsburgh. The back-breaking work gave him a robust physique and an iron will. The short, neatly trimmed gray beard and silver laurels contrasting against his walnut-colored skin lent the noble bearing of a Roman senator. Barely visible beneath his left ear was half-moon scar, punched there by the end of a broken bottle neck wielded by a poor loser who had been unlucky in a late-night card game in a rough waterfront tavern long ago. Before he could continue the slash around Sephus' throat, the lout was repaid for the gash with a broken arm and a permanent limp, and he wisely decided to give up gambling and flee town right after that. Sephus Walker was a force to be reckoned with.

Now, nattily dressed in a starched white shirt and black tie with a handsome beige silk brocade vest, with pressed black trousers and polished boots, he was lounging in the empty barber's chair a grateful customer had recently vacated. Alternately scanning the day's newspaper and peering through the plate glass window at the comings and goings on the street outside, his piercing black eyes appeared to be searching for someone who owed him money.

176

Tightly clenching a short, fat, smoldering cigar in his beefy fingers as if it was trying to escape, he was summarizing the news for Solomon, who wasn't particularly listening as he finished trimming his customer's hair.

"Humph," Sephus grunted. "Says here, dem Irish boys is kickin' up a storm dere in New York City; goin' crazy in the draft riots." Not waiting for a response, he continued. "I reckon 'cause they're poor folk who can't pay their way out of the draft - like them rich white boys, uptown." He glanced over at his paltry congregation. "Oh, yeah, I been to New York City - I know what I'm talkin' about here," he insisted - though no one was disputing him.

He rattled his paper like a Sunday morning preacher shaking a tambourine before returning to his sermon. "Even burned down a colored orphanage," he murmured incredulously. "Them dirty low down good for nuthin' dogs," he growled. "Had to call out the Fed'ral troops to put'em down! Seem like we at war everywhere you turn," he said somberly. The congregation wisely decided to remain silent.

Solomon untied the apron from behind his customer's neck and turning aside, gave it a sharp snap like the crack of a whip. After brushing off the shoulders of his customer's coat, the gentleman stood up, nodded his satisfaction in the mirror behind them, and flipped Solomon a coin. Solomon caught the coin in mid-air with his left hand, making it disappear like a magician. "Thank you, Solomon. Fine job, as usual."

Solomon nodded politely adding, "thank you Mr. Shackleford, grateful for your patronage, sir." Solomon dropped the coin into the cash box with a "clink" on the counter behind him, then deftly began stropping his straight razor back to a sharp and polished edge.

"See you next month, Shackleford," growled Sephus, his eyes still glued to the paper like he was trying to memorize his times tables. The elderly customer tipped his hat and quietly headed for the door as if trying not to disturb a bulldog mulling over his bone.

Taking another quick look to check the pulse of activity on the street, Sephus grunted again. Like a hawk setting his sights on a rabbit running for cover, he frowned at the young white man hurrying toward the door of the barber shop. Keeping his eyes on his prey, he turned his head slightly and spoke to Solomon out of the side of his mouth in a gravelly voice, like a frog with a sore throat.

"Solomon, here come that white boy again, keeps pesterin' you about the army." Solomon turned toward the door as the young man entered the shop.

"Good morning, Solomon," the young man politely hailed. "Hello James," Solomon replied, with proper civility. Sephus cleared his throat, intimidating the rabbit into saying "good morning Mr. Walker."

James Ferrill was agitated and still huffing from trotting down the street. Droplets of sweat slid down the sides of his face from somewhere in the forest of thick hair under his hat. Nervous and trembling, he held out a piece of paper that looked like it was trying to wriggle out his hand.

"Solomon, have you decided yet?" Ferrill implored; his voice just above an urgent whisper. "I can't wait any longer, I have to know today." Solomon nodded his head thoughtfully, still not speaking, but his inquiring eyes encouraged Ferrill to continue his report.

178

Waving the paper as proof, Ferrill continued. "I got the draft notice and I have to reply today." Sephus looked up from his paper, annoyed at this distraction. His hawk eyes were sizing up Ferrill as if he was trying to decide the quickest way to dispatch this rabbit.

"If you can't do it, I've got to find someone else right away – today. My wife's about to have a baby and my folks are too old to run the store by themselves. I can pay you $250 if you enlist in my place," he said feverishly.

Sephus grunted. His thick fingers had choked the life out of his cigar and he could easily have done the same to this pest who was interrupting his morning break. Turning the page, then snapping the paper with both hands like the reins on horse, he growled: "Cost *three hunnerd* dollars to hire a bounty man, boy. *Everybody* knows that," he said with a flash of lightning in his eyes. Sephus was a seasoned poker player and could see through this bluff like the plate glass window of his barber shop. His eyes, smoldering more than his cigar, glared down at the newspaper like he was angry with it. His menacing silence made Ferrill feel even more uneasy. Solomon looked disinterested.

"Oh yes, that's right," he confessed. "Yes, I'll make it $300, even – but that's all I have Solomon. Please." He looked like a man doomed to walk the gang plank in shark-infested waters. Solomon thought for another moment while the plea for salvation hung in the air like the cloud of smoke from Sephus' cigar.

Caveat emptor, Sephus warned Solomon in Latin, with a voice like a Roman oracle. But Solomon had already lost all hope for the life he had once longed for. After nodding his head thoughtfully, he replied. "Then you have yourself a deal, James."

The young man's face immediately transformed from cloudy to bright and a sigh of relief escaped his lips. He grasped Solomon's hand so quickly it startled the young barber, shaking it vigorously.

"Thank you, Solomon, thank you, thank you," he repeated several times. Sephus, looked up from his paper, rolling his eyes like it was the worst performance in a play he'd ever seen. Sucking his teeth with disdain, he turned to the page of the box scores of the baseball game and rattled his paper again, trying to chase out the wrinkles.

Ferrill nearly forgot to let go of Solomon's hand as he turned to walk out the door. "By Jupiter, I'll have that money for you tomorrow, Solomon. I promise you." His stream of thank-yous trailed behind him as he walked out the door still talking to himself.

The menacing hawk eyes lifted up from the newspaper, looking more like inquisitive owl eyes, now. The raspy voice spoke. "Solomon, why you wanna fight dis white man's war? They only lettin' colored boys in 'cause they need'em now. They wasn't good enough to fight an' die before."

Solomon shrugged but remained mute. Sephus continued in a voice uncharacteristically compassionate. "Look son, I know you still hurtin' - it ain't been but four mont's since Mary died, but..." His words trailed off unfinished because he didn't want to inflict more pain on the young man he thought of much like a son. Solomon eased down into the empty chair.

"I know, Sephus. But I can't get her out of my head. Not here. Not now. Everything reminds me of her. The memories haunt me when I'm awake and asleep. They bring me no comfort. They just make me miss her all the more. I can't drink enough to make'em go away. It hurts somethin' awful, Sephus," he said in a plaintive voice.

180

"Some days, I wonder if life's worth living at all. So I guess I have to go find out. And that $300 will give me good stake to buy a house when I muster out. It'll only be two years. And I'll get a monthly pay while I'm in the army." He paused. "They opened up a training camp for colored troops near Philadelphia. That's as good a place as any to start my life over again."

Sephus nodded. "Okay, son. I understand. I been through a lot in my life, too." Sephus had other scars, many of which were on the inside. "You gotta earn your stripes some time. But you keep safe now, boy. I want you to come back here and be mayor of this here town someday. Help keep people like me in line," he said, with something approaching a smile on his poker face. "An' you can have your job back anytime you want."

"I will, Sephus. I'll come back. You been like a second father to me, and I'll never forget that." Sephus re-lit the old stogie in his big fingers, making puffing sounds and clouds of blue smoke that camouflaged his misty eyes. The two barbers sat in their chairs, quietly watching life go by through the shop's plate glass window.

CHAPTER 24

Johnny has gone for a Soldier

A few days later, 23 year old Solomon Clifford, was on the train from Pittsburgh to Philadelphia to report to Camp William Penn in the Chelten Hills just outside the city. There he would become Private James Ferrill of Company D, of the 6th United States Colored Troops. He didn't know it at the time but he had just signed a pact with the Devil, and the Devil would try his best to collect his due.

He stared vacantly out the window, not really seeing the familiar sites for the first few miles of the 300 mile trip to Philadelphia. Instead, he was looking into the past, still suffering from the pain of his broken heart. He had to leave Uniontown, because everything reminded him of Mary. It seemed as though he had known her all his life and believed they would always be together.

Well-meaning people had told him that happy memories of her would give him peace, yet the opposite was true. Somehow, he managed to make it through the days, but the nights were unbearable. He couldn't drink enough liquor to dull the pain - in fact, it seemed to have no effect at all except to make him drowsy with the false promise of elusive sleep that only briefly came. It did nothing to stop the dreams. He would drag himself to bed at night and lay there with his eyes shut, sometimes for hours, waiting for a reprieve from the pain like a governor's pardon. All he could think about was Mary and how much he had loved her, how much they laughed together, and loved being together. Now the world was a far crueler place than he had previously known.

He hid his grief poorly. Friends and family tried valiantly to comfort him, but nothing could ease the heartbreak of losing the person he had loved so long and so dearly. People kept asking if he was OK, and he feebly lied in response. No, he wasn't OK and never would be. Even in the darkened room with his eyes closed tightly he could see her face, and the memories of her swept over his defenses like a mighty wind bending back the trees. He had walked around his rooms muttering to himself and talking to her for days. When he broke down crying one afternoon after the last customer had left the barber shop, he knew he had no choice but to leave. The army would take him far away to new places with new people, and maybe two years and a thousand miles on the road would allow him some measure of relief. He didn't know what else to do, and he couldn't bear seeing his sad face in the morning anymore as he shaved before heading to the shop. Now, in the reflection of the train's window, he saw a young man with a *café-au-lait* complexion, black hair and blue eyes. At 5'5" he was not a tall man, but he was sturdy from climbing hills and mountains in his youth.

He had always loved the train. He felt safe inside the belly of this iron horse. The gentle rocking was soothing, and the rhythm of syncopated beats and rattles of the cars racing down the track was hypnotic, prompting restful reveries. The air streaming in through the windows and between the cars felt cool, even for July.

The train chugged along toward the eastern side of the Allegheny Escarpment, part of the oldest mountain range in America. This was the edge of his known world. He couldn't read or write, never having books to tell him about what natural wonders lay to the east. This was an odyssey of discovery. He had lived his life thus far in the southwest counties of Pennsylvania - Fayette, Cumberland, Allegheny, and Greene - where he was born. He had been as far south

183

as Negro Mountain in Somerset County on the Maryland border, and had traveled to the western part of West Virginia to visit relatives with his father, but east was a new direction in his life.

Traversing valley after valley, with stops at little stations along the way, the train sailed into the heavenly Blue Ridge Mountains appearing every bit as soft and blue as a September sky. Still the train rolled on toward the Kittanning Gap and the great Horseshoe Curve near Altoona. He was mesmerized as he stood up, holding onto the frame in childlike awe at the wonders he spied through the window. He had heard of this horseshoe but had never quite believed it existed, only a hundred miles from home. The conductor smiled as he witnessed this young man, flabbergasted by one of the man-made wonders of the steam-age.

"Never saw the curve before?" the conductor asked. Solomon could only answer with a silent "no," by slowly moving his head from side to side, never taking his eyes off this monument to human ingenuity, strength, and perseverance.

"It was built about ten years ago, but others had tried for twenty years or more before they could finally get it done." The conductor smiled again as he walked down the aisle like a sailor on sea legs, which had come from years of navigating the platforms of wobbly trains in motion.

The Horseshoe Curve was built with the sweat and stamina of burly Irishmen who swung their picks with a fury. Their stalwart and sure-footed horses hauled miles of steel track up the grade and tons of rock debris away on their trip back down. Solomon's reverie was soon broken as he saw Union pickets stationed above the tracks, and remembered that the Battle of Gettysburg had just taken place a fortnight ago. There, Confederate General Jubal Early and his troops had routed a command of Union infantrymen, chasing them toward the city of York and the Susquehanna.

Solomon immediately grasped the strategic importance of this engineering marvel, and how the Confederates might want to invade the North. Like two opposing trains on the same track, war was coming to him, just as he was going to meet it. And that brought to mind his younger brother, Jacob, who was following in his footsteps by enlisting in the 11th U.S. Colored Troops Heavy Artillery. He admired his brother's courage but he feared for Jacob's life.

Solomon's face stayed glued to the window, trying the catch a final glimpse of the leviathan structure, as the train completed the curve. "I'll see you again on the ride home, my friend," he thought to himself. But it would be a very long road home for him and he would be greatly changed – more than he could imagine at the present time.

The train rumbled on past the Piedmont, crossing the Juniata River, and heading toward the state capitol at Harrisburg. He thought about a young brown-skinned woman named Cassey Turner from West Virginia, who always had a tender look in her eyes when she set her sights on him. Cassey had an enchanting voice, and he once heard her singing the old Irish lament *Johnny Has Gone for a Soldier* - a sweet and mournful song about a young farmer going off to war and the woman he leaves behind. He could almost hear it now. However, he blocked the thought because it also brought up memories of his late wife, Mary, that made his heart ache like an old war wound.

Yet another marvel was waiting to amaze him, just miles around the next bend. At first, he wondered if he was dreaming. He had never seen the mighty Susquehanna before, named after a

185

great warrior tribe that once ruled its banks and lengthy valley. He knew it eventually flowed into the Chesapeake Bay - another natural wonder he hoped to see while in the army. The Susquehanna stretched toward him like a giant blue snake - deep, wide, and powerful with gentle curves that belied its strength. He had heard people back home speak of this river and he had longed to see it with his own eyes. The surface of the water was as smooth as looking glass, mirroring the deep blue of the sky above. On the eastern bank lay the shining city of Harrisburg - the state capitol.

He had always loved the old Pennsylvania that he had known all his life, and this glorious eastern half made him love his homeland even more. "It is something worth fighting for," he told himself. It lifted his spirits to think that he hadn't even reached Philadelphia, yet he felt that he had seen and learned much already.

CHAPTER 25

City of Brotherly Love

The rest of the trip was a blur, passing through the lush farmlands of Lancaster County, seeing Amish people dressed in black and riding in little carriages like they did back in Ohio, not far from home. He suddenly awoke in the bustling City of Philadelphia, in the midst of hundreds of other young colored men in civilian clothes, all marching up the street to the beat of a fife and drum, heading toward Camp William Penn just outside the northerly city limits.

The camp had just opened on the Fourth of July and though no talking had been permitted on the march, Solomon would soon learn the names and stories behind the faces of colored men of a dozen different shades and walks of life. Nearly 11,000 men from eleven regiments of United States Colored Troops would be trained at Camp William Penn - named after the kindly Quaker best remembered for launching his "religious experiment" of tolerance in the state that now bore his name; and for his fair and enlightened treatment of local Indians.

At camp, Solomon met other men in Company D, of the 6th USCT, like Nathan Hickok, Alexander Kelly, and George Grueb. He also met men from other companies like Edward Ratcliff and Miles James. Some stood out from the rest - like the scholarly and genial Christian Fleetwood, who had graduated from Ashmun Institute (later renamed, Lincoln University) in Oxford, fifty miles away; and the handsome, aspiring actor Powhatan Beaty.

There was a close-knit group from Chester County. The oldest - James Boggs - was 41 years old, and the youngest was John Miller, age 20, both from West Caln. There was 24 year old Jacob Hammond of East Brandywine, and Peter Richmond of West Goshen, who was 29 years old. Each one vowed to look after his brother.

Some recruits - like Powhatan Beaty - had been slaves, and some like Solomon had been born free. Some were Southerners and others, Northerners. Some were educated and others illiterate. Some were reserved while some were rowdy. Not everyone in the throngs of people crowding the sidewalks were cheering the recruits marching by. Philadelphia may have been called the *City of Brotherly Love*, but in the summer of 1863 it seemed a misnomer. Some whites in the crowd jeered at the motley crew of what they called "monkeys" and "misfits," outraged by the thought of black men being trained to carry guns. They wouldn't have it in *their* city. Consequently, Camp William Penn was built just outside the city limits in the Chelten Hills section.

This mosaic of men in the nascent process of transforming into an army had ardent supporters, too; for Philadelphia was also a hotbed of abolitionists who wrote fiery editorials in local newspapers and raised funds to organize the Colored Troops. And William Still and places like Mother Bethel Baptist Church served as important components of the Underground Railroad. The men may have been marching to camp as raw recruits, but they would depart as soldiers who would prove themselves equal to any others, North or South.

Watching the men march into camp with great enthusiasm and admiration from the window of her nearby home was Lucretia Mott - "the little lioness," - as she was sometimes called; an outspoken critic of slavery and a tireless proponent of women's rights. She was

188

considered equally important as her husband James – if not more so – who had been a co-founder of the Pennsylvania Anti-Slavery Society.

She regularly baked cakes and pies to give to the men at camp, and to help raise funds to support the troops. Accompanied by other abolitionists or various dignitaries, she occasionally visited the camp to give rousing speeches to the troops. However, because of her diminutive size, the soldiers would gently lift her off the ground and place her atop a large drum so she could be seen by all. On this pedestal she would rally the troops with exhortations to fight for the cause of freedom. To the men, within the breast of this lamb-sized lady beat the heart of a lioness, and it inspired them immensely.

Many knew the story of the 1838 burning of Pennsylvania Hall near 6th and Race Streets 25 years earlier by an angry white mob, incensed that the Anti-slavery Convention was meeting inside. After smashing the windows, the rioters set the magnificent building ablaze. Armed with nothing more than the courage of her convictions, Mott told the delegates – white and black women together – to lock arms and they pushed their way through the raging mob outside.

Solomon was wide-eyed as he marched through the gates of the camp, guarded by stern black soldiers carrying loaded muskets with fixed bayonets, ready to respond with vigor to any sign of trouble. One of the first stories Solomon heard at camp demonstrated the character of the battle-hardened camp commander, German-born Colonel Louis Wagner. Wagner insisted that his soldiers sit next to him on public transportation, ignoring local segregation policies. When a black sentry shot a belligerent white man trying to force his way into camp, Wagner stood by his soldier.

Although the enlisted men and a few of the sergeants were blacks, the officers of the US Colored Troops were white, and not all shared Colonel Wagner's commitment to equality. Some could be as harsh as Southern overseers, and others - including some white abolitionists - could be patronizing and racist in their own right. But Solomon's favorite was a white infantry officer, Lt. Nathan Huntley Edgerton. Edgerton was an Ohio Quaker with dark hair and beard, and piercing black, soulful eyes, whose reserved demeanor camouflaged great courage under fire and his egalitarian willingness to risk his own life for the Colored Troops under his command.

Wagner insisted on military discipline, but discouraged severe physical punishment because he thought this reminded former slaves of the brutal treatment many had experienced in the past. Not only did it promote a negative association with white officers, Wagner believed it actually encouraged rebelliousness among these troops. To the contrary, he wanted them to have pride in and loyalty to their regiments - an *esprit de corps* - rather than view the camp and its officers as merely an extension of the plantation system.

Instead, he wisely subscribed to a system of minor punishments, strictly enforced, that made the transgressor feel isolated from the ranks and realize that he was dishonoring his brothers in blue. Wagner's goal was to transform dehumanized former slaves into well-trained, disciplined soldiers who would fight to the death to protect their comrades-in-arms, the Union, and the honor of the flag.

The more intelligent and adept soldiers and sergeants willingly policed their own ranks, and helped the others to adapt and succeed. The educated troopers often assisted in teaching illiterate ones to read and write. Overall, the Colored Troops were generally

190

cooperative and orderly, and "church meetings" were a common sight in USCT camps. These soldiers weren't only fighting to win a war, they were fighting for equality; and to be viewed as soldiers who were the equal of the white troops wearing Union blue or Confederate gray. They could not merely aspire to be "almost as good as."

Inside the gates, the camp was methodically planned like a small city; with barracks, a blacksmith shop, laundry, shooting range, garden, fountain, stables, church, school, guard house, prison, quartermaster, hospital, dining room, ice house, parade grounds, and daguerreotype gallery. Like a railway engineer, Colonel Wagner made certain the camp ran according to schedule as smoothly as his Swiss timepiece. He spoke with a German accent and walked with an obvious limp, because he had seen death close-up at the Battle of Bull Run in August of 1862, serving as a Captain in the 88th Pennsylvania Volunteer Infantry.

In the midst of heavy fighting his right leg, below the knee, was shattered by a Confederate musket ball. After the battle, he and 16,000 other dead and wounded troops were left behind by the retreating Union army, resulting in his capture and confinement in a Confederate prison camp. Later, coalescing from his wounds in a Philadelphia hospital, he had learned of Camp William Penn and requested the assignment of camp commander.

He was a brave and capable officer, and a combat veteran who had risen steadily in rank. He believed these black men deserved the best training possible since many of them would meet certain death on the battlefield. He knew that if wounded, they would be summarily and brutally executed by the Rebels who viewed the Colored Troops as traitors, and not as enemy soldiers to be treated as prisoners of war.

Wagner strongly disagreed with the decision reached by some members of Congress who had originally determined that the Colored Troops should be used only as laborers, and therefore should be paid less than their white counterparts. But the Colored Troops in the field refused their pay until the order had been rescinded and they were paid the same as white soldiers.

At Camp William Penn, the new recruits were lined up, in formation, on the parade ground and organized into units. They were assigned to the barracks where they were given bunks, equipment, weapons, and uniforms. Now, late in the day, they were marched to the mess hall for a hot meal – decent by army standards but some of the best food many of the former slaves had known. After supper, there was a little time for meeting and talking among the recruits, before organizing their kits for the next day.

As he lay in his bunk, "Private James Ferrill" – as Solomon Clifford now had to call himself – found it hard to sleep. His mind was racing with thoughts and images from this long but remarkable day. Soon, the weariness of the road caught up with him, knowing that tomorrow would be another very long day, beginning at dawn with a bugle blowing reveille.

CHAPTER 26

Rally 'Round the Flag

Each day flowed into the next, according to the strict schedule set by Colonel Wagner. First came days of calisthenics and endless drilling - lining up in order and marching in formation until the squads wheeled about as one. Next, came mastering the manual-of-arms and how to shoulder and carry their muskets. Learning how to care for their weapons and kit was paramount because a properly maintained musket would mean the difference between life and death. Most infantrymen were issued the 1861 Springfield - a musket with a rifled barrel for greater accuracy over the older smooth-bore muskets. Accurate up to 200 or 300 yards, with a burst of smoke and flame it spat out a deadly .58 caliber minié-ball that could shatter a bone so completely on impact that amputation was often the only practical form of triage medical treatment under the circumstances.

Although, it was still a muzzle-loader, the addition of a percussion cap was a major improvement over the old flintlocks used during the Revolutionary War. Because of the renown of the French army's use of the bayonet, the troops were also instructed in the art of close quarter fighting - which was invaluable when wet weather conditions dampened gunpowder, or when a soldier ran out of ammunition. Skillfully wielded in the hands of well-trained trooper, a musket with fixed bayonet was a fearsome weapon.

Drill, drill, drill. It never stopped. Target practice followed target practice, and later, even more target practice. Then still more practice loading and reloading the musket. A seasoned soldier could fire four rounds a minute – a harrowing lesson that the 6th USCT would learn in battle.

Solomon's time in boot camp passed quickly and he learned much. Although he still could not read or write, he had a quick mind and quick hands. He easily mastered the rapid loading and firing of his musket, due in part to his experience hunting with his father back home in the hills of western Pennsylvania. He was also affable and made friends easily despite his quiet manner.

After roll call on Saturday morning, July 18, 1863, Colonel Wagner announced that a special visitor would arrive that afternoon to inspect and address the troops. Shortly before the appointed hour, a small black carriage was admitted through the gates of Camp William Penn. The driver was white, the passenger black. Both were smartly dressed. As the pair exited the carriage the height of the black passenger was striking, as was his bearing. Some of the troops, already waiting in formation, thought he had an aristocratic air. His skin was the color of burnished leather and adorning his head was a shock of thick black hair streaked with gray and roughly combed to one side. The men were greeted by one of the officers and escorted toward the parade ground.

As he strode swiftly on long legs, his attention was drawn to his right where two black troopers were being punished. They had been ordered to sit astride a split rail – the kind used for fences – suspended several feet off the ground. It was an extremely uncomfortable position and it appeared as if they were riding stick horses, hence the name "riding the saw buck" for this particular punishment. A cloud of controlled anger flashed across the black man's face like heat lightning. He said something to the civilian walking next to him, but he never broke his stride. For those times, he was a near giant of a man, at over six feet tall and 200 hundred pounds, and he loomed large as he approached the small speaker's platform in front of the troops. In unison, the ranks snapped to attention as the Master Sergeant barked: "ten-hut!" ("Atten-tion!")

Colonel Wagner addressed the troops in the heavy German accent they had grown accustomed to hearing. "At ease, men." On cue, the lines snapped to the "parade rest" position. "You are fortunate to have a prominent visitor today who would like to speak to you. He and others have been fighting their own battles to organize and support the United States Colored Troops. You are evidence of their success. However, that is only half the battle for acceptance - you must fight for the other half - not just with guns and cannon, but with courage and grit." He paused to collect his thoughts.

"There are those who say that you are not the equal to any white man and never will be. And that you will run at the sound of the first shot fired. But I have watched you transform from raw recruits to solid soldiers. And I do not believe you are inferior or else I would not be your commanding officer. So you must fight two wars with two enemies. The first: to preserve the Union. And the second: for equality and recognition. And you men will be among the vanguard to blaze the trail. But I will let our distinguished visitor - Mr. Frederick Douglass - speak to you directly. Mr. Douglass?"

Douglass stepped forward and scanned every face for a moment before his thunderous voice broke forth, reaching even the very last lines of the formation. "You are a spectacle for men and angels! You are in a manner to answer the question, can the black man be a soldier?"

"Sir, yes sir," the troops shouted as one.

Douglass continued, "That we can now make soldiers of these men, there can be no doubt!" His fierce stare scanned every eye, holding the troops spellbound.

"I know that many of you men were once slaves - as was I. And I know the vicious bite of the whip every bit as well as you do. For, I still bear the scars of that brutality on my back. But this is no plantation and you are no slaves! You are now free men - you are now *soldiers!*" He briefly paused again, giving the men a moment to feel the full weight of his words.

"I did not like what I saw when I passed through the gates of this camp - black soldiers riding the rail - being punished like common thieves," he admonished. "I am well aware that freedom does not immediately grant equality. I am also well aware that freedom may not always be fair, and that all may not share the belief that you are men of equal talent and bravery. Not every white officer believes in you as your honorable Colonel Wagner does. And many will not only question your abilities, but your right to be here and bear arms for this great nation." His words rolled down like thunder.

"It is for you to justify that reply, which I certainly believe you will do, but in order to do this, you will have to prove that you cannot only parade and drill, but equal the white soldier, in neatness of person, in the brightness of your arms, in orderly deportment, and scrupulous obedience to orders.'"[xiii] He paced back and forth briefly like a captain on the deck of a ship as he gathered his next words.

"As I said, this is no plantation and every white man is not your enemy. Many are your friends and advocates - like the esteemed gentleman standing next to me. And there is a great difference

196

between humble submission and obeying lawful military orders," he lectured.

"I believe in this great cause, and two of my own sons are in Union blue. On this very day, one is marching with the 54th Massachusetts on its way to assault Ft. Wagner on a beach in South Carolina. And I hope the angels up above are watching over him," he said, looking up toward Heaven, and holding his giant palms upward as if to catch blessings falling down from above. "So, as you can see, I am giving the cause of freedom more than mere words. I am offering up my own sons as Abraham offered up Isaac to the will of the Lord. And I am as proud of you men, you *soldiers* in blue, as I am of my own sons who are your comrades in arms.

"God and history will be witnesses to your actions in this just cause. And whether you live or die, it is how your fight for the honor of your flag - and the honor of your people - that will echo down through the generations, and blaze a trail for other men - *free* men - to follow! Rally 'round the flag boys, 'rally 'round the flag," he exhorted. The troops erupted into cheers.

Some weeks later, on a warm October day, the 6th USCT left camp and marched down the length of Broad Street in Philadelphia, eventually passing by the Union League where high-ranking military officers and civilian dignitaries stood on the steps of the beautiful building proudly watching the United States Colored Troops march by. There were abolitionists like James and Lucretia Mott, financier Jay Cooke, poet John Greenleaf Whittier, black artist David Bustill Bowser - who designed the regiment's beloved flag - and black scholar, baseball player, and activist Octavius V. Catto, who nearly eight years later to the day, would become a martyr for the cause of freedom. The soldiers were resplendent in their dark blue tunics,

197

shiny brass buttons, and white gloves, lock-stepped with eyes riveted directly ahead, marching the tune of *The Battle Cry of Freedom* as the blaring brass instruments and big base drums echoed through the streets of the city.

The Christian Recorder - a contemporary newspaper published by free blacks reported the momentous event. "As the regiment passed the Continental Hotel, a city tough ran out from the crowd and snatched the color (flag) from the sergeant, who knocked the intruder down, rescued his flag, and resumed his place in the ranks, to the cheers of many of the spectators."[xiv]

Eight months later on the night of Saturday, July 23, 1864, as soon as it was good and dark, a family of shadows took off into the night from their cabin on the Fortsville Plantation in Greensville County, Virginia. They were traveling fast and light, with only a little water, a loaf of bread, a small piece of smoked meat, and two rolled up blankets tied and slung over the man and woman's shoulders. Andison Parham had a large leather wallet, somewhat like a backpack, in which he carried two young girls - his 3-year old daughter Sarah, and his 2-year old niece Rachel Ann - his sister Martha Jane's child.

Martha Jane carried a few more supplies bound up tightly in a cotton sack, and beside her trotted her 9-year son, George. For two years after Cornelius had escaped, they had waited for this chance. And they had to cover at least 20 miles by night, across fields, farms, hedgerows, and the Nottoway River - to reach the Union picket lines, as the 6th United States Colored Troops and other regiments were marching toward Petersburg, some 40 miles away. Even though it
198

would be Sunday morning with the first light of dawn, in the daylight they could easily be spotted so far afield from the plantation.

They set a punishing pace, stopping every five miles to rest briefly. The toddlers had been given a sedative tea prepared by Mama Rue to keep them sleepy and quiet. Andison and Martha Jane were big and strong, and her son George was as tough as any soldier - scanning the horizon, listening for dogs and horses, and helping every step of the way. The skies were black as pitch, which made the moon and stars burn all the more brightly, as if especially for them. "God's fireflies," Andison whispered as they crossed an open field.

Each time they rested they were breathing deeply and bathed in sweat. Yet the danger, fear, and excitement they felt at the real possibility of escape drove them ever onward. There was no turning back now. Crossing the Nottoway in the dark had been their greatest challenge, but they knew a narrow ford where it would be shallow and they crossed over around midnight. That lifted their spirits because if dogs were tracking them, the river would present a temporary obstacle. Trackers would be hesitant to cross their horses in the dark and dogs would have to roam the other bank trying to pick up their scent, delaying any pursuit.

About 3:00 a.m., they took their final break, allowing themselves just a few extra moments to finish the food they needed for fuel to carry on. Just before dawn, the moon set and the stars began to fade like dying embers in the slowly lightening sky, casting the shadow family in deep azure light. Fear was beginning to harry them because they were uncertain if they were lost. They did not have a watch or a compass, and they had been navigating by the stars and recollections of three elderly people. They tried to block out of their minds what would happen if they were caught. It would go hardest on

199

Andison. When she could repress her fear no longer, Martha Jane turned to her brother and pleaded, "Andison!"

The tone of that single word sent a chill down his spine, and he looked directly into her eyes, fearing what he might see - because he had seen that look once before and he knew what she was prepared to do. She would rather die with her children in this field than be forced back to a hellish life on the plantation. He dearly loved his sister and he knew the torment she had suffered for years - perhaps better than anyone else. He also loved her husband Cornelius like a brother; because, despite years of degradation and abuse, he had chosen this tortured woman for his wife. Yet, there were secrets Cornelius did not know, and these two conspirators vowed long ago never to tell him - but not because he was not worthy of their trust, or their love. To the contrary, Cornelius was infinitely worthy of both.

The siblings had painfully kept some of these traumas from him because they occurred in the past and they knew how deeply those sufferings would have hurt him - not so much for himself - but for his wife, Martha Jane. Cornelius would have not only absorbed her pain, but like many slave husbands, he would have blamed himself because he had been unable to protect his wife from such misuse.

Furthermore, he would have felt even guiltier because by comparison, his life and treatment as a slave had been infinitely better. When the truth offered only excruciating emotional pain, the siblings thought it was a greater act of love not to dig up these miseries that had been buried long ago. Out of love for his sister, Andison would not prevent her from doing anything she felt in her heart and soul that she had to do. There would be a better life after this one, he believed.

Bewildered, Andison searched the horizon, rubbing his forehead. "I ain't never been this far, Martha Jane," he was ashamed to admit. But fear meant nothing to the Spartan little slave boy. George scanned the landscape with angry eyes, forcing it to give up its secrets. As if yielding to his will, he suddenly saw a few tiny fires twinkling in the distance.

"There!" the boy with the eagle eyes whispered excitedly, pointing the way. Where the family summoned the strength to continue on, they would never know. Fifty yards from the fire, Private James Ferrill who was on sentry duty, saw shadows moving toward him in the pale light of dawn. "Halt, who goes there?" he demanded, pointing his musket at the trespassers and drawing the attention of the other sentries on duty. Nearly out of breath and waving a white cloth, a woman gasped: "Help us, sir; for God's sake help us!"

As the group materialized in the light of the clearing, he was astounded by what he saw. He had expected to see Rebs - not runaway slaves. His blue eyes grew wide with wonder, because this group was soaked with sweat and looked like they had just swam an ocean in darkness. Three other colored troopers came over and the family collapsed in their arms. Martha Jane couldn't help crying.

"You're safe now, ma'am; you're all safe," the soldiers assured them. "I don't know where you came from," Pvt. Ferrill said, still awed by the sight, "but you'll be safe now. But quickly - come with us."

201

CHAPTER 27

Battle of the Crater

Trench warfare is among the worst forms of fighting. During the day, the men melted in the sweltering heat of a Southern summer. Their coarse woolen uniforms made the suffering worse, and nightfall seldom brought significant relief. After a cooling rain, stagnant water collected at the bottom of the trenches, quickly making them muddy and putrid - perfect conditions for fostering typhoid fever, dysentery, and cholera. While providing a measure of protection, the trenches made it more difficult to evacuate the dead and wounded after a battle, adding to sanitation problems. Many tens of thousands of soldiers died of diseases and infections during the course of the war, and over 620,000 were killed in total.

At first, it seemed like an ingenious plan, largely developed by the Argentine-born Lt. Colonel Henry Pleasants, a former railroad and mining engineer from Pottsville, Pennsylvania, who was now commander of the 48th Pennsylvania Infantry. Pleasants, whose troops included several Pennsylvania miners reportedly heard one say: "We could blow that damned fort out of existence if we could run a mine shaft under it."[xv]

To break the stalemate of the Siege of Petersburg, Pleasants' plan was to dig a tunnel over 500 feet long under the Confederate lines, which would end with a horizontal gallery - forming the shape of a "T" - packed with 8,000 pounds of gunpowder, twenty feet under the enemy's fortifications. If the Union army couldn't overpower the Confederates with a direct assault, it would blow the fort to "Kingdom

Come." Unsure and uneasy of what was underway, some of the Rebels could hear the sounds of pick and shovel in the days before the attack.

Solomon Clifford - now known as Private James Ferrill of Company D, of the 6th United States Colored Troops - rose early along with the rest of his company about 3 a.m., and prepared silently for the attack at the crack of dawn. The men were nervous but determined to demonstrate the pride and valor of the Colored Troops. The whole camp was a flurry of quiet activity. Always a light sleeper, George Washington Parham - the tough, wiry 9-year old runaway who had recently arrived in camp with his family peered out the end of their tent with eyes open wide.

U.S. Colored Troops, including the men of the 6th were part of General Ambrose E. Burnside's IX Corps, and were originally intended to spearhead the attack by Union troops into the fort after the explosion. However, these orders were changed by Major General George Meade and the Commanding General of the U. S. Army, Ulysses S. Grant the day before, because they were doubtful of the plan's success and reluctant to risk a massacre of Colored Troops and the political repercussions that would surely follow. Brigadier General James H. Ledlie's 1st Division was chosen instead to lead the assault, but Ledlie apparently failed to give his troops adequate instructions and reportedly spent his time during the battle drunk, far from the action, providing no leadership. He was dismissed from his command.

At 4:44 a.m. on July 30, 1864, the fuse was lit and the charges exploded with the impact of what must have seemed like a meteor striking the Earth. The blast created a crater approximately 170 ft. long, nearly 80 ft. wide, and 30 ft. deep. Private James Ferrill (also known as Solomon Clifford) stood among the ranks with his comrades in arms, watching the unfolding of events in horror as tons of rocks, dirt, body parts, and weapons were flung into the air.

Although they had already fought in a number of battles, one soldier in line doubled over and retched uncontrollably at the macabre sight. The Confederate troops were stunned and disoriented. After a puzzling delay which allowed the Rebels to regroup, for some inexplicable reason the Union troops poured directly down into the now alien landscape of the crater instead of strategically charging along its rim where the footing was far superior.

These two actions proved fatal to the Yankees as the Confederates, under the command of brilliant civil engineer and Virginia Military Institute graduate Major General William Mahone, quickly reorganized and began pouring a fusillade of rifle fire and artillery shells down onto the first waves of attacking Union troops. Mahone later called it "a turkey shoot."

The Confederates swooped down like raptors, engaging in fierce hand-to-hand combat, using rifle butts, bayonets, and bare fists to annihilate the invaders. Union soldiers caught in the crater were doomed, and many of the black troops were killed immediately when they tried to surrender.

Although the 6th was ordered to stand firm and hold a section of the line to prevent the enemy from flanking them, they watched in abhorrence as other Colored Troops from eight other regiments were ordered to follow the first white soldiers into the crater from which there would be no escape, no rescue, no food or water, and no shade from the blazing summer sun. The sound of the explosion had been overwhelming and would contribute to the loss of Solomon's hearing later in life.

The rising shouts, screams, curses, cries, and moans emanating from the monstrous pit melded with the explosions of artillery rounds and relentless gunshots formed a cacophony of

204

sounds. It was savagery on a level he had never before witnessed nor would have imagined. His company was ordered to fire upon the Rebels, but it was not effective for fear of hitting their fellow soldiers. He fully-cocked his musket, took careful aim, and pulled the trigger.

The powder flashed in his face, burning his skin with a shower of searing granules, as a piece of the brass percussion cap blew back directly into his left eye, temporarily blinding him. The force of the explosion knocked him backward off his feet, and amid the darkness all he could see were sparks splashing everywhere - as if a blacksmith had just struck a red hot piece of iron on an anvil. He thought his eye had been blown out and instinctively patted his face blindly to feel if it was still hanging from its socket.

He cried out in extreme pain, and the fear of being a blind black man in Union blue on the battlefield brought a sense of unbridled terror into the darkness. A trooper next to him - he didn't know who - dropped to his knees and told him to stay down while calling for a medical corpsman. Solomon writhed in agony, feeling as though his optic nerve had been struck by lightning. The vision in his right eye slowly began to return, and with the help of the corpsman, he was able to struggle to his feet and stagger back behind the lines. However, the battle had been etched in his mind by fire, and he would never be able to erase the dreadful carnage of what he saw that day.

The fighting dragged on needlessly for hours due to the incompetence of Union generals. It was a devastating loss for the North. The Union Army suffered 4,000 killed, wounded, or captured. The South had a mere 1,500 casualties. Ulysses S. Grant would later write: "It was the saddest affair I have witnessed in the war."[xvi]

On a hill by the hospital tents behind the Union lines, a black man dressed like a preacher watched the slaughter through a spyglass. He lowered the spyglass, and with a look of anguish and contempt in his eyes, turned and walked away – disappearing among the tents where surgeons were busy with their bloody work. He had heard there were new runaways in camp, and he was determined to find them and to try to help them if he could, as he had once been a runaway himself.

CHAPTER 28

Fee for the Ferryman

Leviticus D. Ferryman was an itinerant preacher and circuit rider who traveled from camp to camp, ministering to the Colored Troops and their camp followers. Since time immemorial, wherever armies marched, a motley group of civilian men, women, and sometimes children often tagged along behind. The men might serve as scouts, teamsters, axe men, wheelwrights, laborers, messengers, or sometimes traders or merchants who provisioned the troops with various supplies and services not provided by company quartermasters. Camp women also provided a number of various and sundry services. Some might be wives or mistresses, others provided nursing, sewing, laundry, cooking, carrying water, or prostitution. Though such women did not actually take their sobriquet – "hookers" – from Union Major General Joe Hooker's brigade, his raucous camps were often blamed for it.

No one knew much about the mysterious origins of "Deacon" Ferryman as he was often called. He claimed to be from nowhere in particular and that he was anointed by some backwoods preacher in the wilderness to spread the Gospel to wayfarers far from home.

He seemed to have no formal education yet he was knowledgeable and literate. He seldom wrote anything down because he apparently possessed an encyclopedic memory; and he was adept at quoting Scripture, which lent an air of legitimacy to his clerical claims. When he preached, he did so passionately and left no one unconvinced or unburdened after listening to him. He could hold a group spellbound with his dramatic voice when he retold stories from the Holy Bible about pharaohs and chariots, prophesies and angels.

In America, where regional dialect is a clue to identity, Ferryman had no accent at all - or perhaps an amalgam of many. He was definitely not from any part of Virginia. At one time, he may have lived a large city like St. Louis or Chicago, Baltimore, or Washington - because there was an air of urban sophistication about him. At times there was an elusive western twang to some of his words or the cadence of down-country delta speech. He could have been from anywhere. And when asked where he hailed from, he volunteered nothing but a smile in response or skillfully changed the subject by parrying a question with another question. He also jealously guarded the secret meaning of the letter "D" that abbreviated his enigmatic middle name; sometimes glibly claiming it stood for "Deuteronomy."

He may have been a colored spy for the Union - like Mary Elizabeth Bowser or Harriet Tubman - although most Southerners summarily dismissed any evidence of such intelligence in blacks. But it was precisely this attitude that allowed house slaves and servants to provide critical surveillance on tactical discussions as they served meals or cleaned the houses of prominent politicians and military leaders who ignored their presence as no threat to privacy. No one knew for certain, but it would not have been a surprise to some if he had indeed been a spy. He was not dishonest but he was not entirely forthcoming, either. He was a genuine character, whoever and whatever he was.

Ferryman was of average height and build with a dark brown complexion, black hair mixed with a little gray, and dark eyes whose twinkle could not obscure that they had seen great suffering. He often wore a dusty black overcoat and bowler hat with a soiled white shirt that he appeared to live in, and was in great need of a vigorous washing. He was quick-witted and spry and no stranger to strong drink, but he held his liquor well. Other than a grin with a rosy glow and a penchant for loquaciousness, the only other sign of his inebriation was a good-natured humming of spirituals, so engaging that he seemed to expect his worn-out horse would join him in song.

He could be sincere or sly, and obviously had a good measure of savvy vagabond within him, but was he was unerringly moderate and well-mannered. By trying to direct colored refugees to friends, family, or abolitionists in safer environs, out of harm's way and out of the Army's hair, he provided a service the Army did not object to and tacitly approved. He traveled an erratic elliptical route going as far south and west as the Union picket lines, or sometimes perilously farther; and as far North as the freedman's camps located in the forts encircling Washington, D.C., which provided safe havens for black refugees streaming north. Along this route, he delivered messages to and from military camps, Quakers, freedmen, and other collaborators, because many of the refugees could not read or write. Trying to gather news of lost relatives was exceedingly difficult during the war, but it would be virtually impossible afterward.

Ferryman was a familiar visitor in the camps, and though most people knew *of* him - no one really *knew* him. He was friendly but seemed to have no friends. He was constantly on the move and seldom slept in the same place twice. The Rebs wanted him because they assumed he was a spy. Whether he was or not, if captured, he would have faced torture and certain death. On one occasion, a Confederate sharpshooter put a bullet through Ferryman's hat when he had strayed too close to enemy lines. So, he carried a small pistol in case he needed to invoke an immediate form of Divine intervention.

He camouflaged his wariness with nervous laughter, but he could smell trouble like the smoke from a cooking fire, miles away. Most people attributed his caginess to the inherent danger of being a free black man traveling the road alone - and with good reason. Since any free black person - North or South - could be kidnapped and sold into slavery despite protest. Slave status was difficult to disprove, and local magistrates and commissioners were paid $10 for a legal finding that a defendant was a runaway versus $5 when determining the person in dispute was free. Ferryman was inscrutable and his kept his own time, like a will-of-the-wisp, appearing and disappearing easily and often. Yet he was always on time wherever he needed to be, and his precise travel plans were known only to himself and his horse, and he wanted it kept that way.

There was a special bond between horse and rider. It was not a master-servant relationship and they were far more than simply partners. They had both been owned and badly mistreated by the same brutal master, and only the horse had witnessed all that had happened one fateful night in East Texas long ago. The horse, an Appaloosa, was no stranger to strife and had seen war before. It had been ridden by a guerilla fighter in the Border War in "Bleeding Kansas," where wild-eyed militant Christian and abolitionist John Brown had fought a holy war against Southern sympathizers ten years earlier. Ferryman and his horse had battle scars from life. They understood each other, cared for one another and to observers, seemed like brothers.

The horse he called "Pony Boy" was Ferryman's confessor, and the preacher had much to confess about his life. But when he spoke quietly to his horse, the animal's eyes reflected compassion and understanding, always offering absolution. Leviticus' penance was to serve his people, which he did without pay or official recognition.
210

It was a way of cleansing his soul - a personal and spiritual duty. And he was unable to resist God's will which commanded him to continue this mission for who knows how long. These two world-weary spirits had been through much and had traveled far together, and they could never return home - wherever that was. The road was their only home now.

≈

Company D of the 6th USCT was assigned to guard the picket line that night between the two armies. Knowing they would be completely exposed and vulnerable to enemy fire on this open hill in the daylight, the troopers dug holes in the ground during the night which served as their only protection. They covered the tops of the holes with canvas to shade them from the merciless summer sun. Confederate snipers did their best to try to pick off any Yankee who raised his head or had to leave his burrow.

To relieve the boredom of endless hours in the rifle pits, occasionally one of the soldiers would raise a boot or cap on a stick above their heads, only to have it immediately riddled with bullets by the enemy. Not only did this provide a source of perverse entertainment - it was an easy way to make the Confederates waste their ammunition. From the Rebs' viewpoint, they just couldn't resist an opportunity to send one of these damned black Yankees to "meet his Maker" back in Africa.

The stalemate produced few casualties, but the humiliating defeat of the Union Army in the Crater demonstrated an atrocious lack of Union leadership and the Confederates' steely resolve to drive the northern invaders from their homeland in what they often called, the "War for Southern Independence" or the "War of Northern

Aggression." After Company D was relieved around noon the following day, Pvt. Ferrill – as Solomon always had to call himself now – set off in search of someone in the camp who could do his laundry.

Behind the main encampment, Ferryman walked pensively among the civilian tents and ramshackle lean-to's that were quickly constructed, so they could be just as quickly deconstructed when the camp was on the move. There was a flurry of activity with women stirring cauldrons of water, boiling lengths of coarse white cloth to be cooled, dried, and cut into strips and used as bandages. But there were never enough, because the "butcher's bill" was never paid in full.

In the woods nearby, black laborers were felling trees to be cut into planks for various purposes – to make coffins, repair wagons, or to be used as cutting boards for the surgeons. Branches were trimmed and cut up for firewood. Many blacks carried buckets of water toward the front lines for thirsty wounded and dying soldiers.

Ferryman periodically stopped a passer-by to inquire about the new arrivals. Although there were several thousand soldiers in and around the camp, the black civilians were a small and well-defined group by their lack of uniforms; and he was eventually directed to the tents of the newest arrivals. When she wasn't caring for her children or carrying water for the Union soldiers, Martha Jane did laundry to earn money, while her brother Andison worked as a laborer at camp. Like many of the refugees and camp followers, they witnessed much of the battle the day before.

As Ferryman made his way through camp, he encountered Pvt. Ferrill, who was now wearing a black patch over his left eye. Ferrill had been on sentry duty the night Martha Jane and her family crossed the Union picket lines. And he was carrying a sack slung over his right shoulder and looking for a laundress, having heard that she

212

might be one. They finally located Martha Jane, who was washing clothes in a large cast-iron pot of soapy water as her children watched.

"Who dese men Mama?" her son George Washington asked suspiciously, sitting crossed-leg on the ground by the fire, poking the hot coals with a stick.

"Hello young man," Ferryman responded brightly. The boy knew Ferrill was a soldier because of his uniform, but he warily eyed the dubious stranger in black.

"Hello Miss Martha Jane," said Pvt. Ferrill, touching the brim of his cap, "you remember me?" She stopping scrubbing a shirt on a washboard, shook the soap suds off her hands and wiped her brow with the back of her forearm before drying her hands on her apron.

"Yes, I remember you Pvt. Ferrill. Oh my Lord, what happened to your eye?"

"Gun misfired and blew a piece of the percussion cap into my eye. I gotta wear this patch for a while," he answered somberly.

"Oh Pvt. Ferrill, I am so sorry. I hope you'll be alright," she replied. "Thank you kindly," he answered. "I expect I will, ma'am," the soldier added. "And I was wonderin' if I could pay you to do some laundry. But first, let me introduce this gentleman," he said, nodding toward Ferryman. "This here is Deacon Ferryman, he's a preacher. And he helps runaways and refugees who are trying to go north."

Ferryman said "Good day to you, ma'am," and tipped his hat. "Please to meet you, Deacon," Martha Jane replied, rising to her feet; politely trying not to notice how rumpled his clothes were or how soiled his white shirt was - for a "deacon."

213

"My sincerest apologies for interruptin' your work on this fine day, ma'am. And since this brave soldier, here, is a man of action and wants to engage your services, I'll kindly allow him to conduct his business first," he said grandiloquently. Solomon glanced at him, somewhat amused, while Martha Jane tried valiantly not to smile.

"Thank you, Deacon," Pvt. Ferrill began. "Miss Martha Jane, they say you're a good laundress, charge a fair price. Can you wash these for me?" He hoisted the gunny sack off his shoulder adding, "What do you charge, ma'am?"

"Mostly two-bits a big load but you don't have that much; so, a little less, for you." Pvt. Ferrill handed over the sack. "Thank you, Miss Martha."

"You need'em in a hurry?" she asked cautiously. "No ma'am," he replied. "I reckon we'll be camped here awhile."

She smiled as she accepted the bag. "I believe we can have'm for you tomorrow afternoon." Her tone was friendly as she looked at George, who gave a nod of approval. He liked this soldier with the eye patch. There was something safe and steady about him. He wasn't like some of the others who could be rowdy and troublesome at times.

"Well, thank you both very much," Pvt. Ferrill replied. "I'll come back late in the day tomorrow, ma'am." He winked at George who winked back. "Good day, Deacon," he said to Ferryman as he turned to walk away.

Little hawk eyes now focused on the Deacon. There was something about this man that made George uneasy. He seemed nice enough on the surface; but like dark water, there was a lot beneath the surface that he couldn't see. The man smiled like he was happy, but

214

his eyes said something different. They looked sad - and a little crazy. The boy was good at "seein' into" people, his mother said. Although he tried hard, he could not pierce this man's many layers, and it reminded him of a Bible story Rev. Asher - the camp chaplain - told at church meeting one Sunday, about a wolf dressed up like a sheep.

Martha Jane motioned to one of the small wooden crates that served as seats. "Please sit down, Deacon." They sat down together. "Some of the others told me about you."

As they began talking, Martha Jane's brother, Andison, arrived from cutting timber in the woods. Ferryman introduced himself again and asked them to tell him about themselves and where they were heading. After listening carefully to their story, he explained how he might be of help to them by relaying messages to his network of contacts or by guiding them toward the safety of the refugee camps near the capitol in Washington City. Against his better judgment, George Washington began to like this peculiar preacher, but he still didn't trust him, and he didn't know why.

"How much do you charge for your services, Deacon?" Andison inquired? Ferryman looked puzzled. "Charge?" he asked. "No charge," he said, sounding as if his feelings were hurt.

"Then, you work for the Army?" Martha Jane asked. Visibly offended, he stiffened up, brushing the trail dust off the sleeves of his coat in a hopeless attempt to make himself look more presentable. Answering defensively, he said: "I do the *Lord's* work, good people. I do the Lord's work and no one else's. I help the Army when I can, and anybody else who needs it. But I serve a *higher* power. I owe the Lord a great debt for lifting me up out of bondage, and I am bound to serve Him in repayment of that debt 'til I am freed of it."

215

There was poignancy to his words that touched them all and overcame their guardedness. It hadn't occurred to them that he, too, might have once been a slave, and like them, may have suffered great hardship. They didn't understand him, but they knew he was speaking from the heart. Martha Jane was speechless and a look of quiet admiration dawned on Andison's face as skepticism faded from George's, who now felt sorry this man, although he didn't know why.

With his eyes a bit misty, Ferryman was slightly embarrassed by his involuntary betrayal of emotion. His was not a soul at rest, and sometimes the well of sadness within him was close to the surface and too easily breached. Whatever this man was hiding, it was probably something bad that happened to him, George reasoned. It was not because he was a bad man. Or if he *had* been a bad man before, he wasn't one now.

Martha Jane broke the silence. "Deacon, we're about to have our evening meal – won't you stay and join us?" Sensing that they shared much in common, he graciously accepted the offer from these fellow sojourners. Sharing a meal with kindred spirits was a sacramental act of communion which he was compelled to honor. He noticed that George was smiling at him now, and he took this as a sign that the question was settled.

"Why, I'd be de-lighted," Deacon Ferryman responded grandly, suddenly sounding chipper. Andison smiled warmly. "And what is your name young man?" he asked the boy. Tall for his age, the boy stood up and proudly replied: "George Washington Parham. But they call me "Washy.""

216

CHAPTER 29

Devil's Horseshoe

It is arguable whether the South had superior military officers, but that sometimes seemed to be the case. President Lincoln was frustrated with the Union high command throughout much of the war. Considering the North's larger population and greater military and industrial resources, it is remarkable that the Confederacy was able to fight so effectively for as long as it did. However, there are a number of contributing factors worth considering in that regard.

First, the South has produced an abundance of outstanding statesmen, soldiers, scholars, authors, architects, inventors, agronomists, and other achievers since before the Revolution. Of the first twelve Presidents of the United States, nine were Southerners – seven of whom were Virginians – and just three were Northerners. Southerners had been instrumental in the founding of the Republic, and many were proud of their ancestral roots across the Atlantic. However, the brilliance of such post-Enlightenment minds could not obliterate the blindness of the South's tenacious insistence on slavery which, like dragon's teeth, sowed the seeds of its own destruction.

For families like the Ridleys of Southampton, values like *duty, honor,* and *tradition* were deeply embedded cultural beliefs for Virginians in particular and many Southerners in general. The commanding General of the Confederate Army of Northern Virginia, Robert E. Lee, not only graduated second in his class at the United States Military Academy at West Point, but based on his intelligence, engineering skills, and distinguished record of service in the U.S. Army during the Mexican-American war, Lee had also served as Superintendent of the United States Military Academy for three years. During his tenure as Superintendent, his eldest son - George Washington Custis Lee - graduated first in his class in 1854.

Robert E. Lee's sterling family history was intertwined with that of the nation. He was son of revered Revolutionary War hero Major General Henry "Light Horse Harry" Lee, III; and he had married Martha Washington's great-granddaughter by her first marriage to Daniel Parke Custis - Mary Anna Randolph Custis.

As an exceptional officer in the United States military for 32 years, Lincoln had been so impressed with Robert E. Lee that he offered him command of a Union army at the outbreak of the Civil War. Although Lee felt the Union should be preserved, he could not take up arms against his fellow Virginians.

One of Lee's most trusted generals was fellow Virginian and West Point graduate Jubal A. Early, Esq. - who invaded Pennsylvania, briefly occupying the city of York. Another prominent Virginian - Colonel George Smith Patton, the paternal grandfather of the notable World War II general sharing the same name - was a graduate of the renowned Virginia Military Institute, which has produced some of the most decorated military officers and generals in American history.

Among the South's military leaders were cavalry officers Colonel John Singleton Mosby, nicknamed "The Gray Ghost" because of his ability to elude capture; and West Point graduates, Generals J.E.B. Stuart and Thomas J. "Stonewall" Jackson. While some Northerners at the time may have presumed Southerners were generally unschooled "country bumpkins," Stonewall Jackson deconstructed that myth and "served on the VMI Faculty as Professor of Natural and Experimental Philosophy & Instructor of Artillery

218

from August 1851 until the beginning of the Civil War in April 1861." [xvii]

Among the Confederate officers who graduated from West Point was standout General James Longstreet, who Robert E. Lee called his "Old War Horse." Several of Lee's classmates were destined to become prominent military leaders of the Civil War – on both sides – including the future General of the U.S. Army and 18th President, Ulysses S. Grant. Grant and Lee also served together in the Mexican-American War under General Winfield Scott – arguably considered by some historians to be the best military commander of his time.

Which side had the ablest officers may never be resolved. But it is noteworthy that a number of the men in the Confederate high command were college graduates with formal state-of-the-art military training and education from the United States Military Academy at West Point in New York. Some of those cadets developed strong fraternal bonds with classmates they would later be forced to meet in combat on bloody battlefields during the Civil War.

Drawing on their European roots, in a cultural sense, Confederate military officers may have identified with the *noblesse oblige* of old world knights and cavaliers, by adopting the traditions of chivalry, horsemanship, and sword-fighting of a bygone era. Southerners believed they were defending their homeland – and a way of life built on slavery – from Northern invaders who sought to destroy that way of life. Perhaps this galvanized among Southerners a sense of cohesiveness and shared vision that was unattainable in the North because of its diversity of ethnicities, plurality of socio-economic groups, and competing political perspectives.

As with any agrarian people who are closely tied to and identify with the land, the rank and file Confederate soldiers held similar personal reasons for their patriotism, even though most did not directly reap the economic rewards of slavery. Regardless of social standing, slavery and the racial superiority of whites were widely considered *givens* – and some might insist, *God-given* rights – that had no place in the intense debate over the soul of the Nation, as Northern abolitionists characterized it. By comparison, Southerners were a more homogenous group, unified by political, cultural, religious, and historical traditions. For the South, the war was about states' rights and property rights – not the serviceable agenda of abolitionist morality.

Contrastingly, there were a number of social, political, and cultural factors in the North that inhibited the same level of cohesiveness and singularity of vision shared in the South. But the North's secret weapon was *numerical* superiority. It had more people, money, weapons, ammunition, trains, and machines than the South, and superior transport systems for re-supplying its troops in the field. Washington, D. C., also enjoyed the recognition of being the official seat of government of the United States, and could therefore diplomatically discourage England, France, and other countries from interfering and supporting the South. Had the South won its independence political alliances across the globe would have been realigned.

In the absence of such a victory, no matter how valiantly Southerners would fight for their "Lost Cause," they could not defeat the leviathan North. Yet, they would try, and pay dearly for it. Bitter memories of that costly defeat would be remembered by some descendants to the present day.

In comparison, it is essential to note there were exceptional officers and soldiers in the Union Army as well. Certainly, men like Brigadier General John Garland - a native son of Virginia; General Nelson A. Miles who was wounded four times in battle; General Philip H. Sheridan; and the incomparable General William Tecumseh Sherman were renowned for their military success and valor. Yet there were lesser known heroes as well, like Congressional Medal of Honor winner Brevet Major General Joshua Lawrence Chamberlain - a college professor and member of Phi Beta Kappa - who fluently spoke nine languages in addition to his native English.

Chamberlain commanded the 20th Maine Infantry at Little Round Top at Gettysburg, where his unit repulsed repeated charges of Confederate troops even after running out of ammunition, overwhelming the enemy with a brilliant flanking maneuver and downhill bayonet charge that forced the Confederates to surrender.

There was also Sergeant Jones Bradbury of Pennsylvania who enlisted for two tours of duty, was wounded, captured, and imprisoned in the horrific Confederate prison camp at Andersonville, where Union soldiers were reduced to barely living skeletons and nearly 30% of them died. After Bradbury was paroled from Andersonville, he returned to his unit and was mortally wounded in battle three days before Lee's surrender at Appomattox. There were many superb Union officers, soldiers, sailors, nurses, volunteers, supporters, and spies too numerous to properly recognize here. Sailors and naval officers in the Revolutionary and Civil Wars are another group of unsung of heroes, who often rest in unmarked watery graves.

≈

In an attempt to build a canal across Dutch Gap, the soil was soaked with the blood of U.S. Colored Troops. Southeast of Richmond, the capitol of the Confederacy, was a horseshoe shaped bend in the James River. At the "head" of the bend, a strategically placed battery of Confederate artillery made that section of the river impassable for Union boats attempting to navigate upstream. Union brass came up with the idea to have troops dig a canal across a narrow neck of land separating the upper and lower stretches of the James, called Dutch Gap, where it could be protected by a battery of rifled cannons to the right, and Union mortars to the left. Initially, it seemed like a simple yet ingenious plan.

Soldiers of the 6th USCT were assigned the task of digging under cover of darkness in the cool of the night. Earning extra pay for their efforts, the soldiers worked quickly and removed the first few layers of topsoil and loose clay, buoyant and laughing at the impotent Confederate battery, stationed too low and far away to do any damage to life or limb, much to the consternation of the enemy.

As they dug deeper, the sides of this wide trench provided protection from the artillery shells whistling harmlessly overhead. To give them added protection from the shells and Rebel snipers, the Colored Troops dug foxholes into the thick sides of the deepening canal.[xviii] And so a game of cat and mouse developed. When Union lookouts saw the silent puffs of smoke from Confederate batteries, they sounded the alarm for the troops to jump into their foxholes. As the sun began to rise so did their trepidation and with good reason.

General Butler became aware that instead of being properly treated like prisoners of war, black Union soldiers were being conscripted by the Confederates to dig fortifications as some slaves were also forced to do. In addition, unlike white Union soldiers, black troopers were often summarily executed on the battlefield and were not permitted to surrender. Now with General Grant's approval, Confederate prisoners were forced into the canal to dig along with the black troops as deadly rounds from newly positioned mortars began to fall on the men. Regardless, the Confederate batteries continued their lethal fire despite the danger to their own soldiers, who had to scurry around trying to find what little protection they could among the exploding shells. Soon, General Grant received direct word from Confederate General Robert E. Lee that the practice of using colored Union troops as forced labor was stopped, and Grant ordered Butler to withdraw the Confederate prisoners accordingly.

As the Rebel mortars continued to rain shells down upon the Colored Troops with deadly accuracy, the mood became somber and desperate. The heat of these August days in Virginia was brutal, and the sides of the canal blocked any occasional breeze. Some men grew mentally stressed and physically ill at the sight of exploded bodies causing blood-curdling scenes.

At midnight on September 27th, as sudden as a summer squall, orders came that the Colored Troops were moving out - unfortunately, not soon enough to stave off this pointless blood-letting. Nevertheless, the order was welcomed and followed without complaint. The men packed up and moved off down the road in the dark to a hill two miles away with their spirits unfortunately rising. It was unfortunate because what awaited them there was a far worse fate - and one of the bloodiest episodes in the Civil War.

CHAPTER 30

I shall fear no Evil

In their dark blue tunics, the soldiers of Company D of the 6th United States Colored Infantry quietly materialized out of the dense early morning fog like apparitions, standing shoulder to shoulder along the tree line atop a hill overlooking their fate. Solomon Clifford - now known as Pvt. James Ferrill - had always loved the cool, thick fog that cloaked the tree-covered mountains of his native western Pennsylvania. Soft and airy, it slowly burned away with the rising rays of the summer sun - whispering the promise of a peaceful day, as a cheerful chorus of birds and insects rose up with the pale light of dawn. But here on this hill clung a different kind of fog - one that was warm and humid, making their heavy wool tunics damp with dew on the outside and wet with sweat inside. It was an eerie, unsettling curtain that slowly evaporated, revealing a little valley and gloom and doom that should have been posted with the warning from *Dante's Inferno*: "Abandon all hope, ye who enter here."

Solomon no longer wore an eye patch, but he had lost some of the vision in his left eye - and the long-term prognosis was not encouraging. Yet he could still sufficiently see the sight that lay before him. From where they stood, the hill rolled gently down into a cool and sparkling stream only inches deep but a dozen feet wide, which the soldiers knew would soak their leather boots thoroughly enough to slow them down, making them better targets while sapping their bodies of warmth and their feet of comfort. Beyond the stream was dank, dismal swamp land thick with briars and mud deeper than the bracing stream. Judging by the somber sight in Solomon's sad blue eyes, that was only the beginning of this gauntlet of death.

At the foot of the hill across the swamp, lay several large trees felled facing in his direction with clusters of branches carefully whittled to the sharpness of arrow points. Since Roman times, this weapon of war known as an *abatis,* was a malevolent and novel invention using the natural shapes of trees for the cruelest intentions. Farther up the hill beyond the abatis were rows of long sturdy stakes forming the shape of an "X," connected through the middle with a long logs. Their weight anchored them to ground, providing a row of stakes held at an upward angle, with ends honed to the severity of spear points ready to impale any attackers.

These deadly and effective barriers dating back to the days of medieval warfare were known as *chevaux des fries* – or *Frisian horses* – and were successful in withstanding cavalry and infantry charges. Should any of the black troops be lucky - or unlucky - enough to proceed that far through a hailstorm of bullets, this last death trap would delay them at point blank range in front of the Confederate rifle pits at the crest of the hill, manned by two thousand seasoned sharpshooters, capable of firing a combined 8,000 rounds a minute.

From somewhere in his memory, Solomon could hear the strains of a hymn not heard since his young bride's funeral – *Nearer My God to Thee.* It crept through him like the chill of the morning air when he walked to church alone at dawn that day.

"E'en though it be a cross that raiseth me,
still all my song shall be nearer, my God to Thee."

As the melancholy refrain passed through his head, he thought of how after Mary's sudden and traumatic death, there were times when he had *wanted* to die. That was part of why he had enlisted - life hadn't held much meaning for him at the time. So, if he died in battle for a glorious cause he would pass on knowing he had died a martyr, ascending to Heaven lifted up by seraphim and the sounds of angels' wings. But he didn't want to die like this - oh my God, not like this - lying face down in the mud at the bottom of a swamp without as much as a shallow unmarked grave to rest in until Judgment Day; helpless as scavengers picked and scattered his bones. Every man there knew there would be no time for Christian burials. This would be a hard and desolate death, and there would be nothing honorable about it.

While maintaining his position, he took a last look at the long lines of soldiers standing on either side of him. So far from home, this was his family now. He wanted to remember - for as long as he could - these good lads with whom he had trained, marched, lived, and was now proud to die. He had grown especially fond of the group from Chester County, in his home state of Pennsylvania.

To his right he could see John and William Miller, both aged 20; and at 41 years of age perhaps the oldest man in Company D, James Boggs - all from West Caln Township. To his left he saw 24 year old Jacob Hammond from East Brandywine and Peter Richmond - a singer with a good voice, who had just turned 29. (Richmond would survive this charge, only to be killed in battle nine weeks later.) As best they could, each man tried to catch sight of the other's eye as a way of saying a silent good-bye.

Surveying the Rebel rifle pits at the crest of the hill opposite them though his spyglass, Captain John McMurray could see the

226

regimental flag of the 1ˢᵗ Texas Infantry - part of legendary Confederate General John Bell Hood's shock troops. He let out a muffled groan and without moving his head muttered to the quiet Quaker, Lt. Nathan Edgerton, standing next to him: "Damnation. It's the 'Ragged Old First.' Plus, I see the colors of the 4ᵗʰ and 5ᵗʰ Texas." Edgerton diverted his eyes away for a moment without betraying alarm. "The Grenadier Guards," he whispered back. He, too, knew what the 6ᵗʰ was in for and paused for a moment of peace-making with the Creator. Everyone knew the Texans were ferocious battle-hardened veterans who would valiantly fight to the last man. They were excellent marksmen, and this would be the very definition of *shooting fish in a barrel.*

The two opposing lines of troops watched each other from across the killing field. Upon surveying the scene, most of the black men in blue took time to make their peace with the Lord, as Reverend Jeremiah Asher - Chaplain for the 6ᵗʰ USCT - recited the 23ʳᵈ Psalm. "As I walk through the valley of the shadow of death, I shall fear no evil, for Thou art with me..." (Reverend Asher would survive this battle, but die nearly 10 months later to the day in Wilmington, North Carolina; where, after ministering to sick USCT troops, he succumbed to illness himself and passed on to glory.)

Those praying with Rev. Asher were also clutching keepsakes and thinking of loved ones they would never see again. One trooper patted his pocket, making sure his last letter to his wife would be found on his body and began reciting the letter silently to himself.

When Lt. Edgerton heard the words, "valley of death," he thought of a poem he once read to his students - which raised a few eyebrows - when he was a teacher at the Quaker Westtown School, in Chester County, Pennsylvania. Throughout the course of recent

227

history, Quakers could often be found on the battlefield, which seems incongruous for members of a religious group for whom peace is a core principle of belief. Yet it is doubtful that very many believed, like the ancient Spartans, that the highest honor was to die in battle. Nor did many likely take pleasure in killing their enemies - as sometimes war is merely an avocation for murderers whose zeal would garner them the gallows in civilian life, instead of ribbons on the battlefield. Perhaps many of these quiet warriors were simply following their leadings from the *Inward Light* - or Inward Light*ning* - believing that God sometimes requires justice as a precursor to peace. And it was their duty to serve God - not to question God's will.

Edgerton recalled a verse from the poem *The Charge of the Light Brigade* by Alfred Lord Tennyson, he had read to his students:

> "Half a league, half a league, Half a league onward,
> All in the valley of Death, Rode the six hundred..."

Same story, he thought ironically - a suicidal frontal assault charging a battery of guns and artillery; except that the Light Brigade had horses - though that made no difference. The horses were slaughtered along with the men. He doubted anyone would remember the black soldiers or their white officers who fell here this day, or that a record of their valor in the face of death would echo through the ages, the way it had for the British troops at Balaclava, ten years earlier and half a world away.

Like many intelligent and contemplative men, Edgerton loved poetry. As he prepared himself for battle, two lines of another Tennyson poem - *Locksley Hall* - came to mind:

"I had been content to perish, falling on the foeman's ground, When the ranks are roll'd in vapour, and the winds are laid with sound."

As the fog lifted, the hard-bitten Texans looked across at the black soldiers with mild curiosity, wondering how many would litter the ground like so many fallen trees. There was little anger in their eyes because these were men accustomed to killing, and doing it well. They appeared cold and methodical, determining their angles of fire and counting their cartridges. One grizzled-looking war-weary Texan of indiscernible age whispered matter-of-factly to the comrade beside him: "Them black boys is studyin' it mighty hard; but they's still a-comin,' ain't they?" His partner stopped chewing long enough to spit a glob of tobacco juice over his shoulder. "Yeah," he responded resignedly, "'cause that wouldn't stop us, neither." Nodding his head thoughtfully, he added: "They got grit; I'll give'm that."

Next, an astonishing order came down the line from Union General Benjamin Butler. The Colored Troops were ordered not to load their guns for the assault! The General didn't want their ammunition wasted by tripping over these obstacles and having their muskets accidently fire. They probably wouldn't have the time or the cover to reload, anyway. To make certain the troops obeyed the order, they were further ordered to remove the percussion caps from their muskets, rendering them impossible to fire. All the way down the line the men could hear the black sergeants like Christian Fleetwood, Alexander Kelly, and Powhatan Beaty quietly barking out the order with deadly resolve to "fix bayonets." In unison, the troopers obeyed, every one preferring to challenge the battle-hardened Texans rather than their steely black sergeants. The next few minutes passed so quickly that it would be difficult for Solomon to later recount the order of events that unfolded.

229

At the moment the command to charge was given, the blue line of soldiers swept down the hill like a rush of water overflowing a levee. At the same time, 2,000 Rebel rifles were cocked in unison. As the long blue wave rolled down the hill, Solomon didn't have a second to look around. Except for an occasional glance upward to maintain his direction, he kept his eyes on the ground to keep from tripping, holding his musket in front him at a slight angle so as not to obscure his vision, since most of his sight had not yet returned in his left eye. A disturbing thought forced its way into his head, beginning as a sinister whisper until becoming an angry shout: "Why aren't they firing at us?" it asked urgently and repeatedly. The Rebs were waiting until the bluecoats got within 150 yards to make every shot count.

Company D completed its gallop downhill, splashing into the cold stream, carefully trying to avoid turning an ankle on the slippery algae-covered rocks in the stream bed. It was then that they heard a sound like a crack of lightning, as if the skies had opened with a cloudburst and a barrage of hot and angry minié balls rained down on them like hornets from Hell, splintering everything in their way.

Solomon kept his eyes on the increasingly treacherous terrain in front of him, but with his peripheral vision he could see troopers falling away to his left and right as the heat-distorted lead cones slammed into them at 650 miles per hour. There were so many Confederate rifles firing at once that it sounded like a battery of Gatling guns were trained on Company D with deadly accuracy. In this narrow and brilliantly focused killing zone most of the shots hit their marks because it was nearly impossible to miss the slow-moving shapes at this distance.

As he tried to make himself as small a target as possible, Solomon began to see splashes of blood, a head exploding over here, an arm flying through the air over there. The dreaded minié balls didn't slice through their targets, they obliterated them. Fear gripped Solomon to his core but still he soldiered on - in the very definition of courage under fire.

As they reached the first abatis, with valiant effort, the troopers with hatchets hastily hacked a path for the column to move forward. The color bearers entered the gap first with officers and fellow troopers following; but as in all wars, the enemy chose the officers and color bearers as their first victims. As the Stars and Stripes lay on the muddy ground, an officer picked it up and was immediately shot dead. Second Lt. Frederick Meyer of Company B picked up the flag and was promptly shot through the heart, his body flung backward. With his free hand, Lt. Nathan Edgerton of Company D pulled the flag from Meyer's death grasp and urged the soldiers onward with his sword in his left hand, but he was suddenly knocked down. Edgerton at first thought he had tripped over briars or underbrush. When he looked down, he saw his hand covered in blood and the shaft of the flag shattered in two, along with his wrist.

Dizzy from loss of blood, Lt. Edgerton was unable to go on, but two black sergeants sprang into action. First Sgt. Alexander Kelly of Company F, picked up the Stars and Stripes from Lt. Edgerton; and Sgt. Major Thomas Hawkins of Company C, who was still recovering from a gunshot wound incurred recently at the Siege of Petersburg, picked up the Regimental Colors. Amid enemy fire, the sergeants brought both flags back to the line to keep them from falling into enemy hands. Instinctively reacting to what he thought was a flash of light, Solomon raised his left hand to shade his eyes when a minié ball ripped through his palm, mangling the delicate bones inside. Fearing his hand had been shot off, he grasped his wrist in agony as he sank into the mud.

231

Seeing the futility of the fight and the enormous loss of men and blood, Major Kiddoo called for an orderly retreat back to the line until more troops could be engaged in the attack. It took all of Solomon's strength and concentration to pick his way back across the field of death, lucky not to get shot in the back or in the back of the head. He scurried from cover to cover – a tree here, a boulder there. Rushing past prostrate and gory bodies, he tried to steal a glance to see if any of his friends were among them. The Rebels would not let up their punishing fire. Musket balls whizzed past him splintering everything in their path, and he zigzagged as best he could to avoid the artillery shells exploding on impact around him.

He fully expected death would strike him at any moment. He prayed for a quick death, a clean death, a soldier's death. He didn't want to lay in the muck for hours, suffering in agony with a shattered spine, or trying to hold in his intestines from a gaping gut shot wound, begging God for a rescue he knew would never come. His left hand was a useless bloody mess and the pain was relentless and unforgiving. He held his musket with his right hand, cradling the barrel in the crook of left arm. It felt God-awful heavy but the pressure of its weight helped to staunch the blood flowing from his hand. By the time he began the return ascent up the Union hill he was gasping for breath but nearly out of range of Confederate rifle fire.

He felt like he was moving in slow motion, for it seemed to take him hours to climb the hill. The sound of the voracious gunfire and deadly artillery shells drowned out the moaning and wailing of wounded men, until all he could hear was his pounding heart and labored breath. He tripped at some point, falling in an exhausted heap on the ground. He could go no farther and lay there waiting for the kill shot that would put him out of his misery. He thought of his

232

beloved Mary because he wanted to die with her image in his mind. When he heard her voice calling to him, he knew then he was dead.

As the air was reflexively sucked back into his lungs, the pain in his hand returned. Looking up, he could see her at the crest of the hill, calling to him. She was lying on the ground with her arm outstretched as if trying to pull him out of a well. He could not comprehend what was happening at that moment. In his grogginess, her pleading slipped through the roar of war like a lifeline to a drowning man. He held out his bloody hand toward her and focused on her voice like a beam from a lighthouse on a dark and rocky shore.

That was all he could concentrate on as he pushed himself up and onto his knees. With a final piercing scream from her, he struggled to his feet and called out her name. His vision was blurred by sweat pouring off his forehead and burning his eyes. With one last burst of energy, he staggered toward her as she slowly evaporated from his sight. When he finally reached the crest of the hill and the Union line, he collapsed and must have passed out because he remembered nothing of the moments afterward.

"The (6th) Regiment entered the battle with 367 rank and file. Of this number, three officers and 39 men were killed, 11 officers and 150 men wounded, and 7 missing, an aggregate of 210, more than 62% of its strength."[xix]

"The most staggering loss of all was suffered by Captain McMurray's Company D. The Captain had gone into battle leading thirty-two men. Forty minutes later twelve of them were killed or mortally wounded, while sixteen others including one officer were sent to the hospital with wounds. McMurray gathered together all of his company's survivors - there were only three (not killed or wounded). The company had lost over 87% percent of its men, the heaviest loss ever reported by any company of Union troops in a single charge."[xx]

A second charge was mounted with more reinforcements. Seeing the slaughter of their brothers-in-arms, many of the black troopers shouted "Remember Fort Pillow!" and poured down the hill like an angry tidal wave. With supporting artillery fire the Union Army took the Confederate high ground and engaged the Rebels in fierce hand-to-hand combat, overwhelming the enemy.

Three black soldiers of the 6th USCT would be awarded the Congressional Medal of Honor for their valor at the Battle of New Market Heights - also known as The Battle of Chaffin's Farm. They were: Sgt. Major Thomas R. Hawkins of Company C, from Cincinnati, Ohio; 1st Sgt. Alexander Kelly of Company F, from Indiana County, Pennsylvania; and Pvt. Samuel Howard of Company K, from Salem County, New Jersey.

Lt. Nathan Edgerton was also awarded the Medal of Honor for his bravery that day. Of the 16 Congressional Medals of Honor bestowed upon U.S. Colored Troops and sailors during the Civil War, 14 troopers were awarded the Medal of Honor for their gallantry at the Battle of New Market Heights. Among them were the amiable, college educated Sgt. Major Christian Fleetwood of Company G, 4th USCT; 1st Sgt. James H. Bronson of Company D, 5th USCT, born a slave in Indiana County, Pennsylvania, before enlisting to fight for the freedom of millions of others; and the handsome and talented former slave, 1st Sgt. Powhatan Beaty of Company G, 5th USCT - who would pursue an acting after the war. Nearly 20 years after President Lincoln's assassination there, Beaty would appear on the stage of Ford's Theater in Washington, D.C., at the height of his career.

234

As he marched back to camp still in a state of shock from pain and loss of blood, Pvt. James Ferrill weighed the merits of his brief military career. He was six weeks shy of his 29th birthday; nearly blind in his left eye and his left hand was mangled - shot through with a musket ball. Neither would ever be the same again - nor would his memory, after seeing such carnage on the battlefield. He had survived a suicidal mission and showed great courage under fire. But his heart still longed for Mary and the soft green hills of Pennsylvania.

He vaguely remembered being in the surgeon's tent and seeing the face of Deacon Ferryman, and Martha Jane may have come to bring him water. Perhaps they had given him laudanum to operate on his hand because his mind was foggy. After two days' rest, he collected his kit and paid a visit to Martha Jane and Andison Parham to bid them goodbye, as he was being shipped to a veteran's hospital in Providence, Rhode Island, where he could receive long term medical treatment for his wounds.

He hugged them all and with his right hand, shook hands with young George. They were also leaving soon. Deacon Ferryman would guide them to Arlington Heights, a refugee camp at one of the forts circling Washington. From there, with God's grace and the help of Quakers, she and her children could make their way north to find Cornelius. The perilous journey would take a week, but with the tide turning in the war, it was now time to move quickly.

All felt as though they were losing a good friend. Pvt. Ferrill had grown fond of this heroic little family and the itinerant preacher who watched over them. Grasping his right hand, because his left was still bandaged and resting in a sling, Martha Jane said: "May the good Lord watch over you, Pvt. Ferrill, and lead you safely back home to Pennsylvania. And may he heal all your hurts and wounds, and give you another good wife someday." He simply smiled in response. "You look enough like my husband Cornelius to be his kin," she remarked. "'Cept he has green eyes, and yours are blue. You a brave man, Pvt. Ferrill, and may God hold you in His hands."

The deacon responded with a righteous "Amen!"

"Thank you kindly for all you done for me, Miss Martha Jane, Andison, Deacon, George – all of you," he said smiling at the children. I'll never forget you – and you're pretty brave, too. And I pray the good Lord – and Deacon Ferryman – lead you out of this wilderness to a real nice home with your husband Cornelius. And maybe God willin,' I'll see you all again someday."

Unfortunately, he would never see them again. As he walked away with hope and tears in his eyes, he could never have foreseen that 55 years later his future grandson, Tom Bolden, and Martha Jane's future granddaughter, Maud Ridley, would meet and marry in 1919 in Media, Pennsylvania. And together they would make the 300 mile drive from Media to Pittsburgh by way of the Horseshoe Curve to attend the old warrior's funeral six years later in October 1925.

CHAPTER 31

Confession and Communion

The little group gathered their belongings and packed up for the trip to Arlington Heights. Deacon Ferryman borrowed an old buckboard wagon and a dray horse from the army quartermaster, sealing the deal with a bottle of contraband white lightning as interest on the loan. He tied his horse, Pony Boy, to the back of the wagon to conserve its strength – so it could be used for scouting and foraging when needed. Fortunately, the group didn't have much to bring. When they crossed the picket lines that night in June, all they had were the clothes on their backs. But after living and working for four months in the Union camp, they had earned a little money and a few extra clothes to take with them. Yet they were puzzled as to why Deacon didn't pack more supplies for the trip. Although they didn't want to ask him directly, he sensed their concern and explained that they had to travel light in case they ran into trouble. Too many supplies would tire the horse faster, slowing them down.

However, he added with his customary twinkling smile, "In the wilderness, the Lord will provide." Not completely convinced, they accepted it on faith.

Deacon Ferryman did a masterful job leading the pilgrims through restless and contested territory without incident. It was apparent he had taken this trek before, because he always knew precisely where to stop and for how long; and where he could find water or parcels of food that would be left for him – sometimes hidden in the crotch of a tree or stashed under a log in a small pit in the ground lined with stones.

Occasionally, he would find a cryptic note with the supplies, which he would study and then burn. They arose every day before dawn, had a quick bite to eat, then pushed hard until noon when Ferryman would seek the cover of a grove of shade trees to give the pilgrims and the horses a chance to rest. While they did, he took Pony Boy out to scout the area, making sure the way ahead was clear. He was a man who could afford no surprises, as he knew there was a price on his head.

The travelers typically rested between noon and 2:00 p.m., during the hottest part of the day. They would then resume the trip until dusk, pulling up in some secluded spot that Ferryman had planned in advance. As Andison and Martha Jane made camp and George scurried about quietly collecting firewood, Ferryman would circle the area to make sure it was safe - and he repeated this precaution once more well after dark.

Occasionally, the group would wake in the middle of the night to find him gone briefly on patrol. They knew he was hunted and haunted by memories that kept him from a sound sleep. Even though they were generally behind Union lines, they knew those boundaries could change at any time without notice. So, everyone had to be very quiet and extremely vigilant. They were grateful for Ferryman's diligence in watching over them, and pondered how many more fugitives had he done this for.

Andison and Martha Jane had wondered why he asked them so many questions back at the army camp, but they never challenged him about the reasons for his actions. They knew there was more to this backwoods preacher than meets the eye. They gathered that his quirkiness and secrecy were in large measure for their safety - because the less they knew, the better, if captured. And correspondingly, the more he knew about them, the better and safer they would be. Yet they liked and trusted him - though they weren't always quite sure why - and that was all that mattered to them.

He was a world-weary traveler who never truly rested. His friendly and easy-going manner belied an ocean of pain brooding just beneath the surface. Though they were deeply spiritual people, they didn't begrudge this battered backwoods Moses a sip or two from his flask at night around the fire, after making sure everyone was safe. It seemed to calm his nerves and provided as much rest as he reluctantly allowed himself.

Late one night near the end of the journey, Martha Jane was restless and unable to sleep. Now that freedom was nearly in reach, something dark and unsettling had been troubling her that she wanted to leave behind on the road before crossing into the Promised Land. Ferryman had been studying some scrap of paper when she got up off her blanket and joined him by the fire.

"Miss Martha?" he asked softly, "You all right?" Seeing her pained expression in the firelight, he asked: "Are you sick? I got some peppermint oil and a little medicine in my bag, but we can get you to a real doctor in a day or two, if you can just hold out 'til then."

She shook her head, looking even more distraught, which concerned him. "You been snake bit?" he asked with alarm. Although tears were welling up in her eyes, she had to smile in response. "Now, Deacon Ferryman," she began with a voice as soft as butter, "don't you think I'd be hollerin' my head off if I was bit by a snake?"

The worried look on his face melted into mere concern, and he responded with a smile of his own. And the two shared a quiet

239

chuckle. "Well, I guess you do have a point there, Miss Martha Jane," he kindly acknowledged. But he inquired again with his eyes.

"It's jus'...it's jus' that..." He nodded gently as encouragement for her to continue. "Back there, on the plantation...I had to do a lot of things. I was a breedin' woman," she said with shame. Ferryman's dark brown eyes responded with a look of compassion and absolution. "Cornelius knows but he loves me anyway. I don't know why," she mused in a voice thick with emotion.

"Because he's a good man and you're a good woman," the Deacon insisted. Struggling to find the right words, she continued, "And now that I might really see him again in Pennsylvania..."

Still perplexed as to the reason for this confession Ferryman quietly probed, "And?"

"What happened back there was terrible," she continued. "It hurt me real bad. I did some things - some real bad things he don't know about. I never lied to him, but I never told him about everything I been through, either. Jus' never was enough time, or the right time. And now, Cornelius'll want to get married, in a *real* church - not like when we jumped the broom - and we'll live in a town where he'll work and people'll get to know us...and, and, what do I say? What do I tell'em? How can I tell'em what all I done - mos'ly before I even met Cornelius - and about what all I been through? I wasn't just no field slave, you know. An' if I don't tell'em, I'll be livin' a lie an' feel more ashamed than I do already. Sometimes I jus' feel so rotten inside. Like an' apple with a worm in it, that's eatin' away at me. An' goin' to a new place, kinda makes me feel worse, 'cause I wanna make a fresh start," she said as hot tears streamed down her cheeks.

Ferryman resisted the urge to prod her on because he knew she had more to say. "I know Cornelius forgive me - at least, for what he *knows*. But what about the rest? I want *God* to forgive me, too."

She was trembling now and using all her strength to hold back the deep sobs that were causing spasms inside her. Across the clearing, wrapped in his blanket, her brother silently awoke, hearing everything; but he remained motionless, pretending to be asleep, for fear of interrupting this time for spiritual healing. A large tear rolled down his cheek.

Deacon was also moved. He divined what she was talking about. He had known women like her, including his own mother; and he knew the heart-breaking choices some slave women were forced to make because of the abysmal things they had to endure. Choices like: whether to bring another child into a world of certain misery; or would it actually be more loving to send them gently on to a better world, a world of everlasting life with Jesus? In some ways, that seemed far less cruel and selfless than keeping those infants in this world, watching them suffer years of extreme, dehumanizing abuse.

As terrifying a life in slavery could be, the one refuge slaves did have was the promise of a better life in the hereafter; a promise made in the Holy Bible itself that was indisputable, even for their masters. It was to be an eternal life where there was no pain or sorrow - only peace and happiness in the arms of the Savior, surrounded by all of their loved ones who were missing or had gone before. This was their heavenly reward for Hell on Earth - this one ephemeral shred of hope they could hang onto in this life. It was the only theological or existential explanation that allowed this tortured existence to make any sense at all - that their suffering was the thorn-filled path to salvation. It was their Appian Way.

Any good mother or father would willingly accept ten times the pain their children had to endure, if it would alleviate their offspring's suffering. So why let them suffer? Countless blacks were raped, whipped, mutilated, worked to death, tortured, lynched, and sometimes burned alive. Was that the kind of perilous and uncertain future slave parents wanted for their babies and toddlers, sons and daughters? Didn't Jesus say: "Suffer the little children to come unto me?" Wouldn't they be safe and happy and at peace in Heaven with Him? Theirs was a purgatory few whites could imagine.

As the words welled up inside him, Ferryman choked back his own tears. "First...God done forgive you already, Miss Martha Jane. He knows you a good woman, and He knows that no slave has any say on what happens to them, or what they have to do."

He swallowed hard to steady himself, because he had been unprepared for the wellspring of emotion and appalling memories this poor woman's anguish had unlocked within him. It was now time for a confession of his own. He began slowly, speaking in a voice she had not heard from him before, as if he was possessed. And his story sounded something like this one...

"I was born a slave. After my master died, 'my sister and me went to his son. His son was a killer. He got in trouble there in Georgia and got him two good-stepping hosses and the covered wagon. He branded us. He brand my mother before us left Georgia...that nearly kilt her. He brand her in the breast, then between the shoulders. He brand all us.

"Then he chains all he slaves round the necks and fastens the chains to the hosses and makes them walk all the way to Texas. My mother and sister had to walk. Emma was my sister. Somewhere on the road it went to snowing, and Massa wouldn't let us wrap

242

anything round our feet. We had to sleep on the ground, too, in all that snow. We never had no quarters. When nighttime come, he locks the chain round our necks and then locks it round a tree... our bed were the ground. All he feed us was raw meat and green corn... I et many a green weed. I was hungry. He never let us eat at noon, he worked us all day without stopping. We went naked, that the way he worked us. We never had any clothes. My sister, Emma, was the only woman he have till he marries. Emma was the wife of all seven Negro slaves. He sold her when she's 'bout fifteen, just before her baby was born. I never seen her since.

"'Massa have a great, long whip platted out of rawhide, and when one the negras fall behind or give out, he hit him with that whip. It take the hide every time he hit a negra. Mother, she give out on the way, 'bout the line of Texas. Her feet got raw and bleeding, and her legs swoll plumb out of shape. Then Massa, he just take out his gun and shot her, and whilst she lay dying he kicks her two-three times and say, 'Damn a negra what can't stand nothing.' You know that man, he wouldn't bury mother, just leave her laying where he shot her at'..."[xxi]

Tears were now streaming down Ferryman's cheeks. As he began to come out of his trance and regain his composure, his voice now resembled the one to which she had grown accustomed. But it was eerily cool and detached as he continued his story.

"Me and Pony Boy, we was the last ones with him. He had sold off or killed all the rest of the slaves, and he beat Pony Boy just like he beat us. But he's a good horse, you know? Never hurt nobody. So one night, Massa got drunk real bad, an' ran outta whiskey. Made me hitch Pony Boy up to the wagon, help him up to the driver's seat and cussed me to get in the back. We was ridin' into town on a dark road

243

along the swamp. There were gators in that swamp - everybody in East Texas knew that. That's why nobody took that road at night.

"He was so drunk he couldn't hardly see. Pony Boy stopped suddenly, 'cause a big tree limb had fallen down across the road - but Massa couldn't see it and he started whippin' Pony Boy to make'im go ahead. So Pony Boy jumped over the log, pullin' the wagon behind'im. But the front wheel snapped and the wagon turned over, throwin' me an' Massa off. The hitch broke, too, and Pony Boy was free - but he didn't run off. I got up off the road lookin' for Massa, but he had been thrown to the side of the road and had slid down the muddy bank into the swamp. An' he was cussin' somethin' awful. He was yellin' at me to come pull him out. As I limped over there and looked down, I heard a splash and saw two yellow eyes in the water movin' toward him an' he heard it, too. By God it was a big, bull gator; like a monster.

"He started yellin' for me to grab a stick and hold it out for him so I could pull'im up. But them big yellow eyes looked jus' like the Devil. Maybe it was. That splashing kept comin' closer. I leaned over the bank and he cussed me again; said he was gonna kill me when he got out, just like he did my momma. He was trying to claw up the bank but it was slick with mud. He clutched onto some tree roots and started to pull himself up, but I grabbed a spoke from the broken wagon wheel and I beat his hands bloody for all I was worth.

"When he slid back down that big ol' gator splashed up outta the water, and in one bite had that bastard's legs in his mouth, up above the knees. Screamin' like a baby, he clawed at the tree roots again trying to pull hisself out of the water. But I beat his hands off even worse than before - broke every bone he had. The look o' terror in his eyes was payment for killin' my momma, and for everything he done to us. He kept screamin' all the while that big bull gator was crackin' his bones like tree branches, with its jaws, until it pulled him
244

down under that dark water an' there was nothin' left to see but bubbles. Everything got real quiet. No crickets were chirpin'. Even the frogs had stopped croakin'. But it had all been music to my ears, and there was a real peaceful feelin' when it was all done," he said with satisfaction, "like somethin' evil had just gone out of the world."

"Me an' Pony Boy looked at each other an' we knew we was free. I rode'im back to the cabin, got his blanket, saddle, and everything we could use, and rode off into the night, headin' north. An' I never looked back." Martha Jane had stopped crying, and her eyes offered nothing but compassion and absolution.

"So, you see, Miss Martha, a lotta us done some ugly things. But they're done now and there's no undoin'em. I made a promise to God that night that if He forgive me, and give me and Pony Boy a second chance, we would help other black folks to be free. An' I been livin' up to that bond ever since." They sat in silence for a few moments, feeling a heavy burden had been lifted off each of them.

Andison got up quietly and joined them by the fire. "Any coffee left?" he asked kindly. Ferryman smiled and poured him a cup. "I know that God has forgiven both of you," Andison testified. "Now it's time for you to forgive yourselves. We paid for our sins. Slavery is the greater sin. But we're not slaves anymore. We're different people. *New* people. *God's* people." Glancing over at the sleeping children, he added, "the Children of God." And he passed the cup to each of them as a sign of communion.

CHAPTER 32

River Jordan

The group made its way past the Union pickets circling the outskirts of Washington, as Ferryman flashed a permit at the sentries that bore some official signature and seal. Neither Martha Jane nor Andison could read, so they didn't know what the paper said, but they thought it odd that one of the soldiers gave Ferryman a quick salute. When young George asked why, Ferryman responded with a warm smile, saying: "Aw, they jus' bein' friendly, little man."

As Ferryman pulled the wagon to a stop, not far from the Capitol on the heights overlooking on the Potomac, they paused and with a sigh of relief savored the sight of what seemed to them to be the edge of the Promised Land. From their vantage point, they could see part of the circle of Union forts surrounding the city, and the refugee camp on the lee shore.

"Well folks, you done made it to Canaan," Ferryman said grandly with a broad sweep of his hat, "and now you gonna cross the River Jordan. But we can't linger here long, because after all – we're still in ol' Virginny. They made their way down to a boat landing on the river, just in time to meet two sturdy USCT soldiers and their female passenger pulling up in a large rowboat.

"Hello Deacon!" the corporal called out. "Hello Corporal!" Ferryman responded good-naturedly. The party got down off the wagon and Ferryman introduced them to the soldiers.

"Andison, Miss Martha Jane: these gentlemen are friends of mine – Corporal Joshua Hawkins and Private Aaron Seaborn.

We've worked together a long time." Cpl. Hawkins introduced the female passenger - Mattie Pritchard. Pritchard, also a former slave, now worked at the refugee camps as teamster and part-time nurse, assisting the camp doctor in processing new arrivals. She was a tall, strong, stocky woman with a big smile. The five adults exchanged greetings. Ferryman continued, "These men will take you 'cross the river to the camp and get you settled there. They're good men and you can trust them just like you trusted me."

"Ain't you comin' too?" young George asked, with his mother and uncle chiming in. "Naw," Ferryman replied. "I wish I could stay a while, son, but I can't." Despite their protests, he continued: "There's a lot more work to do. I gotta git back on my circuit, 'cause they's some more folks I gotta help along the way. An' they're countin' on me. It's the Lord's work and you know I can't break my bond. But you in good hands now," he promised.

Ferryman and the Corporal exchanged slim, leather-bound packets of papers, and then he continued. "These good people'll get you to your new quarters and see you get food. An' they'll make sure you meet the Quakers who can help you further on your way north.

"Don't worry folks, we've walked in your shoes," the Corporal said. "And there's a bunch of young boys just like you over there, and they be happy to make a new friend," Pvt. Seaborn assured George.

"And I'll see that you meet some of the other ladies in camp," Pritchard said to Martha Jane. Pritchard then climbed onto the buckboard. "I'll meet you at the medical station after I get this wagon to the livery stable. They gotta pack it full of supplies and send it back to the 6th, with the rest of the wagon train." Martha Jane waved as Pritchard pulled away.

The little family encircled Ferryman, hugging him. "How we ever gonna thank you for all you done for us, Deacon," Martha Jane asked as tears welled up in her eyes. "Deacon, you delivered us from bondage," Andison added, obviously emotional. "An' you're my bestest friend," George insisted. Ferryman nodded to the soldiers who placed the family's belongings onto the large rowboat.

"Now, don't you folks be gettin' me all misty-eyed," Ferryman said. "First of all, the *Lord* delivered you from bondage - with a lotta help from yourselves. I'm jus' the one that *drove* you here. You'll be safe, and protected, an' free over there. There's a big community of freedmen. It's a clean place and they's good people there jus' like you. They even got a preacher too," he said as he ushered them to the waiting rowboat.

"My flock, well you know, they're all spread out along the road behind the lines - like you folks was. An' I gotta help as many of 'em as I can to get to where you're goin'. But don't worry, we're all gonna meet in Heaven someday, if not before," he said with a genuine smile.

Martha Jane and Andison nodded silently in assent. "You helped us; you saved us," they said. "No, *you* saved *me*," Deacon Ferryman countered. "An' you know the Lord moves in mysterious ways, so, who knows that I might not see you again someday after the war?" They knew it was a cheerful lie but it buoyed their spirits nonetheless.

Andison and the children climbed into the boat. Before stepping in after them, Martha Jane pulled a small tightly wrapped package out of her bag and offered it to Ferryman. "Here, Deacon, this is for you," she said with a beatific smile.

Nonplussed, and at a rare loss for words, he stammered: "For me, why, but what for, Miss Martha?" It had been many years since anyone had given him a gift. She responded with a gentle kiss on his cheek and a broad grin as she stepped into the boat. "Open it," she prodded him.

Still baffled, he pulled open the package to find a clean white officer's shirt. At first, he didn't know whether to be delighted or offended in comparison to the threadbare, soiled old shirt he perpetually wore. "What, where, how…" he sputtered.

"I know you can use a new shirt," she replied, "since I won't be around to wash the one you're wearin' anymore." The children giggled as the wonderment on his face burst into shout of joy.

"Well, Hallelujah, sister! How did you…?" he began. With everyone seated in the boat, the Corporal pushed off into the water.

"The Quaker - Lt. Edgerton - he helped me," she explained. I giv'im the money and he bought it at the commissary. I knew they wouldn't sell it to *me!*"

"But where did you get the money from?" he asked, perplexed.

"You think I washed all that laundry for free?" she responded saucily. "I ain't no slave no more Deacon," she added proudly.

It was the first time they had ever seen Ferryman truly laugh. With his face beaming like sunshine, he shouted again: "Hallelujah!" then did a few frenetic steps of a jig, much to the delight of the children. "God bless you, Sister Martha! God bless you all," he shouted with a vigorous wave of his dusty old hat as the strong soldiers began to row the boat away.

"Good-bye Deacon Ferryman, good-bye Pony Boy!" George yelled out. "Deacon, you a good man, an' we'll never forget what you done," shouted Andison hoarsely. Martha Jane called out last. "God bless you, Deacon. God has forgiven you and holds you in His heart for all you done for His people. You're free now too, Deacon!" she said with tears streaming down her face, "you are free!" she affirmed with a voice cracked with emotion.

He replied with formal bow and a wave of his hat as he climbed onto his horse. "We *both* free, Miss Martha Jane," he called back. "We *both* free now, an' don't you never forgit that! You hear me?" he insisted. "You lissen to ol' Deacon Ferryman, now. God done blessed you! He delivered you from Pharaoh. He blessed you all!"

She nodded with a look of grace he carried in his memory for the rest of his days. He circled the horse around, back toward the road. With tears in his eyes, he said to his horse, "Ol' Pony Boy, maybe it's time for you an' me to think about settlin' down." Pony Boy nodded his head and nickered in agreement, picking up his pace. Ferryman couldn't bear to turn around because he feared it would make his heart ache even more. As their boat was rowed toward the distant shore, they watched Deacon Leviticus D. Ferryman ride off with a cloud of dust trailing behind – or maybe it was his guardian angel.

CHAPTER 33

Patches on the Quilt

Getting settled in at the refugee camp was a little overwhelming at first for the Parham family, but they soon fell into a routine and learned their way around. The camp was efficiently organized and well-laid out, with the more established areas looking like the beginnings of a permanent community. They first had to see the camp doctor to ascertain their health and to make certain they were not carrying infectious diseases.

Next, they were assigned a large tent; and a welcoming committee, of sorts, came to orient them to camp life. Andison found work right away and there was a make-shift school for refugee children like George, taught by Quaker women. There was also a kind of nursery for younger children staffed by a nurse and some of the mothers, and once the family got adjusted to their new quarters, Martha Jane's daughter, Rachel, and Andison's daughter, Sarah, were placed there during the day so that both adults were free to work.

After they learned her story, a pair of Quakers visited often and advised Martha Jane that they were in touch with Friends in Pennsylvania who had provided a home for Cornelius. Martha Jane yearned to know more about how this was possible. While not wanting to divulge too much about their network, they explained that Friends throughout the South kept in regular contact - and that included the Quakers at Blackwater Meeting in Southampton County. But there were too many lives at risk to say much more about this underground network - as there were Southern spies and sympathizers everywhere. Although General Robert E. Lee was somewhere around Richmond at the moment, his home - Arlington House - was less than four miles away. But it was in Union hands, and adding insult to injury, part of the property was now being used as a cemetery for Union soldiers. There was also a nascent Freedman's Village on another part of the grounds.

However, nowhere in the South was completely safe - not even the Capitol itself. And slavery was still legal in the nearby border states of Delaware and Maryland. Since the Federal Fugitive Slave Act remained in full effect, they risked capture. So, the less one said, the better. But they assured her that Freedmen, free blacks, and Friends were also everywhere. And that some Quakers even posed as slave owners, buying slaves at auction in the South and then spiriting them north to freedom. They begged her patience and understanding, as it would take some time to complete all of the necessary plans and arrangements before sending her and the children northward, as this would be more difficult for a family than it was for a single man traveling alone, as Cornelius had done.

Time dragged on in her heart but for the others it passed quickly. This new life of freedom was a balm to their souls. To live and work amongst other free blacks who could now hold their heads high and look toward the future was a far different world from the one they had left behind. Andison loved his job as a gardener at the new military cemetery where the sweat from his brow and the labors of his hands created beauty and profit for himself instead of his master. He also met a kind and fetching woman named Hannah, ten years younger, who had lost her children and husband when they were auctioned off separately from her old master's estate. Fortunately, Hannah was quite fond of Andison's daughter, Sarah.

252

When Martha Jane finally received word that it was time to start her journey northward, Andison decided to stay behind with plans to marry Hannah. He had a good job at Arlington cemetery and Sarah needed a mother. For the first time in his life he was earning wages, and he had his eye on a little piece of property about 8 miles away on the Potomac River in Alexandria. In a couple of years, he would have enough money to buy it. Until then, they could live safely and comfortably in the Freedmen's Village. His decision pulled at her heartstrings, but his sister knew it was the right one for him and his little girl. She also knew that it would certainly be possible to see him again, given the proximity. After a round of tears of joy and sorrow, she said good-bye to her brother and his happy little family, and turned her eyes north - "boarding" the Underground Railroad with her children. But in years to come, she would never divulge the secrets of this part of her journey, as she had promised the daring people who had risked their lives, and their own freedom, to help her.

Reuniting with Cornelius was like a dream. It was the happiest time in Martha Jane's life, and the aura of those first days in the green, little country town of Media would stay with her for a very long time. And Cornelius could not have been happier. It had been three lonely years without his wife, with only a few scraps of information about her and the children to sustain him during the entire time. Yet he had remained steadfast - never losing hope. He had kept busy, staying productive, and was also able to acquire a rudimentary education at the Blue Hill School in Upper Providence.

Isaac and Elizabeth Smedley Yarnall - the courageous Quakers who had provided a home for Cornelius - gave her and the children a warm welcome. Martha Jane had never known white people like these two before. After becoming accustomed to life in the North, and saving their money, Cornelius and Martha Jane were eager to establish a life on their own.

They first moved into the County's new almshouse, which was clean and close to Cornelius' job. But they eventually wanted more privacy and independence, so they rented a little house a local blacksmith had just vacated on nearby Providence Great Road - just across from Providence Friends Meeting House. This allowed them to see Isaac and Elizabeth often, as the Yarnalls were members of that Quaker Meeting.

The tragic news of President Lincoln's assassination was a dreadful reminder of the violence and enmity in the South. The granite columns holding up the marble portico of the county court house were draped in black, reflective of the somber mood of the townspeople and the rest of the nation. The trial of the conspirators was avidly covered in the local papers. But their capture and execution were cold comfort, particularly for former slaves who viewed Lincoln as a living saint, and this was a national tragedy of historic proportions.

Cornelius continued to succeed at his job as the delivery wagon driver for Hawley & Snowden's Hardware Store on State Street, and Martha Jane earned money by taking in laundry and whitewashing houses. Rachel Ann and George Washington - "Washy" - as he still preferred to be called were old enough to accompany her. On Christmas Day, 1866, 12-year old Washy got the present he had long been wishing for - the exciting news that he would soon have

254

another sibling. He hoped mightily that it would be boy like him, and on June 10, 1867, he got his wish - in the form of a little brother named William Henry Ridley.

The years passed quickly and like weeds in the garden, Rachel and Washy grew tall and lanky for their ages, but "Willie" was not faring as well. He was a bright and inquisitive little boy but often sickly and quieter by comparison, causing his mother great concern. When the two older children were in school, Martha Jane would bring Willie in the yard with her to hang up the laundry, but she had to tie a rope around him to keep him from wandering off. Everything seemed to fascinate him and he appeared to become lost in his own little reveries following a frog or marveling at a fluttering butterfly.

Three years later in April of 1870, a fourth and final child was born; another daughter - Rosa Ann - named for Cornelius' long lost sister. Cornelius never knew what became of his beloved sister Rosa - where she went or who she was sold to - presenting him with the impossible task of even knowing where to begin looking for her. The war had dragged on too long and the widespread death and destruction across the South had uprooted hundreds of thousands.

As stated earlier, well over half a million soldiers, blue and gray, had died and there were more missing, wounded, amputees, and unmarked graves. Many of the government buildings that had housed official records had been by damaged by fire or destroyed during battles. Masses of blacks on the move had passed through refugee camps, and all over the South countless former slaves roamed the countryside searching for lost loved ones.

Even if Rosa had somehow managed to return to Bonnie Doon after the war, there would have been no trace of Cornelius remaining in that area indicating where he had gone; nor any news about him for years, because the Underground Railroad had been too successful in covering its uncharted tracks. Rosa's fate remains a mystery. Although it was a tragic and traumatic loss, she would never be forgotten.

Ten years after his escape, the family with four children had outgrown the little blacksmith's house and needed a home of their own. In 1872, they bought a new, two-story brick house at 308 North Olive Street, on the other side of town.

The Media Ridleys prospered and the South now seemed a world away and far behind them. Not only was Cornelius a valued employee at the store, he was developing significant standing in the community. His polite and friendly manner was appreciated by customers and neighbors alike, and those who knew him marveled that this affable apparently "white" man could have ever been born a slave. The couple found a group of members of the African-Methodist-Episcopal Church with whom they felt a sense of connectedness. For the present, the group had been holding services in the local school house on Sundays. However, they were well-organized and determined to raise enough money to build a church of their own, which they planned to call "Campbell." African-Methodist-Episcopal congregations in the region traced their roots to "Mother" Bethel AME Church in Philadelphia, founded in 1794 by Bishop Richard Allen, who had also been a former slave.

While their other children were healthy and active, Willie continued to struggle with long bouts of illness, which delayed the

256

start of his schooling for years. After a series of particularly high fevers, his vision was significantly impacted and he was forced to wear glasses at an early age. Fortunately, his parents were earning enough money to afford them. Washy was always protective of his younger brother, as the bond between the boys was unbreakable. Being strong and sinewy for his age, Washy seldom had trouble with other local youths and under his vigilance, neither did Willie. By this time, Washy was 17 years old and an imposing young man, living on his own and working for a local building contractor.

As the years passed Willie slowly grew stronger and was finally able to progress in school. His sister Rachel became a secretary in a business office and Rosa would soon begin training as a nurse at the Woman's Medical College, founded by Quakers, in Philadelphia.

In 1887, Willie graduated with honors from Media High School. After losing the tip of a finger in a saw mill accident one summer a few years earlier, he had decided that physical labor was not suitable for him. Sitting next to his father on the delivery wagon, each time they rode past the court house he marveled at the majestic building with the Latin inscription across its portico: *omnes viri boni ipsam aequitatem ipsum amant*, which loosely translated means "every good man loves justice for itself."

Willie saw that the judges and attorneys who served in court appeared to be well-dressed, influential, and learned men. He knew of the bitter injustices his parents had suffered during slavery. So, upon graduation from high school, he began studying for a career in law in the office of a prominent local attorney, Louis H. Richards, Esq.

CHAPTER 34

The Case of W. H. Ridley

The Chester Times, September 4, 1889

"RECKLESS SHOOTING"
"Several Mediaites Come to Chester
and Try to Paint the Town Red"

"Last evening, two carriages were driven to Chester from Media. They contained, among others, a young colored man named Ridley, who is studying law in the office of Horace Manley, Esq., and a son of Morris Hannum. At the Colonnade Hotel the party engaged in a wrangle and exchanged a number of revolver shots. The men then ran out of the hotel, hastily entered one of the carriages and drove down Third street.

"Officers Meath and Williams were at the bridge when the shots were fired, and both started on a run toward the hotel. Their attention, however, was directed to the carriage and they ran out into the street, Meath seizing the horses by the heads. He had no sooner done this than the occupants of the carriage opened fire upon him, whereupon he released his hold, the driver used his whip freely and the team was soon lost to sight.

"Young Hannum, who was seated in the other carriage, was arrested and taken to the lockup, and the other offenders will be secured.

"Young Hannum was discharged this morning, the evidence showing that he was not a party to the shooting. This morning, Officer Campbell arrested the other parties, Cornelius Ridley, colored; John Armstrong, son of the County Commissioner; and Thomas Strickler. Mayor Coates gave them a hearing and held them for their appearance in court. One of the horses was shot in the neck and in two places in the body, and the cushion of the carriage was riddled with bullets. All the parties are young men and treated the whole matter as a huge joke.

"Ridley was shot in the leg, though the wound is not serious. All these young men were serving circulars for the nomination of [John B.] Robinson for the [State] Senate. Packer, the electric light man, struck one of them in the mouth and the other [Jesse] Baker men jumped on the youths, which was the cause of the shooting. When Officer Meath caught the horses by the head, the young men thought their antagonists had pursued them and fired."[xxii]

The Chester Times
(mid-September) 1889

"THE RIDLEY SHOOTING CASE"

"The Grand Jury have returned true bills against Cornelius Ridley for carrying concealed deadly weapons, shooting with intent to kill and assault and battery. Cornelius Ridley will probably be able to show that on the night before the election, when the shooting affair occurred, he was home in bed. His son William probably knows more about it, but he is not at present under indictment.

"Will Stiteler, the Media liveryman, says the published report that he intended to sue young Ridley for the value of the horse shot, is not true. He says he did not hire the horse to Ridley and holds him in no way responsible.

"The witnesses in the Ridley case were all discharged in court yesterday until Friday morning. The charges against John Armstrong and Theodore Strickler, arrested with Ridley for being implicated in the election row, were settled early this week without going to the Grand Jury, and the indictments were withdrawn."[xxiii]

The Chester Times
September 25, 1889

"RIDLEY'S CASE ON TRIAL"

"The Ridley shooting case was called up at 9:30 this morning and is on trial as we go to press, with the prospect of lasting most of the day. Well-known young men of both Media and Chester are witnesses in the case. William Ridley, the defendant, is a young colored man, a graduate of the Media High School, and at present a student in Lawyer Richards' office, Media. His friends are much interested in the outcome of the case, but they believe the young man will be able to show that he was not altogether to blame for the trouble. The shooting occurred the night before the recent exiting election and the details are already well known to the Times readers."[xxiv]

The Chester Times, September 26, 1889

QUARTER SESSIONS COURT

"The Case of W. H. Ridley Occupies the Time of Court and Jury"

"The case of William H. Ridley, of Media, charged by Officer Lewis Meath, with assault and battery, carrying concealed deadly weapons and shooting with intent to kill, occupied nearly all of yesterday's session and was not concluded when court adjourned last night at nine o'clock.

"The prosecutor, Lewis Meath, was the first witness called, and he told of being on Third street bridge on the night or early morning of the occurrence and hearing two shots fired in front of the Colonnade Hotel. He says he and Officer Williams started up the street, where a team came toward them at a rapid gait and a man named Mason called to the police to stop that team. He undertook to stop the team when someone in the wagon fired a shot at him and he went down to escape being shot. The team then went up Edgmont avenue and he and Officer Williams emptied their revolvers after the fleeing team and its inmates.

"Officer Williams corroborated Officer Meath as to the team coming down the street and the latter's efforts to stop it.

"William Mason, who called to the officers to stop the team, says he did so because of the shots heard at the Colonnade. He heard Meath call 'halt' and then go down, but rather singularly he says he heard no shots fired. On cross-examination Mason said that he saw Ridley earlier in the evening at Abbott's and he was pointed out to him as a man who was down from Media distributing circulars in favor of John B. Robinson.

CONFLICTING TESTIMONY

"The remainder of the Commonwealth's testimony was conflicting, but taking the story of the most disinterested and reliable witnesses, the trouble started in front of the Colonnade hotel about one o'clock by a number of members of the Hanley Hose Company, who were favorable to Baker, attacking the defendant, William Ridley and George Hannum, who were with him, for distributing the objectionable circulars.

"John Armstrong and Theodore Stickler stated that they were sitting in their wagon in front of the hotel waiting for Ridley and Hannum, whose team was there, and that when Ridley and

Hannum came out that they were attacked and knocked down. Ridley was knocked down twice, the second time right in the gutter with four or five men on top of him and that the first shot came from the gutter. When the first shot was fired they [Armstrong and Strickler] started with their team down Third street and when down near Edgmont avenue Ridley came running down with the bullets flying, and saying he was shot, jumped into their wagon. Both the young men say they saw no one they took for a policeman, but supposed the man who tried to stop them was part of the mob.

"Nelson Duncan, another commonwealth witness, corroborated Strickler and Armstrong, and that Ridley was not the aggressor but that he was attacked and would probably have been killed had he not used his pistol when the crowd got on him and the shot was fired and the crowd scattered.

"The testimony of Peter McGonigle, George Wheaton and Peter Cunningham, members of the Hanley Hose gang, was in direct conflict with [the] above, and they all told a very unlikely tale that when a man named Packer struck young Hannum in the face Ridley walked into the crowd and fired the first shot before he was touched. Wheaton's testimony was also in conflict with that of the officers. When asked

263

about the number of shots fired he said: 'Well, I am on my oath and don't want to make a mistake, but I think there was at least fifteen.'

THE DEFENSE

The defense in the case opened by putting young Ridley himself on the stand. He said that on the night of the trouble he went to Chester to make a speech for Hon. John B. Robinson and distribute circulars. He had heard of people being stopped between Media and Chester and put his revolver in his pocket for protection. In Chester he met Hannum and accepted an invitation to ride home with him. They stopped at the Colonnade Hotel and came out on the pavement with a crowd of fifteen or twenty when the house closed about one o'clock [in the morning]. 'Someone hit George Hannum in the face,' said Ridley, 'when I stepped up and said, *That is not right, gentlemen,* I was immediately caught around the body and thrown to the ground, and a crowd of four or five were upon me in a second. I considered my life in danger and drew my revolver and fired upward. The crowd scattered and I ran down the street and jumped into the wagon of Armstrong and Strickler. In the excitement I saw someone grab at the horse's head, but I didn't know it was a policeman, but thought it was some of the mob pursuing us. I fired in the air and also fired one shot after the team had turned up Edgmont avenue. We were fired upon by the officers and those in the rear and five shots struck the wagon and two hit the horse.'

"Ridley also said that his glasses were knocked off in the scuffle, and as he is near-sighted, he could see very little without them. The young men with him bear him out in the statement that he did not know the man who called to him to halt was a policeman. They say they saw no police.

"R. E. Ross, the well-known Third street merchant, was a good witness for Ridley, and corroborated his statement in regard to the scuffle and the number of shots fired on Third street. He is a boarder at the Colonnade and saw the fuss from his room window.

"Charles Sweeney, watchman at the Saving Fund, and Frank Olmstead, watchman at the Chester National Bank, also said there were at least six shots fired on Third street, if not more.

"Theodore Strickler, a Commonwealth witness, was called to contradict Officer Lewis Meath as to the number of shots fired before Ridley got into the wagon. He said there were at least six and that Ridley called out 'fellows, I am shot, let me in,' as he crawled into the wagon.

"Ridley's revolver given up the day after the occurrence showed three chambers discharged, which goes to corroborate his statement and also that of Armstrong and Strickler as to the number of those fired.

"To prove good character for the defendant almost the entire bar were summoned, but after calling John T. Reynolds, W. Roger Fronefield and William L. Mathues, the District Attorney said they did not question Ridley's character, and Judge Clayton said it was not necessary to call any more if good character was admitted.

"William L. Schaffer, who defended Ridley, spoke to the jury for an hour and a half last evening and was followed by District Attorney Hannum in a speech of an hour. It was then nine o'clock and the court adjourned until ten o'clock this morning, when Judge Clayton charged the jury and they were sent out to prepare their verdict. The opinion prevails that Ridley will be acquitted of all the charges.

Two Shots Only.

"George Wheaton, one of the witnesses in the Ridley shooting case, says that his testimony was not correctly reported. He says he only heard two shots fired, not fifteen.

RIDLEY FINED

"Result of the Election Eve
Shooting Scrape in This City."

"William H. Ridley, of Media, the young colored law student who was engaged in the shooting fracas in this city on the night preceding the late Republican primary election, was yesterday sentenced by Judge Clayton to pay a fine of $25 and costs of the suit on the charge of carrying concealed deadly weapons. On the more serious charge of assault and battery and shooting at a policeman the jury had acquitted him. [xxv]

"Before sentence was passed on him Captain Isaac Johnson, although not employed as counsel in the case, addressed the Court in his behalf, arguing that to imprison this young man would probably blight his prospects forever and prevent his entering the legal profession, for which he is studying. Judge Clayton also took a merciful view of the case, and, after a fatherly reprimand, discharged the defendant upon payment of the fine and costs."[xxxvi]

CHAPTER 35
Wedding bells

With the trial now behind him and his forthcoming legal career fortuitously not derailed before it began, nor had his life been tragically shortened by a hail of bullets - William could focus on his upcoming wedding less than two weeks away on October 10, 1889 in Washington, D.C. He had met his betrothed - a beautiful and mysterious woman from the Danish West Indies - on one his frequent trips to the city. Like other successful doctors, lawyers, and professionals who were first-generation descendants of former slaves, he was making important and influential connections in Washington that could help further his career.

These periodic trips also gave him an opportunity to visit his cousin Sarah, as well as his Uncle Andison and Aunt Hannah who lived in nearby Alexandria - just 7 or 8 miles south of the capitol. Living in the same neighborhood as Cousin Sarah, was the Thomas family, who were old friends of her parents. It was on one of these visits that Mrs. Thomas introduced William to a lovely young seamstress who resided just up the street, with the elegant name of Josephia Constantia Philips. She was the daughter of a wealthy New York merchant and diplomat who had spent much of his life in the West Indies but who eventually returned to New York, where he had passed away four years earlier in 1885, according to his obituary in *The New York Times.*

In 1887, two years after his death, Josephia boarded the S.S. Advance - built in Chester, Pennsylvania - bound for New York, arriving at Ellis Island, alone. Contrary to her naive expectations, her father's old New England blueblood family was shocked and dismayed to meet this previously unknown island beauty born out of wedlock, and she was not warmly welcomed. Envisioning no future there, she traveled to Washington where her only other relative lived – a West Indian-born woman reputed to be Josephia's half-sister. Other than this putative sister, Anita, who bore no family resemblance, Josephia was alone in the world – or so she said. And the dashing young law student was all too happy to remedy that.

However, there was much he did not know about her, and that she spoke primarily Spanish and some broken English only made her more exotic. She was reportedly a clairvoyant who could read one's fortune by examining a cup of tea leaves or the palm of one's hand.

Josephia was an attractive and graceful woman who had apparently lived a privileged life in the islands. She spoke of having a governess and living in her father's mansion on Government Hill on St. Thomas, where he had been a member of the Colonial Council. There, they had servants, beautiful flowers, and many important visitors like Antonio Guzmán Blanco, the Dictator of Venezuela. Because of her father's position and thriving shipping business – and to keep her out of harm's way and political intrigue – she was safely ensconced at a Danish boarding school in Frederiksted on the west end of St. Croix. There, she had survived a Caribbean hurricane by lashing herself to a tree; as well as the October 1878 Fireburn rebellion during which peasants rioted, attacking forts and burning many of the island's sugar plantations. Yet there were large pieces of her past about which she was evasive; and despite the gift of clairvoyance she often exhibited, unbeknownst to her she also carried a family curse.

William had much to learn about Josephia in the coming months and years. Some of the obscure details of her colorful life would take decades to uncover, and had he believed in fortune-telling,

270

he would have been wise to have had his own fortune told. But the ardor and exuberance of youth and the promise of a professional career as a bright and distinguished attorney gave all too rosy a hue to his vision of the world. Foremost at the present time, was preparing for the upcoming nuptials and the many details and decisions that would occupy his thoughts for the fortnight ahead. Somehow he would have to keep up with his legal studies; and in the spring term, take a course at the University of Pennsylvania to further his knowledge of the law. But everything else would have to wait for now.

EPILOGUE

Delaware County Bar Association

Minute and Resolution on the Death of William H. Ridley, Esq.

In the Court of Common Pleas

in and for the County of Delaware, Pennsylvania.

Court Room No. 3. Friday, February 9, 1945.

Before Presiding Judge Albert Dutton McDade

and Judge Henry G. Sweney.

"William H. Ridley was born in the Borough of Media, the son of Cornelius Ridley and Martha, his wife, highly respected residents of the said Borough. Cornelius Ridley was born and reared as a slave in Virginia and during or following the Civil War moved to Media where he was employed for years by Samuel W. Hawley and later Hawley & Snowden, hardware merchants. No man stood higher in the estimation of the people of the County than Cornelius Ridley..."

My earliest known maternal ancestor, Cornelius Ridley, was once a runaway slave who escaped his plantation and his master-father by walking 300 miles north via the Underground Railroad to our hometown of Media, Pennsylvania, in the early 1860s. Given refuge by local Quakers, he worked and patiently waited for three or four long years until the "train" eventually brought three other passengers - his wife Martha Jane and her two children - ten year old George and two year old Rachel Ann.

272

The history of the Ridleys of Southampton County in Virginia - the owners as well as patriarchs of my ancestor - is too long and detailed to be faithfully recounted here. Their story is not mine to tell, anyway. For the sake of historical context and out of respect for my esteemed friend and Ridley family historian Bromfield B. Nichol, Jr., who co-authored *Ridley of Southampton* (1992) with his kinsman Lyndon H. Hart, III, I am compelled to share a small part of their history since it is a confluence to ours.

Bromfield Bradford Nichol, Jr., was born in 1929, and graduated from the venerated "Virginia Military Institute, Class of 1951. He was awarded the Distinguished Service Cross and the Bronze Star Medal while serving as a platoon leader with the 140th Tank Battalion in Korea...He is a member of the Society of the Cincinnati[xxvii] in the State of Virginia...On 15 September 1951, in the Anchorage Presbyterian Church, he married Nancy Hope Boone."[xxviii] In congratulating me on earning my doctorate at the University of Pennsylvania, he wrote to me on August 14, 2007:

"Dear Sam,

I can't tell you how very proud I am for all you've accomplished. You're a credit to the Ridleys. The very best of luck to you on your future career. Keep in touch. Your cousin, Brom.
Pensacola, Florida "

To acknowledge the bond of humanity, kinship, and scholarship between a descendent of slave holders and a descendent of a slave held by them is a tribute to the fraternity of man. I am greatly honored by my friend and kinsman's recognition. I am equally honored by the recognition of my kinship with the descendants of Ridley slaves who remained in Southampton County after my ancestors fled 150 years ago.

273

The other thing that Cousin Brom's courageous act of kindness accomplished was to allow me to finally give myself permission to accept my white ancestry, which I had never truly done before. Although I have always been proud of my other ethnic ancestors, and have always considered myself to be of mixed race; perhaps like many descendants of slaves, I could never bring myself to recognize my white ancestors who likely became members of my family through conquest, rape, or subjugation - and I harbored deep and immutable resentment toward them for doing so.

However, after reading the landmark work, *Ridley of Southampton*, and particularly the notations concerning my cousin Brom Nichol - a bright, distinguished and enlightened man, a father and a war hero - I could no longer find a reason to hate an entire clan of people I had never met. I reasoned that if such remarkable people could produce a scion like Brom, then there must have been others like him with whom I would have felt a spirit of kinship. They could not all have been money-grubbing, racist slaveholders, who beat their bondsmen, raped slave women, exploited black children, and broke up families forever. With this chance encounter on the leviathan Internet, I became worthy of the Ridleys, and they became worthy of me. Brom's simple act of benevolence liberated me from decades of anger and resentment. It was an act of emancipation for one who had never been a slave, by one who had never been a slave owner. It was a peace treaty long in coming yet well worth the wait. And I believe it meant as much to him, as it did to me.

As I wrote in my doctoral dissertation for the University of Pennsylvania, "In the stories handed down to me by my grandmother Maud, 'Bonnie Doon,' 'Buckhorn Quarters' (the slave quarters for Bonnie Doon), and 'Fortsville' (the plantation where Cornelius' wife, Martha Jane lived) were just names of near mythical places that no

274

one in my family had ever visited nor knew their locations. To my knowledge, no one in my family had ever visited those plantations after Cornelius and Martha Jane escaped from slavery in the early 1860s."[xxix] One of my lifelong goals had always been to find these sites.

In 1997, as I was diligently conducting genealogical research on the Internet, I met a fellow researcher and distant relative named Morgan Munsey, an architect in New York City; who, like me, is his family's historian. Morgan is a descendant of another mulatto Ridley slave - Wilson Hubbard Ridley - born about 1824 in Southampton County, Virginia. He lived on the Rock Spring plantation owned by Robert Ridley, which was not far from Bonnie Doon. According to Morgan, Wilson Ridley's putative father-master may have been Colonel Thomas Ridley II; and Wilson's mother was a slave named Hannah Maclin (1795 - 1882). Since Colonel Thomas Ridley II was the father of Robert Ridley and Colonel Thomas Ridley III (sometimes referred to as "Major Ridley" to distinguish father from son), it is possible that Wilson Ridley was a paternal uncle to my ancestor Cornelius. My distant cousin Morgan spent his summers growing up on the farms of his grandparents in Southampton County. It was through him, that a maternal aunt and I were able to find and visit Bonnie Doon plantation on Thanksgiving weekend, 1998. I am eternally grateful to Morgan for helping me to achieve the goal of a lifetime, which I also described in my dissertation - *The Construction of Ethnoracial Identity within Situational Contexts* © 2007 (University of Pennsylvania, UMI/ProQuest).

"Finding the dilapidated old plantation of Bonnie Doon was a moving experience for us - coming face to face with such an ugly part of our family history. In locating Bonnie Doon, I had once again found physical evidence of something that had previously only been a part of my family's oral tradition, the accuracy of which has never failed me. The sky was overcast and a steady, cool wind was blowing through the tall grass. The wind produced an eerie sound, providing an atmosphere that each of us admitted later in the car had been unsettling. We walked around the once magnificent but now decaying antebellum mansion. Some glass remained in the upper windows, which seemed to stare out at us like the eye sockets of an empty skull. I sensed a feeling of malevolence. We walked around the building taking photographs. I then gathered some cotton from the other side of the dirt driveway, which I imagined Cornelius might have walked or driven down hundreds of times during his years there. I also gathered some soil from that same driveway.

"Finally, before leaving, I wanted to get a closer look into the basement to see if there were any remnants of the jail cells. I crept in close and peered inside a large hole where the bricks had fallen away. This concerned my aunt because the building – as the posted sign attested – was in dangerous condition. I could see no cells, bars, or shackles. Though I was powerfully tempted to drop inside and explore further, the weakened condition of the foundation worried me, and rightly so. Instead, I placed my hand against the foundation for a moment" (which gave me the impression of sensing "vibrations" and a fleeting image of a gray-haired man with bronze skin, wearing a straw hat and muslin shirt, laying bricks at that spot). "As we headed to the car we turned and looked once more at the sad structure, imbibing the atmosphere of that place. I felt as though I was being watched, but said nothing to my companions until we drove away in the car – and they then shared that they had experienced the same feeling."[xxx]

Over Labor Day weekend in 1999, twenty-five members of my family and I visited distant relatives in Southampton County, to attend an annual reunion hosted by Morgan Munsey's family.

276

On Thanksgiving Sunday, we attended Morning Star Baptist Church – the traditional "home church" of other descendants of former Ridley slaves and free people of color. The pastor introduced me and gave me an opportunity to make some briefs remarks about our trip and our ancestors, and to display a poster board of old family photographs and to show Cornelius' cane. A month later, I received a very warm letter from the church dated October 18, 1999, which said in part:

> "We would like to thank you and your family for wanting to come here to greet the other family members. Your coming made the Ridley family feel like the prodigal son. On behalf of the descendants of Jordan Ridley, Pastor, and Morning Star Church Family, I would like to thank you for taking time out to come to unite with us. Your visit will never be forgotten. On behalf of the descendants of Jordan Ridley, we believe that you are family and we are glad and excited that we were united. Thank you and your family.

> "With all our Love,
> Morning Star Baptist Church
> Rev. Arthles H. Lynn, Sr., Pastor
> Mrs. Deborah Ridley Freeman, Church clerk."

Joseph "Jordan" Ridley, his sister Ambrit, and their siblings were the children of Cornelius' uncle, Wilson Ridley. This validation of our identity and kinship with people of this region was evidence enough for me that we had found our homeland. Having a homeland to look back to is not just a cultural luxury; it is an integral part of the history, psychology, and culture of diasporic peoples. It gave us a feeling of legitimacy as descendants of an illegitimate infant who never knew his mother, and who was born and raised during the evil institution of slavery. I am truly a Ridley.

According to the esteemed historian John Hope Franklin, there were nearly four million slaves at the time of the Civil War[xxxi]. It is impossible to know how many of them successfully escaped - but most of them were young males. However, conservative estimates suggest that number was at least 50,000[xxxii], which is still less than 2% of the overall number held in bondage.

Cornelius said that his father was his master, and by the time Cornelius was born at Bonnie Doon in 1839, his putative father Colonel Thomas Ridley, III (1809 - 1875) was arguably among the richest planters in Virginia, if not the entire South. He was also a Colonel in the Southampton County militia that captured Nat Turner, leader of a slave rebellion in 1831, which sent shock waves across the South. Ironically, although Turner himself visited Bonnie Doon to try to enlist the help of Ridley slaves, they refused to join him. Instead, they helped to fortify and defend Bonnie Doon and Rock Spring plantations from the rebellious slaves. Looking back in time with a jaundiced and anachronistic eye, one might scoff at Ridley slaves, considering them merely cowards, but this is unlikely and overly simplistic - especially considering what occurred afterward.

Eight years after Nat Turner's Rebellion, Cornelius was born at Bonnie Doon; probably in one of the cluster of slave cabins called Buckhorn Quarters, to a mother he would never know, and who may have died shortly afterward.

On the 1850 Slave Schedule for the U.S. Census in Southampton County there are over 300 slaves listed as belonging to Thomas Ridley. Of those slaves, only a handful are designated as "mulatto"; all others are designated as "black." On that schedule is a 12 year old male mulatto. Of the slaves listed as belonging to Thomas Ridley on the 1860 Slave Schedule for the county, there is a 22 year old male mulatto. Although I have no evidence to prove it

278

conclusively, I believe that person to be my ancestor Cornelius; because he was in the right place, at the right age, at the right time in history, with the right racial designation.

Although Cornelius reported that he never knew his mother, he did say that he had a beautiful sister named Rosa, who was sold to someone in New Orleans. He never saw or heard from her again. But I continue to search for her and have visited New Orleans twice to do local research, trying to find her. Given his fair complexion, red hair, and green eyes, it was likely that Cornelius' mother was a quadroon or octoroon. We may never know the complete genealogy of my ancestors who were born into slavery, but what we do know - we are proud of - and preserve it through family oral tradition and memory. Those who were lost or have passed on are not forgotten. The search to find them continues because in finding them we can find ourselves.

This book is based on my doctoral dissertation, which I intentionally wrote first because I wanted this work to rest on solid academic and genealogical research. While it was necessary to create some characters and events for the sake of continuity, the majority of this work involves real people and actual historical events, as viewed through the interpretive lens of my family history. Archival sources, documents, and photographs were used in a supportive role.

I would like to acknowledge many friends and family members whose ongoing interest and support enabled me to complete this book, as they had the devotion and patience to listen to my disjointed ramblings about this work for years. Among the educators who helped and inspired me on my academic and artistic journey, I am extremely grateful to my dear friend and mentor, the late Ward H. Goodenough, Ph.D., Francis F. Burch, S.J., and chairman of my dissertation committee at the University of Pennsylvania, John L. Puckett, Ph.D., who immediately discerned the cultural and historical significance of my work. Without the support and dedication of these mentors and scholars I would not have succeeded in becoming the first person in my family to earn a research-based doctorate.

Finally, I am deeply indebted to and thankful for my ancestors whose love I feel each day, who I have always strived to be worthy of; and for whom I labored long to tell their remarkable stories in a way that would honor them and do them justice. I hope I have done so. And I dedicate this work to my beloved grandmother, Maud Ray Ridley Ortiga - my first hero - who kept this history alive long enough to share it with me, and without whom none of this would have been possible.

I, in turn, leave this history of my family to my daughter Noelle and those descendants who will come after us. But it is far from complete, and there is much more of this remarkable story yet to be told.

Samuel M. Lemon, Ed.D.
Thanksgiving, 2013
Media, Pennsylvania

End

Cornelius Ridley (April 10, 1839 - February 21, 1922)

Above: Cornelius Ridley with horse, circa 1890. Below: Cornelius (left) driving a mule-team delivery wagon for Hawley & Snowden's Hardware Store, circa 1890. Photo courtesy the late Frank Lees.

Martha Jane Parham Ridley, circa 1900, at about 60 years old.

Picture at right is from a tintype style photograph taken circa 1860, at about 20 years of age, or possibly even earlier. Why it was taken, and by whom, remains a mystery – since it was almost certainly taken while Martha Jane Parham was still a slave, which is curious. If so, it may have related to her being a breeding woman on John Y. Mason's Fortsville Plantation.

Although pictures of slaves are not uncommon, it is still interesting that Martha Jane appears entirely alone in this photograph, and not a part of a family or household picture.

Lt. Nathan Huntley Edgerton (1839 - 1932) a 1st Lt. in the 6th U. S. Colored Troops. Awarded the Congressional Medal of Honor for valor at the Battle of New Market Heights, VA, Sept. 29, 1864; where he was wounded. Edgerton was born to a Quaker family in Barnesville, OH. He attended, and later taught at, Westtown Friends School in Chester County, PA. After the war, Lt. Edgerton had a distinguished career in business, science, and electrical technology. He later retired to a farm near Agness, Oregon, with his wife and family. Edgerton died in 1932.

Maud Ray Ridley Ortiga, born on April 29, 1891, and died on December 4, 1985). Daughter of William Henry Ridley, Esq., and Josephia Constancia Hall Ridley. Maud was the only grandchild of Cornelius and Martha Jane Parham Ridley, and the author's maternal grandmother. The accuracy of Maud's memory was remarkable, and the stories and vintage photographs she shared with the author made this work possible.

Marriage certificate of Cornelius Ridley and Martha Jane C. "Maceson," February 17, 1883.

George Washington Ridley (1855-1933) with his children Lillian E. Ridley and Edward C. Ridley. Right: George's sister Rachel Ann Ridley (1861-1944) from a tintype photograph. George was 9 years old and Rachel Ann was 2 years old when they escaped from slavery with their mother Martha Jane.

BROMFIELD B. NICHOL

August 14

Dear Sam,

I can't tell you how very proud I am for all you've accomplished. You're a credit to the Ridleyz. The very best of y luck to you in your future career Keep in touch

Your cousin

Brom

MORNING STAR BAPTIST CHURCH

≡||≡||≡||≡||≡||≡||≡||≡||≡||≡||≡||≡|||
REV ARTHLES LYNN, PASTOR • DEBORAH FREEMAN CHURCH CLERK • 14502 RIVERMILL RD. P.O.BOX 68 • CAPRON, VIRGINIA 23829 • 804 658-4313 / 757
549 0494 CHURCH /PASTOR • Telephone 757-653-9201 CLERK

October 18, 1999

Dear S. Lemon and Family,

Let me first apogize for a delay response to your card. *Pastor Rev. Lynn,church family and the Ridley family received your card and we are still excited about what took place on Sepember 5, 1999. We would like to thank you and your family for wanting to come here to greet the other family members. Your coming made the Ridley family feel like the prodical son. On behalf of the descendants of Jordan Ridley, Pastor and Morning Star Church Family , I would like to thank you for taking time out to come to unite with us. Your visit will never be forgotten. On behalf of the descendant of Jordon Ridley,we believe that you are family and we are glad and excited that we were united.*

The Morning Star Baptist Church, Pastor Lynn and the Ridley Family would be more than glad to have you to come each year to unite,fellowship and worship witth us. Let us know the time of the year as soon as possible or if if it will be the same time in September.

As for me {Mrs. Freeman,] I am still excited about your first visit . I would like to thank you for such a wonderful picture of your family. I will share it with my family, the Ridley family
Looking forward in hearing from you as soon as possible.

Thank you and your family,

> *With all our Love,*
> *Morning Star Baptist Church*
> *Rev. Arthles H. Lynn,Sr.,Pastor*
> *Mrs. Deborah Ridley Freeman,Church clerk*
>
> *Mrs. Deborah R. Freeman*
> *The Jordan Ridley Descendants*

Letter from Morning Star Baptist Church, home church of descendants of Ridley slaves, commemorating the 1999 visit by the author and his family.

Far left: Solomon Clifford (alias "James Ferrill") of Company D, of the 6th U. S. Colored Troops. Middle: probably daughter Louisa M. Clifford Jones. Man at far right is likely Louisa's second husband, Harry Jones. Photo circa 1920, in Uniontown; or Pittsburgh, PA. Solomon Clifford died on Sept. 29, 1925.

Dilapidated Bonnie Doon mansion, Southampton County, VA; home of Col. Thomas Ridley III. Picture taken by author in November 1998. The building collapsed soon afterwards. Historical marker at right notes that Buckhorn (slave) Quarters, once visited by Nat Turner was located a short distance away.

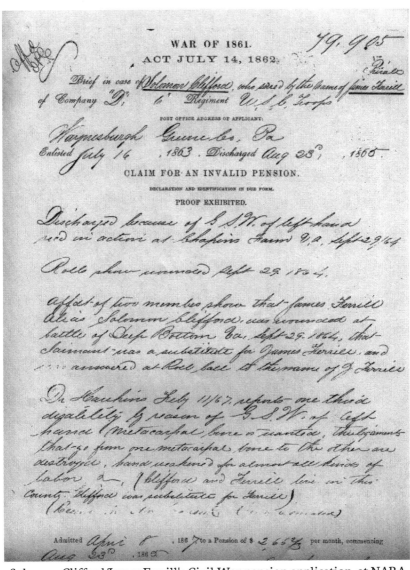

Solomon Clifford/James Ferrill's Civil War pension application, at NARA.

The author, age 4, great-great-grandson of Cornelius Ridley and Martha Jane Parham, taken at Rose Valley School, in Rose Valley, Pennsylvania.

THE WHITE HOUSE

WASHINGTON

September 8, 1997

Mr. Samuel M. Lemon
Apartment 108
421 West State Street
Media, Pennsylvania 19063

Dear Samuel:

Thank you for your letter regarding the suggestion by some members of Congress that the United States Government apologize to African Americans for slavery.

I believe that a formal apology at this time would not be a constructive first step as we begin a nationwide conversation on the difficult issue of race relations in our nation. Instead, I believe this initiative should begin by focusing on substantive issues that will affect the descendants of slaves today -- and other racial and ethnic groups as well. However, I have asked my Advisory Board on Race to look at the question of an apology as the board pursues its work over the coming year.

I appreciate your getting in touch with me on this sensitive and complex issue.

Sincerely,

Bill Clinton

Letter to the author from President Bill Clinton, September 8, 1997.

ENDNOTES

---

[i] William Shakespeare, *The Tempest,* Act II, Scene 1 (1610-11).

[ii] From the eponymous old Negro spiritual.

[iii] Long before I ever saw a picture of Fortsville, I saw it in my dreams. During the mid-1960s when I was living in Cornelius' house, in addition to witnessing the periodic late-night visits of an apparition, I also had a series of vivid, recurring nightmares. One in particular was exceedingly disturbing to me. As I later described it, "In it I was walking around at night in a place I had never been before - an assemblage of a few old, wooden, clapboard houses. And walking along the paths around these houses were black people, who I interpreted to be slaves, because some of them were wearing shackles. But these people had an otherworldly aspect to them. They seemed like walking dead, like zombies. Their vacant eyes seemed to see nothing. This dream frightened me terribly and more so than most of the others I had during this time period." About three decades later when I was pursuing genealogical research, I happened to obtain a drawing of the main house at the Fortsville Plantation, located on the border of Sussex, Greensville, and Southampton counties in Virginia, which is where my great-great grandmother Martha Jane Parham and her brother Andison had been slaves during the Civil War. This drawing looked remarkably like the houses I saw in my dream decades before. And I was startled when I saw it.

[iv] My great-great grandmother, Martha Jane Parham - the future wife of Cornelius Ridley - was born on Mason's Fortsville Plantation on March 12, 1840. On the 1850 Slave Schedule for Sussex/Southampton County, only eleven slaves are listed as the property of John Y. Mason. Of the eleven slaves listed on the schedule, two females are 21 years old, while nine are children from 11 years to an infant less than a year old. Two slave children are male. One is a ten year black female, who may be Martha Jane. Although the U.S. Slave Schedules only record the age, sex, and color of slaves, the ten year old girl listed there is at the right age, at the right place, and the right

time in history to be my ancestor. And I believe it is likely her. Unlike Cornelius, Martha Jane had a nuclear family: a father – George Day, a mother – Mary Moore, and a brother – Andison Parham. The origin of her surname, Parham, is uncertain, but it is an old Virginia name in that region.

[v] From the eponymous old Negro spiritual.

[vi] Ida Hutchinson, Library of Congress Slave Narratives. *To Be A Slave,* by Julius Lester, Scholastic, Inc. (1968), 38.

[vii] *Ridley of Southampton,* 65.

[viii] From the eponymous old Negro spiritual.

[ix] From the eponymous old Negro spiritual.

[x] From the eponymous old Negro spiritual.

[xi] From the eponymous old Negro spiritual.

[xii] Charles Edward Stowe, *Harriet Beecher Stowe: The Story of Her Life* (1911) p. 203.

[xiii] "Camp William Penn: Training Ground for Freedom," by Donald Scott. In: *America's Civil War Magazine,* November 1999.

[xiv] Ibid.

[xv] National Park Service. http://www.nps.gov/history/history/online_books/hh/13/hh13f.htm

[xvi] Frances H. Kennedy, ed. *The Civil War Battlefield Guide.* 2nd ed. Boston: Houghton Mifflin Co., 1998. ISBN 0-395-74012-6.

[xvii] Virginia Military Institute. http://www.vmi.edu/archives.aspx?id=3747

[xviii] James M. Paradis, *Strike the Blow for Freedom: The 6th United States Colored Infantry in the Civil War* (2000), White Mane Books, Shippensburg, PA, ISBN 1-57249-191-4.

293

[xix] *6th United States Colored Regiment Pennsylvania Volunteers* (http://www. pa-roots.com/~pacw/6thuscrorg.html)

[xx] James M. Paradis, p.76.

[xxi] "Ben Simpson: Georgia and Texas," in: *Lay My Burden Down: A Folk History of Slavery,* edited by B.A. Botkin, University of Chicago Press, 1945, (pp.75-76)

[xxii] *The Chester Times,* September 4, 1889, page-1; Chester, Pennsylvania.

[xxiii] Ibid. September 1889.

[xxiv] Ibid. September 25, 1889.

[xxv] $25 in 1889 would be worth approximately $625 in 2012.

[xxvi] *The Chester Times,* September 27, 1889.

[xxvii] An old and distinguished fraternal organization founded in 1783 by American Revolutionary War officers and French officers of rank. Membership is passed down to the eldest son after a member dies. The first president of the Society of Cincinnati was George Washington.

[xxviii] Lyndon H. Hart III, Bromfield B. Nichol, Jr., *Ridley of Southampton,* privately printed, (1992), 235.

[xxix] Samuel M. Lemon, *The Construction of Ethnoracial Identity within Situational Contexts,* University of Pennsylvania (2007), 157 - 160.

[xxx] Samuel M. Lemon, ibid.

[xxxi] John Hope Franklin, *From Slavery to Freedom, A History of Negro Americans,* 4th edition, Alfred A. Knopf publishers, (1974), 239.

[xxxii] John Hope Franklin and Loren Schweninger, *Runaway Slaves, Rebels on the Plantation,* Oxford University Press, (1999), 282.

REFERENCES

Ancestry.com

Pvt. Joe Becton, Co-founder, 3rd USCT re-enactors, Philadelphia, PA

"Fort Strong on Arlington Heights, by Anne C. Webb, 34-39. In: *The Arlington Historical Magazine*, Vol.5, No.1, October 1973.

Freedom's Soldiers: The Black Military Experience in the Civil War, Ira Berlin, Joseph P. Reidy, and Leslie S. Rowland, eds., Cambridge University Press, 1998.

"From Gettysburg to Oregon: The remarkable life of a Quaker Civil War Hero," by Randy Fletcher. In: *Oregon Magazine*, 2009. http://oregonmag/FletcherCiviWar809.html. Courtesy Mary U. Brooks, Archive Librarian, Westtown School, West Chester, PA. 19382

William C. Kashatus, *Just Over the Line: Chester County and the Underground Railroad*, Chester County Historical Society, West Chester, PA; and Penn State University Press, University Park, PA, 2002.

Mark Lardas, *African American Soldier in the Civil War: USCT 1862-66*, Osprey Publishing, N.Y., 2006.

Robert Seeley, a direct descendant of Thomas Garrett

Julius Lester, *To Be A Slave*, Scholastic, Inc., New York, 1968

Mason Family Papers, Virginia Historical Society. Manuscript #MSS1M3816b75.

6th United States Colored Pennsylvania Volunteers, http://www.pa-roots.com/pacw/usct/6thusct/6thusctorg.html

6th USCT Company D, http://www.pa-roots.com/pacw/usct/6thusct/6thusctcod.html

Sixth Infantry USCT, Commanding Officer Colonel John W. Ames http://www.usct.org/6thinfantryregiment/6thinfantryregiment.htm

Kenneth M. Stampp, *The Peculiar Institution: Slavery in the Ante-Bellum South*, Vintage Books and Random House, New York, 1956

William J. Switala, *Underground Railroad in Pennsylvania*, Stackpole Books, PA, 2001.

Susie King Taylor, *Reminiscences of My Life: A Black Woman's Civil War Memoirs*, Patricia W. Romer and Willie Lee Rose, Eds., Markus Wiener Publishing, New York, 1988.

J. Leitch Wright, Jr., *The Only Land They Knew: The Tragic Story of the American Indians in the Old South*, The Free Press, New York, 1981.

"The Underground Railroad," Historic Pennsylvania Leaflet No. 29, 1-4., Division of Public Records, Historic Pennsylvania Leaflets: No. 21 - 30, Pennsylvania Historical and Museum Commission.

U.S. Census

U.S. National Park Service

en.wikipedia.org

PHOTOGRAPHIC INDEX

P-2: Maud Ray Ridley, author's grandmother, about age 12, circa 1903.

P-3: William Henry Ridley, Esq., Maud's father, about age 24, circa 1891.

P-6: 308 North Olive St., Media, PA; purchased by Cornelius Ridley in 1872.

P-281: Cornelius Ridley - the author's great-great grandfather, circa 1890.

P-282: Cornelius Ridley with horse, second photo with mule team.

P-283: Martha Jane Parham, about age 60.

P-284: Martha Jane Parham, circa 1860; *Lt. Nathan H. Edgerton, 6th USCT.

P-285: Author's maternal grandmother Maud Ray Ridley Ortiga; 1883 wedding certificate of Cornelius and Martha Jane "Maceson" Ridley.

P-286: George Washington Ridley with his children: Lillian E. Ridley and Edward C. Ridley; and George's sister Rachel Ann Ridley; Note from Bromfield B. Nichol, September 14, 2007.

P-287: Letter from Morning Star Baptist Church, Capron, VA, Oct. 18, 1999

P-288: Solomon Clifford (aka James Ferrill) with family; Bonnie Doon Mansion and historical marker near Capron, Southampton County, VA.

P-289: Solomon Clifford/James Ferrill's Civil War pension application.

P-290: The author, age 4 years, at Rose Valley School, Rose Valley, PA

P-291: Letter to the author from President Bill Clinton, September 8, 1997.

* Courtesy of the National Archives and Records Administration.

** All other photographs and documents courtesy of Ridley Family Archives, Samuel M. Lemon, Ed.D., Curator.

Made in the USA
Charleston, SC
26 July 2014